Texas

Mexico

Big Spring

El Paso

Ciudad
Juarez

Fort Hancock

Sierra Blanca

Rankin

Fort Stockton

Van Horn

Fort Davis

Alpine

Austin

Del Rio

San Antonio

Eagle Pass

Carrizo Springs

Cotulla

Laredo

Nuevo Laredo

Zapata

Roma

Map of Texas-Mexico Border

Working the Border:
A Texas Ranger's Story

Doyle Holdridge

ISBN
1-933177-25-X (10 digit)
978-1-933177-25-0 (13 digit)

Library of Congress Control Number: 2009934616

Printed in the United States of America
Published by Atriad Press LLC
13820 Methuen Green
Dallas, TX 75240
(972) 671-0002
www.atriadpress.com

Dedication

"Courtesy, Service, and Protection," the motto of the Texas Department of Public Safety, became engrained into my soul and I tried to live by those words for thirty-two years. The men I have known, living and dead, who made the choice to serve the people of Texas working for the DPS understood this motto. I dedicate this book to the officers of the DPS who gave their lives in protecting the lives, rights, property, and privileges of the people of the state.

"Greater love hath no man than this, that a man lay down his life for his friends." John 15:13

Table of Contents

Foreword

Friend, you're holding a collection of stories you will truly enjoy. As you read this compilation you will get to know Doyle Holdridge as he takes you from his days as a young boy in Rankin, Texas to the beginning of his law enforcement career as a Highway Patrolman, his promotion to Narcotics agent, and finally his selection to the position of Texas Ranger stationed in Laredo, Texas. The Texas/Mexico border is where Ranger Holdridge spent twenty-two years defending and upholding the values and laws of our great Lone Star State.

At the beginning of Doyle's law enforcement career he had many opportunities to work hand in hand with active, long-time Texas Rangers. Doyle was privileged to be mentored by well-respected Rangers like Clayton McKinney, Joe Coleman, Tol Dawson, Pete Montemayor and Captain Jim Riddles. Those men made Doyle Holdridge not only a better cop, but when all was said and done, a better Texas Ranger.

Reading Working the Border: A Texas Ranger's Story takes you on a greatly satisfying, exciting, and sometimes humorous ride chasing bad guys up and down the border. Read about the drug dealer who sold him drugs while he worked in an undercover capacity to the drug smuggler he chased along the Rio Grande River, as well as his negotiating with the leader of a prison riot, and finally how he obtained a successful confession to the brutal stabbing of his good friend, the Dimmit

1

County sheriff. With each story you get a peek inside the friendships and working relationships that are made during the most interesting of times. And, it is great to laugh with Doyle even when he is the punch line of the joke.

Doyle is a lawman's lawman who is well-respected on both sides of the border. His work was so well received the Mexican officials gave him police credentials for the State of Tamaulipas.

A successful Texas Ranger understands that everyone has value, and that you can learn something from everyone you meet. Doyle also knew the environment and culture in which he worked. And he discovered what was important and in many cases what was not important to the bad guys.

As you read these stories of Doyle's distinguished career you will have an understanding of what it was like to work as a Texas Ranger on the border.

I have known and worked with Doyle for more than twenty-five years from our days together in DPS Narcotics and then into the Ranger service and finally as his Ranger captain. He never lacked the desire or the tenacity to put the bad guy in jail, or do what was right.

The Texas Rangers have adopted this saying: *El es muy bueno para cabalgar el rio*. Doyle is my true friend, and as that old saying goes in English, "He will do to ride the river with."

Clete R. Buckaloo
Captain, Texas Rangers (Ret.)

Acknowledgements

I wish to thank my wife, Lety, for the endless hours she spent trying to make sense of my West Texas way of expressing thoughts and correcting my fourth-grade spelling. Without her help I would never have been able to put this book together.

I would also like to thank my friend and editor, Mike Cox, whom I've known for the last twenty years, for his invaluable assistance in providing guidance, advice, suggestions and expertise. Without his help this book would have never been printed.

And last, but not least, I wish to express my gratitude to Trish Garcia for being my first reader and providing me with the encouragement to see the project through to the end.

Preface

I decided to write this book to give readers an inside look into what a Texas Ranger does as he performs his duties. Now that I am at the end of my career as a police officer, I realize that when I and the other officers I've worked with over the past thirty-six years die, few people will know anything about the cases that we have worked.

The sacrifices made by law enforcement officers and their families are innumerable. Worked holidays, interrupted meals, and missed family events and vacations take their toll. So does being on call twenty-four hours a day, seven days a week, and three hundred sixty-five days a year. As part of this group of men who have spent their lives working for the greater good for the people of Texas, I feel a responsibility to leave some of my experiences in writing, lest they be lost forever.

The stories in this book really happened, and I have told them to the best of my recollection, although I have changed a few of the names. Bear in mind that these experiences happened to me over the last fifty-seven years. If I have made any mistakes with events or people's names, please remember that I have relied solely on my recollections of these incidents. Of course, all the criminal cases presented through the court system are a matter of public record. Some of the stories are funny; some will break your heart when you read what one human being can do to another.

Serving as a Ranger from 1982 to 2004, I worked thousands of criminal investigations. This book contains

4

examples of the types of cases a Ranger works on a daily basis. My hope is that after you have read the book you will have a better understanding of what a Ranger really does for the people of Texas.

One thing in particular that I want to make sure people understand: There was nothing, and I mean nothing, special about me or the way that I did business. I was just one Ranger, a one-time sheepherder from Rankin, Texas, lucky enough to have been a Texas Ranger. Each Ranger in the state is an expert in his assigned area. I'm sure that they have as many good stories as I do. You can't do this kind of work for nearly four decades without having a few good stories. I hope you enjoy mine.

    – Doyle Holdridge
    Laredo, Texas
    June 2009

The Beginning

The first time I can remember ever actually seeing a Texas Ranger, I was somewhere around 10 years old. My Dad and I were in his faded, red 1952 Chevrolet pickup. We had stopped at one of those gas stations like you see in the movies in the middle of nowhere to get something to drink. We had gotten out of the pickup and were inside the station when a man dressed in khaki pants, white shirt, and cowboy hat walked through the front door. To me at the time, he looked seven feet tall. Everyone in the station snapped-to and really started paying attention to this man. I was very young, but I could tell he was some type of law enforcement officer since he carried a large handgun. No one said much while he was there, but he clearly commanded everyone's respect.

"Who was that guy?" I asked my dad as soon as we got back into the pickup. Dad told me the man was a Texas Ranger and that those men were not the kind of men someone wanted to mess with. If he could be anything in the world that he wanted to be, Dad said, he would want to be a Texas Ranger. I have never forgotten that. Dad was from the oilfields of West Texas and for him to say something like that about anyone was really out of character. Tough as my dad was, I could tell that he had a lot of admiration for the Rangers and that really made an impression on me.

I was born in Big Spring, Texas in 1952 to Doyle and Moodean Holdridge. My mother and father were working-class people, and we did not have a lot when I was young. Dad married my mother when both of them were pretty young, and neither of them had finished high school. My mother,

Moodean, never worked outside the home.

Dad was not around most of the time when I was growing up, because he was always working. When I got up in the morning he had already gone to work. I would go through my day and come in for supper. I would eat supper and settle down to watch some TV. Most of the time he wouldn't show up at the house until just before I went to bed.

Dad worked for most of his life in the West Texas oil patch, and I was moved around a lot when he changed jobs. Oil field work was both tiring and dangerous. The hours were long. I could tell when Dad came home that he was worn out. I watched him work like this all my life.

From time to time Mom, Dad, and I would go to DeLeon in Comanche County to visit Dad's parents. I loved to go see my grandparents on the Holdridge side of the family. My grandpa, Jess Holdridge, would tell me stories about my great-great-great grandfather, John Henry Holdridge.

John Henry served in the Confederate Army during the Civil War. He had enlisted into the 14th Alabama Infantry and fought for the South the entire war. Though wounded twice, he still returned to the fight. At the end of the war he was in the 14th Alabama under Generals Cadmus Wilcox, James Longstreet and Robert E. Lee in the Army of Northern Virginia. When General Lee surrendered at Appomattox, John Henry Holdridge stood nearby. He is buried in DeLeon, along with most of the other Holdridges.

While I was growing up I stayed part of every summer at my grandparents', so I spent a lot of time with Grandpa Holdridge. The Comanche County Holdridges were very religious people. Grandpa took me to church at least three times a week.

He also taught me about hard work. He paid me a dollar a week to do chores around his place. When I got that dollar, he would take me to town in his truck so I could find something that I thought I needed.

Grandpa Holdridge was probably the best man I have ever met. I never sat down at the table with him that he didn't say a prayer before we ate. He always stayed to himself and never had a bad word to say about anyone. I have often thought about him during my life, and I have strived to be like him as best I could.

My parents would drive me to Grandpa's house for my summer visits. Mom always packed short pants for me to wear in the summer. Grandpa didn't like short pants on boys, so he always took me to town and bought a pair of boots and several pairs of blue jeans for me to wear while I was staying with him. That suited me fine. I still dress that way to this day.

My other set of grandparents lived near Denton. From the time that I was very young I remember visiting Grandfather and Grandmother's ranch northeast of Denton. Grandma Johnnie on my mother's side was the love of my life. She spoiled me, and I knew that she was the one person I could go to if I ever needed anything. Whatever she had she split with me and my mother.

Grandfather Ernest ran a small herd of cattle, and Mom and Dad often went to the ranch to help him out. I never really did like staying on the ranch because my grandparents did not have a TV. The house they lived in consisted of two bedrooms, a kitchen, and a living room. The thing I hated most was that the house did not have indoor plumbing. To go to the restroom I had to walk about forty yards out back to the outhouse. I remember that it was always cold in the winter months, and I hated to go out in the weather to use the restroom. At night there were the bedpans to deal with.

The up side to our visits was that I got to help the men work cattle. They always put me on a horse, and I got to push the cattle into the squeeze chute. I thought that was a really big deal. I started doing this at about six years old. I was also trusted with an old .22 caliber single-shot rifle. I was allowed to walk the entire ranch and hunt whatever I wanted.

There was a large stock tank located several hundred yards behind the house, and that's where I spent most of my time. That tank had lots of turtles and snakes, and I nearly burned the barrel out of that .22 trying to thin them out. I think that's when I started to have a love affair with firearms. I really liked messing with guns.

Grandpa Ernest had an old single-shot Long Tom shotgun that I was allowed to shoot as long as he was with me. The gun was far too long and heavy for me to hold up, so when I did get to shoot it I had to prop it on something. Grandpa also carried a double barrel .410 shotgun with a pistol grip. He kept that gun in the front seat of his pickup and took it everywhere he went. The gun was about ten inches long, and I know now that it would be illegal to possess today, but Grandpa didn't worry about its length.

When we got down near the river that ran through his place we always found a lot of snakes. I was scared to death of snakes, and Grandpa felt the same way. When he ran across one, it didn't take him long to dispatch the thing with his sawed-off .410. He just pointed it in the general direction and the problem was solved.

When we were working cattle we always went back to the house for lunch. I remember one day when we were all sitting around the table. I finished my lunch and got up to leave. I looked over and saw one of the hot shots that my father had been using to move the cattle.

A hot shot is a small tube with batteries that produces an electric shock when pressed into the side of cattle – or some other object. It is used to move cattle through the chutes as they are being worked. I was not allowed to touch the hot shots, but everyone was too busy eating to notice that I had it in my hands.

I remember that Dad was sitting at the table with his shirt off, still eating. I decided that I was going to play a joke on him, so I buried that hot shot in the middle of his back, right

9

between the shoulder blades. He screamed, jumped up, and turned the table over. I could tell real quick that he failed to see the humor in my joke.

I hit the back door on the run and headed for the river down in the pasture. I stayed away from the house the rest of the day. When I finally came back, I found that most of the family thought that it had been really funny. Dad learned that he had better not leave one of his hot shots lying around where his six-year-old son could get his hands on it.

My father was always looking for a better job and a way to provide us with more of the things people want in life. For a while we lived in the Denton area and he got a job working in a bomb factory in Dallas. Grandma Johnnie and Grandpa Ernest couldn't afford to hire help, so while we lived in the area, my parents spent a lot of time helping out around the ranch.

As much as Dad worked, we never really lived in a nice place. At one point he tried to branch out from working for someone else and bought a used dump truck. He worked at that for a while until he finally went flat broke. We lost our house and sold everything we had to be able to move back to an area where Dad could return to the oil field where he could get the kind of work he knew best.

I can still remember moving from Denton to Odessa in that old red '52 pickup. We had everything we owned loaded in it. A good friend of Dad's, John Pippen, helped him get a job with Western Oil Company and let us live with him and his family until we could get enough money together to get our own place. I'll never forget what the Pippens did for my family in our time of need. I can still remember drinking powdered milk when we could not afford to buy fresh.

From this point until the day he died, Dad worked in the oil field. To this day, I have never seen anybody work so hard. Though I could not know then that he would end up with nothing at the end, I made up my mind when I was ten that I was going to get some kind of job that provided me with a good working environment, a steady income and some kind of retirement. Even at this young age I was very aware of what Dad was going through trying to support our family.

One day when I was about twelve my dad came home from work and told my mother and me that he had gotten a new job in Rankin. Apparently Western Oil was moving its operations from Odessa to Rankin, a one-time boomtown in Upton County. When we moved there in the early 1960's, it was a new start for my family.

I had never been to Rankin and I had no idea what it was going to be like. When we drove into town I noticed that there really wasn't much to it. At the time I think the population was somewhere around twelve hundred people, though it had been much bigger than that in the mid-1920s when the Yates Field first came in. Dad drove us around to show us where we were going to live. It took us about ten minutes to see the whole place. There was no good side of town or bad side. There was just Rankin.

When we pulled up in front of our new rent house the first thing I noticed was that it needed a coat of paint. The house consisted of a living room, a kitchen, one bedroom, and one bathroom. I found that my "room" was a folding bed set up behind the kitchen table at night. At this stage of my life, I really didn't think about the fact that we were poor. I had never known anything else.

West Texans are hard working and tend to take care of their own problems. Most of the people in Rankin either worked in the oil field, the school, for the county, or in ranching. The people tended to be close-knit and it took a long time before they accepted newcomers into the community. The folks around town all seemed to be in the same position in life that we were. Everyone was trying to get by, working as hard as they could to provide for their families. The only people in town who seemed to have a lot of money were the people who owned land and had worked hard for what they had.

11

The people around Rankin actually cared about each other and took the time to help their neighbors. No one ever locked their doors and most everyone left the keys in their car. After living there a short time, you knew most everyone in town. It was a good place to be a kid.

Not long after we arrived I began to notice that most everyone in town seemed to know the Highway Patrolmen who worked the area, Vic Atwood from Big Lake and Sammy Long from McCamey. They stood out in their community and everyone looked up to and respected them. Those two officers handled whatever came up. They worked wrecks, enforced the traffic laws, assisted the local sheriff's office, and at times helped raise the young people, like myself, in the communities where they served. There wasn't much to talk about in Rankin, so most of the people in town really kept up with what the local Highway Patrolman was doing. After I got a driver license and began looking for female companionship, I started to have encounters with Sammy Long.

We all took our girlfriends to the drive-in movie until a storm blew it down. After that, there was not a lot to do. The town's standard joke was that "Gone with the Wind" was always playing at the local drive-in. I ran with a bunch of young boys who had the same basic values as I had. We all played football and we liked to drink beer and chase girls, not necessarily in that order. As young men will do, I made every effort to party, fight, and get into mischief on a regular basis. In those days you could actually get into a good fistfight with someone and not get shot full of 9mm holes.

Instead of cruising the highways, on Friday and Saturday nights Sammy spent most of his time in town. He would often catch me and my friends with some kind of alcoholic beverage, parking with a girl, fighting, drag racing or doing something else we thought was fun. I was certain that Sammy would end up putting me in the county jail for minor-in-possession of alcohol or something else, but he always hauled me back to my house and turned me over to my dad. Most of the time I would plead with Sammy to just put me in jail, but he always took me home. In my mind that was the worst thing that he could do to me. I understand now that Sammy was doing me a huge favor by not getting me a criminal record for some offense that was a direct result of the growing pains of just being a young man.

The town took great pride in our football team. Nearly everyone in Rankin went to the home games. It was the social event of the week, and everyone took advantage of it to get out and spend time with their friends. The wives and their young children always sat with their female friends in the stands, and all the men stood near the concession stand along the fence so they could talk during the event. Most of the men found time during the game to walk to the parking lot to their cars to get something a little stronger than soft drinks to drink. Even now it still brings a smile to remember those days, when I was so very young and did not know the bad things that could happen to good people.

Home games were important, but the biggest deal of the year was the homecoming game. All the boys I ran with would save their lunch money to pay for the homecoming party that was to take place after we had beaten whomever we were scheduled to play. This event was always planned with great detail.

One year, my high school buddy Gary Glosser and I were the chosen ones to go to McCamey to make the beer run (That's *everyone's* beer and wine for the after-game party). No one in Rankin would sell us beer because everyone knew we were under age.

We had collected everyone's lunch money and had decided that we would make the run during the week, in the afternoon, because Highway Patrolman Sammy Long usually did not work on Tuesday or Wednesday. The party depended on us being able to get by Sammy and getting the beer successfully back to Rankin without getting apprehended.

13

Over the years, we had found a bootlegger in McCamey who would sell us whatever we wanted at an inflated price because we were under age. On the day that we made the run, we left Rankin just after football practice. We had collected the money and made a list of requests. We drove the eighteen miles to McCamey and were on the lookout to make sure that Sammy was not between the two towns. So far so good. We knew where Sammy lived, and we drove by his house in McCamey to make sure his patrol car was at home and he was not out working. Bad news. Sammy's patrol car was not at his house.

We decided to proceed with the plan and go ahead and pick up our party favors. We made contact with our bootlegger buddy and loaded the trunk with beer, cherry vodka and wine. "Man," we thought, "this is really going to be a good party!"

The road between Rankin and McCamey is straight for about ten miles as you leave Rankin. There is really only one major curve as you get near McCamey, and that was the area Sammy always worked. We headed back to Rankin, being careful to obey the speed limit in the event we ran into Sammy. We had driven about eight miles back toward town and had just gone around the curve. From that point, you could actually see Rankin about ten miles away. To my horror, I saw Sammy in his black-and-white patrol car about two miles ahead of us, slowly moving east toward Rankin. He was driving about thirty miles an hour. I knew if I turned around he would stop me, so I slowed down in an effort to stay as far away from him as I could. When I slowed, so did Sammy.

It was about five miles to the Iraan highway so I decided that I would stay behind Sammy until I could turn south and get away from him. I knew a back way into Rankin that came out at the town cemetery south of town, and I knew that if I could make the Iraan highway I was home free. I just had to make it to the highway crossing at the Mule Train Bar so I could turn right. I knew that Sammy kept an eye on the Mule

Train because a lot of the local cowboys and oilfield hands used it as a watering hole. I was hoping that he would stop in there to check it out and I could get around him and on into town.

As I drove on, Sammy slowed even more. He knew my car well, and I knew if I got close to him he would know something was up. There was no reason in the world for me to be between Rankin and McCamey on a school day. Sammy had stopped me numerous times before, and he would know that I was up to no good. So I followed Sammy for what seemed to be forever. I finally got to the Iraan highway at the Mule Train and turned south toward Iraan. Sammy went on down the highway toward Rankin. I thought *man I got it made.* I worked my way down several dirt roads, knowing that I would end up south of Rankin near the cemetery. Then it was just a short distance on into town. *Boy*, I thought, *I am good.*

As I drove up to hit the paved road back into town, you would never guess who was parked on the side of the road by the cemetery waiting for us. Trooper Sammy Long. Sammy just got out of his car and waved me over. He had known all along what I was up to! I pulled over and got out. Sammy told me to open the trunk of the car. I opened the trunk and Sammy just looked at me and said, "Homecoming!"

Sammy then made us open every single beer and pour it on the ground. After that, he made us pick up all the cans and bottles and put them back in the trunk. Then he told us to go throw them away. Sammy then just got in his car and left us standing on the side of the road, in a puddle of wasted beer.

I had a lot of explaining to do to all the friends who had asked me to get their Friday night refreshments. We managed to have somewhat of a party anyway, but it was not as big as it would have been if Sammy hadn't ambushed us with our load of beer on the way home. That's just the kind of guy Sammy was. He found a way to enforce the law, but no one got their life screwed up in the process.

15

My mother was a religious woman, and she would throw a fit if she found out that I was running loose in the world. She would get my Dad stirred up and he was the one who always found the solution to the problem at hand. When he got involved, that's when I suffered life-changing events. Dad always found a lot of work for me to do around the house for the next six weeks after some infraction on my part. He would also take my car away from me for that period of time, and he would have my mother take me to high school each day.

She would drive me up in front of the school where everyone could see that my mother was bringing me to school. It just killed me to have all the good-looking girls see me being brought to school by my mother. Well, this would go on for the full six weeks until finally I would get my car back. Most of the time I would not mess up again for at least two or three weeks.

In my defense, in a small town there was not much else to do but to get into some kind of mischief. I was really good at that. I never did ask my dad what the deal was with the six-week punishments. I think now that it was just the first number that came into his head, and until I left home that was the standard length of time I got for one of the numerous offenses against the Holdridge House Rules.

Like I said, in West Texas the one sport that really matters is football. You live, breathe, and eat football. In Rankin all the people in town felt the same way. You could run through Main Street naked on Friday night and most likely no one would see you if it was a home game night. Most of us played the other sports as well, but the only reason we did was to stay in shape for football. I played football all four years in high school and to this day I can still remember the games and what we went through every Friday night in the fall. Those were some of the best times that I can remember. I made friends that I still have to this day. Also, some of the things that I learned from the coaches have stayed with me. For one thing, they taught us to

16

work hard together, and the physical and mental hardships that were put on us as football players helped me later in life.

Coach Bill Beasley taught me more about what it took to succeed in life than any one else. He taught me that you had to work really hard at whatever you were doing to get to the top. He told me more times than I can remember that at some point in life the only thing that would get you over the hump was that you had to try harder than the next guy and you had to get mean. Those few words told to me many years ago by an "old fat football coach," as he referred to himself, have continued to serve me. It has made the difference many times in my life: get mean and try harder. I live by those words even now.

Over the next few years I continued to live my life as young men will do. I attended school, played sports, and worked around town to make money to support my social life. At the end of my senior year Dad came into my room one night just before graduation and told me that he had provided for me the last eighteen years and it was time for me to move out into the world. I had family in San Angelo, Texas, and my girlfriend, Dana Jo Brown planned to attend Angelo State University. That made it easy enough to decide that I would move to San Angelo to get a job and try to go to college, too.

College

I moved to Angelo—as West Texans call it—in the summer of 1970 to work and start college. I had not yet made up my mind what I wanted to be. The Vietnam War was going on and I had registered for the draft on my eighteenth birthday. Dad had told me that I had the honor of living in the best country in the world and that if that country asked me to fight for it, that's exactly what he expected me to do. I knew what was expected of me, but what I had in mind was getting some book-learning in San Angelo, where, incidentally, there happened to be a lot of good-looking girls. As a result, Dana Jo and I didn't last long after I moved to Angelo. I would have to say that it was my doing and not hers that ended our courtship.

I knew one thing. I did not want to work in the oilfield. I had watched Dad work seven days a week just to get by. In the summer he burned his ass off and in the winter he froze. I had worked on a pulling unit myself during school breaks. The job is grueling and you can lose a limb—or your life—during a moment's distraction. That's not what I wanted to do with my life. My father was a very proud man. When his health started going bad and he had a hard time paying his bills, he told no one. I did not know that he had no retirement or insurance benefits until after he had passed away. He had been living on $800 a month.

I had started my college courses as soon as I had gotten to San Angelo, but I also needed to find a job. I had been a lifeguard while in high school, and I found that the experience helped me land a job. I worked the first summer as a lifeguard, but as the summer came to an end I had to find another job for fall. I had a friend that worked at a stockyard and he was able to help me get a job at Producers Livestock.

The stockyard handled cattle and sheep sales for most of West Texas. At times we sold as many as thirty-five thousand sheep a day. Sheep are the worst animals in the world to try to work with. They were born looking for a place to die. We would work all day getting the animals through the sales ring, and at night before we left work we had to count all the sheep that had gone through the sales ring.

The facility was three or four times as large as a mall parking lot and consisted of pens, alleys, and gates to move cattle and sheep from one area to the other. Located above the pens was what we called a catwalk. It was a walkway built about eight feet above the ground so that buyers could walk above the yard and look over the stock they intended to buy.

When we arrived at work at six in the morning, we had to feed all the livestock before the day's sale started. Sheep are the hardest animals in the world to work with. You can't try to push them from behind. You have to start moving them from the front of the herd, and once you get them moving, you have to constantly keep them moving, or the whole herd will just stop and stand there and look at you. Once they do that, it's a real chore to get them started again. I would find out later that jail inmates are a lot like sheep in some respects.

The thing about working at Producers was that in the winter we froze our ass off and in the summer we burned up. Kind of the same thing my dad had endured his whole life. We spent most of the days moving large groups of sheep from one area to the other. One guy would have to go ahead of the herd and set all the gates so the sheep ended up at the intended location. One or two other guys then brought the herd to their respective pen, so they would go through the sale ring.

All sheepmen understand the importance of having a lead

19

goat. A lead goat was trained to push his way into the sheep, then turn around and lead the herd back in the desired direction. This may sound strange to non-ranchers, but the lead goats worked really well. When the goat walked into a pen and then walked out, the herd of sheep would just follow him out of the pen. As long as the goat kept moving, the sheep would follow.

The goat we used was called Old Pete. He always started the day working really well, helping us move thousands of sheep from one location to another. But during the afternoon he would start to get tired. We had to watch him real close, or human like, he would make a break for it and disappear.

The old white goat had worked around the alleys and gates so long that he had learned how to walk up to a gate, hook it with his horn, turn around and catch the front of the gate with his ass. Pete then backed up through the gate. In a flash, he'd scramble up the stairs of the catwalk.

Sometimes when I was working the alleys I would see Pete getting near the catwalk gate. In the blink of an eye he'd be on the stairs! We'd yell at him as he made his break, but that always seemed to make him hit overdrive. Once he reached the catwalk he would run for hundreds of yards all the way across the facility.

Eventually Pete would jump off the catwalk and hide under a water trough. He always seemed to find a leaky trough so he could lie down in the mud to cool off. Sometimes we'd spend an hour or so looking for him so we could put him back to work.

The old goat fought you every step when you were dragging him back to work. We found that if we filled his bottom lip with Copenhagen snuff, he got a nicotine rush and would work well for the next hour or so. Most of the time by mid-afternoon he gave out, and we had to put him back in his pen. We all thought Old Pete was a lot smarter then we were, because he had the good sense to quit when he got tired.

I don't know how much Pete cost, but I was always told by the foreman that I better not let anything happen to him when he was in my care. It's funny the things that you remember in life. If I told this story to some city folks they'd probably think I was lying. When that old goat was working well, he saved us lots of time and a lot of walking.

I would go to the stockyard early in the morning and work until it was time to go to class. After class I would return to the stockyard and work until everything was done. Sometimes I would not get home until ten or eleven at night. I did this for what seemed like a long time, making only about $400 a month. I knew I had to find something that was better than that.

Partly inspired by my high school experiences with Trooper Sammy Long, it had crossed my mind to try to go to work for the Department of Public Safety, but I had no idea what it took to get a job with them. I had a roommate by the name of Jim Phillips who had just gotten back from Vietnam. Jim was a little older than I was and he was the one who first went to the San Angelo DPS office to find out about getting a job. Jim was also attending college classes with me, and over the next few months we talked about putting our application in with DPS.

I stayed at Angelo State for about two years, and finally realized that I was not cut out for that. I never got drafted, so I knew that it was time for me to find a way of making a living. I had always noticed that people in the community seemed to really respect the Highway Patrolman who worked in the area. Don't get me wrong, they usually liked the sheriff and the area police, but there seemed to be something special about the DPS officers. So I decided to ask about getting a job. I went to the DPS area office on South Chadbourne Street and got a Highway Patrol application.

Over the next few days, I got my new girlfriend, Cindy Buchanan to fill out the application for me, since my handwriting was not nearly as pretty as hers. I took the

21

application back to the Highway Patrol sergeant at the DPS office. He looked at it for a moment and asked me if I had filled it out myself. I told the sergeant that I had my girlfriend fill it out for me because my handwriting was not very good. He tore the application in half, handed me a blank one, and told me to fill it out myself unless I intended to have my girlfriend ride around with me in my patrol car to do all my paperwork—if I was lucky enough to get the job. I filled out the application and turned it in.

The sergeant told me the department got a lot of applications for only a few openings and that they would call me if I made the cut. I went on with my life. A few weeks later, I was told to report for the physical and agility test. I passed both, and it was time for me to get fingerprinted for a criminal history check.

While fingerprinting me, the same sergeant who had torn up my first application asked me if I had ever been printed before. Well, some of my college buddies and I had been arrested for minor-in-possession of alcohol a few months earlier. I really thought hard about not telling the sergeant about the incident, but I decided that I had better go with the truth. When I told him, he reached over and opened a folder that had my mug shot and the report of my arrest for the Class C offense. I know that if I had lied, I would never have gotten the chance to be part of the DPS.

November 1972 was a month full of life-changing events for me. For one, I had decided to get married. I really don't remember asking Cindy to marry me, but I came to realize that I was getting married on Thanksgiving Day. It was this month, also, that I received some assets that were distributed from my great-grandmother's estate on my mother's side of the family. This unexpected income was a welcome surprise. I was also contacted by DPS and advised that I had been accepted as a recruit, and I was to report to the DPS Academy in Austin on November 28.

A week or so before the wedding, I was messing around with some of my buddies and we decided to go to what we called a bull-riding buckout in Midland. A buckout is an event where every rider puts up a set amount of money and the best rider gets all the money. Well, we went to the bull riding and I was having the time of my life.

But during my ride, a bull stepped on my right leg and broke it. As my friends and I were leaving to get my leg taken care of, the daughter of Midland's mayor backed into my car with a big Ford pickup. The guys with the mayor's daughter did not want to call the Highway Patrol to investigate the wreck, so we ended up in a fight with them. I guess we won because eventually, we got the accident worked by the Highway Patrol and my leg fixed up.

Over the next few days I got married and took my wife to San Antonio on our honeymoon. As soon as we got back to San Angelo, I left for Austin and the DPS Academy. I could hardly walk due to the broken leg.

The Academy

I had never been to the capital city before. To tell the truth, I didn't even know how to get there from San Angelo. In addition, I had a broken right leg that I did not intend to tell anyone about because I was afraid that the DPS would not let me stay. But I needed the job because I was now a married man and needed some way to put food on the table. When I finally found the DPS headquarters at 5805 North Lamar Boulevard, I went to the Driver's License office at the corner of Denson and Lamar to see where I was to report. I did not realize that the DPS complex took up several city blocks. Someone at the driver's license office directed me to the training facility, where I was greeted by a very unfriendly drill instructor-type guy in full trooper uniform who told me to go down the street and get my hair cut. I was told to get a burr.

When I got back to the Academy, they told me to take off my boots and hat and to step up on the scales so they could weigh me. I pulled off my boots, and with my hat in one hand and the boots in the other, stepped back up on the scales. One of the officers getting us checked in looked at me and told me that if he had wanted to know how much I weighed with the hat and boots he would not have told me to take them off. I dropped them like they were on fire! About this time another cadet walked in with his boots and hat and did the same thing. The cadet would turn out to be one of my best friends and we would later become Highway Patrol partners in El Paso.

Guys from all over the state had shown up to attend the

school. I felt really out of place because San Antonio was the only other big city I had ever been to and I didn't know a soul at the school. I had not been in the military and was not used to living such a regimented life. From the time we arrived we were told exactly what to do. We did nothing of our own free will. If we wanted to go to the bathroom, we had to ask. We spent the next two days getting all the paperwork done to be a state employee. I could have never dreamed then that I would work for the DPS for the next thirty-two years.

Nor did I have any idea what was in store for me when the training class started. I thought, *These people have got to be out of their mind!* We all had to wear khaki shirts and pants and a black tie. It nearly killed me to have to wear a tie. I had not worn one very often before, and I did not feel comfortable in one.

Then the normal routine started. We would get up in the morning at 5:30 and would do about an hour-and-a-half of physical training, what DPS referred to as P.T. Before I got to Austin I might have gotten up one time at 5:30 in the morning, but I took a leak and went right back to bed. They would work us so hard that most of us could hardly walk by the time we had to go for "a little run." DPS always had a strange idea of what they called a little run. In my mind a little run was where you ran a few blocks or a few laps around a track. It seemed to me like DPS's definition of a little run was running from one town to the next. I don't really know how far we ran, but I always thought that if we had to go that far we should have taken a bus.

When they had first told me that we were going to have to do P.T. I thought, "No big deal." I had played football four years and I was used to working out. Little did I know that the guys running the academy were nuts. It appeared to me that they were not trying to get us into shape, they were trying to find out how far they could push us until we died. When we were done with the run they allowed us to go back upstairs to take a shower so we could eat and get ready for class.

Class was from 8 a.m. until noon. We then ate lunch and had to be back in class at 1 p.m. We stayed in class until 4 p.m. Then it was time for more physical training. This lasted until 5 p.m. at which time we were allowed to take another shower and go to supper. At 6 p.m. we returned to class until 8 p.m. We got two hours for study and then it was lights out at 10:30 p.m.

Once the lights were out I had to find a way to sleep in a building with 140 other men. About the time I got to sleep, someone would start snoring, coughing, farting, or get up to use the restroom. Most of the time it would take me until about Wednesday night to get to the point where I could actually get some sleep.

After a few weeks of this daily regimen, I finally found out why they wanted us to weigh in that first day. They put all the cadets into weight categories. Those classes consisted of small, medium, big, and really big guys. We were told that we were going to do a little boxing to help get us into shape. I still remember the overpowering smell of the alcohol when we walked into the gym.

DPS had done this before. They had put out two white pans like you would see in a doctor's office. One pan was full of mouthpieces in alcohol. The other held water. When it was your turn to get your brains kicked in, you were instructed to reach into the alcohol and take out a mouthpiece. You then took the mouthpiece and dunked it in the water so you could stand to put it in your mouth. Then the fighting started.

I would not call what we did boxing. It was more or less street fighting. It was very obvious that DPS was trying to see which of the cadets would stand and fight and would take care of their partner if they ever got out on the street. Every week each cadet had to be weighed to see what class they had to fight in during that week. I was in the medium class, just under the bigger class. Now when it was my turn to weigh in, I would take everything out of my pockets to make sure that I did not have to fight in the Big Guy class. Anyway, we all had to fight three or four fights. We lost a lot of people out of the class because they could not cut it when it came to protecting themselves.

Around the sixth week of the academy it became obvious to the people around me that there was something wrong with my right leg. I had been wrapping and taping it to be able to run on it, but the leg got so swollen that my calf was bigger around than my thigh. I was sent to the DPS physician, who determined that the big bone in my lower leg was cracked, and the little one broken.

I was given the option of dropping out and joining the next class, or continuing with my class. If I continued, I would still have to do PT. The one concession was that while my classmates ran, I could do sit-ups and push-ups—continuously. After all, I was supposed to maintain the same level of activity as the rest of the group. I opted to stay with my class.

Did I mention that spelling was never one of my best subjects? DPS gave us a list of thousands of words, and each week they gave us several tests. I had to try to stay several hundred words ahead on the list to pass.

As the weeks went by, more and more people left the training. You would be in class and the back door would fly open. Someone's name would be called and they would stand and leave, never to be seen again.

The $50 a month we had to pay for uniform cleaning nearly cost my career. When I got my paycheck, I would take it to my new wife so she could put it in the bank while I was in class the next week. Back at the academy after a weekend off, I was sitting in class when Floyd Hacker, then head of the DPS Academy, barged in and yelled for Doyle Holdridge to get his books and come with him.

I went to Hacker's office, and he told me that the check I had written for my cleaning had bounced. I never have

27

forgotten what Hacker said. He asked one question: "How do you expect the State of Texas to let you handle their business when you can not even handle your own?"

I was allowed to call my wife and learned that she had forgotten to put the check in the bank. It was still on top of the icebox. For the rest of the academy I cleaned out the bathrooms to help me remember not to write hot checks to the DPS.

When I first went to the academy I did not even know that the Texas Rangers were part of the Department of Public Safety. As our training got more specific several Rangers came into class and gave some lectures related to criminal investigation. I learned that it was possible to promote up through the ranks and at some point have the chance of making Ranger. That's when I decided I wanted to be one of those guys with a silver star on his chest. I remembered what Dad had told me all those years before and I could not believe that I had put myself in a position where I might actually have a shot at being a Ranger. I made up my mind that I was going to do whatever it took to reach my goal. I knew that I was going to have to work a lot more than the next guy because I didn't feel that I had the educational background. Like my high school coach taught me, I would have to get mean. From that day forward that's what I tried to do.

I had never tried as hard to do well at anything as I did in the DPS Academy and it paid off in the long run. We started the class with about 140 men and 83 graduated. My mother and father came to the ceremony in Austin and at that point in my life I thought I had it made. I had a job where I would be warm in the winter and cool in the summer. On top of that I would be paid nearly $700 a month. I was ready to make the world safe for democracy and everything else.

Texas Highway Patrol

My class graduated from the academy on April 6, 1973 and I was assigned as a Highway Patrolman at Fort Hancock, a small community fifty-five miles east of El Paso just off Interstate 10. They could have put me in Houston and I wouldn't have been farther from home. Highway Patrol Captain Hugh Shaw had chosen me for the Fort Hancock duty station because Cindy and I lived in a ten by fifty-foot trailer house. There was no housing available in Fort Hancock, so the fact that I had a trailer made me overly qualified to be the new guy at that duty station. I had five days to report for duty.

Cindy and I went back to San Angelo to make arrangements to move. We hired a trucking company to pull our trailer the three hundred miles to Fort Hancock, and I called my soon-to-be partner to get his assistance in finding a lot to park the trailer. When we got there, I found that my partner had made arrangements for me to park the trailer on a vacant lot on the old highway that ran through town, U.S. 90. Fort Hancock, named after an old cavalry post abandoned in the 1890s, had one service station, one café, a motel, and a general store. My wife was not impressed.

After we set up the trailer I discovered that there were no sewage lines in the area. I had a backhoe operator dig a six-foot-deep hole, covered the hole with tin, and I ran a line to it from the trailer. This worked well as long as the wind blew the right direction.

My wife and I did not have a washing machine, so we had

29

to make weekly trips to Fabens to use a coin laundry. A person could get the basics you needed to live at Fort Hancock, but we had to drive to El Paso for groceries, medicine, or entertainment. I really don't know how Cindy put up with the living conditions. She was twenty and had been a city girl all of her life. I worked most of the time and she just stayed around the house waiting for me to return. On my days off we almost always went into El Paso for no other reason than to get out of Fort Hancock.

The state pays its employees once a month. It takes a while to get your life in sync with that program, but after thirty-two years I finally got the hang of it. Toward the end of the month DPS people always watch what they spend their money on. It's just the DPS way. If your wife doesn't work, you have to find a way to make it to the end of the month.

In those days people didn't depend on credit cards. Either you had the money to buy something or you did without. That's just the way it was. We didn't have the money, so we did without things most of the time. My grandmother had given me a small part of her oil royalty when I got married, but the money was nothing to get excited about. I had a little more than the other DPS officers who I worked with, but we still just got by. We spent everything we made each month and never really thought about trying to save for a rainy day.

The day I turned twenty-one Cindy and I went to a café in El Paso and I bought my first legal beer. I thought I had really put my life together. I had a job that I was proud of, I was making a lot more money than my dad, and I had just turned twenty-one. How could things get any better? After Cindy and I got our housing arrangement set up and got into a living routine I began to learn how to be a Highway Patrolman. (After the department started hiring females, the DPS started calling its uniform officers troopers.)

My first partner was a lot older than I was. His name was Mike Greer, and as I later found out, one of the best officers who I ever had the honor of working with. Mike had been a Highway Patrolman for several years and was very good at what he did. He had already led the state in stolen car apprehensions. Mike could read a VIN number off a car, wait a while, and still remember it to run it through NCIC (the National Crime Information Center) and TCIC (Texas Crime Information Center) to see if was stolen. It always amazed me how he could do that.

My first day on the job came on the night shift. At one point after driving me around a while showing me the area he pulled over and turned off the lights. "Where are we?" he asked. I had no idea. Mike told me that it might be good to keep my head out of my ass in case we got into trouble so I could tell someone where to come to help us. That's another one of those things that I have never forgotten.

Those first few months as a Highway Patrolman were very stressful. I was trying to learn what I needed to do my job well. Mike spent most of the time trying to teach me things that would keep me alive while doing that job. One of the biggest dangers in working traffic on a major highway like Interstate 10 is the possibility of getting run over by a passing motorist. In those first couple of years I cannot remember the number of times I had to run for the ditch or jump on the hood of a violator's car to keep from getting hit. After a while, you just got to the point that you accepted the risks as part of the job.

A few weeks after I got out of the academy, Mike and I were working traffic on the interstate about 10 miles west of Sierra Blanca in Hudspeth County. I was riding shotgun with Mike in the lead. I hadn't even got to the point that Mike trusted me enough to let me drive or write tickets.

As we drove toward Sierra Blanca both of us noticed that a driver on the westbound side of the highway was trying to wave us down. We pulled over next to the motorist to see what was up. A man neither one of us knew said he had been driving just past the U.S. Border Patrol checkpoint when he saw a

31

vehicle parked along the fence line. The witness told us that he watched a guy unload several bundles of marijuana from the trunk of his Ford, pile them in a low spot in the ditch and then drive off toward the checkpoint. The witness told Mike and I that he thought the guy was going to see if the Border Patrol had the checkpoint open and then return for the dope if it was not staffed.

We thanked him for the information and got back into our patrol car as fast as we could. Mike decided we would try to catch the guy when he returned to pick up the marijuana. We were about eight or ten miles from where the dope had been hidden so we drove to the area as fast as we could.

When we pulled up I saw two vehicles, two men and a large pile of dope in the ditch. I opened the door and stood up out of the patrol car. I noticed that one of the guys had a pistol in his hand and stood facing us. The other man had this look on his face like he had just shit his pants. Mike yelled at me that the man had a gun, but I had already seen it.

I looked the whole thing over and it was clear to me that another John Doe citizen had affected a citizen's arrest and was holding the doper until the law arrived. I ran up to the guy who didn't have the gun, turned my back on the one who did and pushed the crook to the ground. All the time I was doing this Mike was taking care of the man with the gun. Sure enough it was just like I thought. A local resident had witnessed the doper start to load the marijuana into his vehicle and pulled a handgun to hold the guy until the police got there.

We arrested the doper, loaded the marijuana and headed to the Hudspeth County Sheriff's Office. I was so excited that I didn't know what to do. This was my first load of dope. I had only been working a short time and I already had helped make a big bust. We put the guy in the county jail and weighed the dope. After we processed the packaged marijuana we took photos to use in court. I thought that I had done everything right. Boy was I wrong.

Mike never said a word until we were on the way home to Fort Hancock. Then he asked me one question: How did I know for sure that the guy with the gun was not the doper? The reality of the situation came to me all at once. *I didn't know.* Not only could I have been killed but I had put my partner in a position where he had to come out in the open to cover his dumb-ass rookie partner while he played Superman. I realized that I had to make better decisions because my life and the life of my partner depended on it. Mike Greer had taught me a lesson that stayed with me the rest of my career: When a law enforcement officer makes a decision people's lives hang in the balance. You had better make the decision based on known facts and not gut feelings. Mike probably doesn't even realize all the things he taught me but I really try hard to remember ways to not get killed.

Of course, it took me years to fully appreciate how much some of the men I first worked with affected the way that I have done business as an officer. When I started with the DPS, it was a lot different than it is now. If they told you to do something, you did it. There was no overtime or comp time for the extra work. DPS wanted a good day's work for the pay that they gave you. If you worked extra and did well at your assignment, you got to keep your job, that's all.

The older officers I was around instilled in me a work ethic that I still have. They were from the old school. They were doing the job because they believed in what they were doing. They were working for the good people of the State of Texas. The way they saw it, someone had to stand up for the good people. If they had to make sacrifices with their personal lives, that's what they did. I think that's the way things should still be.

During my career with DPS, if I heard people bitching about bad working conditions at the department, I would tell them that I couldn't really complain because I had been herding sheep before I hired on. I don't think they really believed me, but that was the truth. After seeing what Dad had gone through, I thought there wasn't a better job in the world than the one I had. I couldn't believe that they actually paid me good Yankee dollars to do something I enjoyed as much as working for DPS.

Mike Greer, Mike Wohleking and Doyle with load of marijuana in Hudspeth County. This was my first load of marijuana, seized in 1973.

When I arrived at my new duty station I was still a young man but the DPS demanded that an officer act like a full-grown man. I went into DPS as a twenty-year-old who still acted like

34

a boy at times. Five months later I was expected to act like an adult. That's where men like my partner Mike Greer, Hudspeth County Sheriff J. C. "Cowboy" Stubbs, Ranger Clayton McKinney of Alpine and Culberson County Sheriff Richard Upchurch came into play. They provided me with guidance and advice on what was expected of me from the day I got there.

There is really no way to explain what it's like to take on the job of being a Texas Highway Patrolman at twenty. For one thing, up to that point in my life I had never seen a dead person. Well, I saw a lot of them after I went to work. The wrecks we investigated were often bad, and the things we saw were a real shock to me. I still remember a lot of those wrecks all these years later. One happened just before Christmas. A whole family, including children, got killed. Christmas gifts had been strewn all across the highway.

You never get used to having to make a death notification. When you have to tell a mother and father that little Johnny is dead and is never coming home, it stays with you the rest of your life. I have been doing that kind of thing all these years and it still bothers me. It's one of the worst jobs a peace officer has to do.

Tommy Powell

After I had worked around Fort Hancock for a while I began to meet some of the people who lived and worked in the area. Fort Hancock had a few local residents and a lot of U.S. Border Patrolmen assigned to the area. My partner had told me the Border Patrol would give us a box of .38 Special wad cutters ammunition for each illegal alien we found and brought to them. At the time Mike was on the DPS pistol team, so he could always use the ammo. I didn't have the money to buy target-shooting rounds, so every time we found illegal aliens, we turned them in to the Feds.

Lots of illegal aliens came through the area, so we always had plenty of ammo to practice with. On our days off there was really nothing to do, so I would go into the desert and practice with my service weapon. I was young and really interested in my job, so I also spent a lot of time looking around my area to see what I could learn about it.

In patrolling our area, at times Mike and I drove out to Tommy's Town, located between Fort Hancock and Sierra Blanca on Interstate 10. Tommy's Town had a total population of two—Tommy and Marie Powell. They were right out of one of those old movies where an old man and woman have a one-pump gas station out in the middle of the desert. Tommy handled the gas station and Marie ran the restaurant, if you wanted to call it that. They didn't really like anyone except Highway Patrolmen and sheriff's deputies. Tommy was somewhere between sixty or seventy at the time, and Marie was about the same age.

Tommy wouldn't weigh 120 pounds with a big rock in each pocket. He only shaved or combed his hair about once a week. Most of the time he looked like he had worn the same clothes for at least several days. He always wore a cook's apron, and he let the part that should have been around his neck hang down the front of his pants. When I first met Tommy, my partner had warned me that he was mean as a snake. Mike told me that Tommy let the apron hang to his knees in the front for a very good reason. He always carried a cocked and locked Colt .45 Model 1911 stuck down the front of his pants, and he had been known to use it on several occasions. The apron covered the old Army-issue semiautomatic.

Marie was also well-heeled, carrying a Smith & Wesson .38 Special in her dress pocket. The gas station and the café were in separate buildings about twenty yards apart. Tommy and Marie slept in the back part of the cafe. Tommy had wired the gas station so when he closed at night, he could turn on a speaker and hear in his bedroom everything that was going on in the station. He was always calling the sheriff's office or the Highway Patrol to tell them he had apprehended someone trying to break into the station.

Mike told me that if and when I got one of those calls, to make sure when I pulled up that Tommy knew it was me, and that I should not just walk up on him. Once Tommy got stirred up, he said, it was really important that I do this. Otherwise, a fellow (meaning me) could get hurt.

As I worked the area for the next few months, I found out a little more about Tommy. I was in the sheriff's office in Sierra Blanca one day when I overheard Ranger McKinney and Sheriff Stubbs talking about the last guy Tommy had killed. I could tell by the conversation that there had been more than one. In the most recent case, Tommy had closed his station and he and Marie had gone to bed. As always, he had turned on his speaker so he could hear if someone was trying to break into his gas station.

Sometime that night, a guy drove up and parked near the station, probably thinking this would be an easy score. He was mistaken. After breaking into the station he was in the process of leaving when he ran right into a little man with a short-barreled 12-gauge. Tommy tried to get the guy to surrender but the burglar figured he could take the scattergun away from such a frail-looking old man. When the intruder grabbed the shotgun by the barrel, Tommy pulled the trigger.

When the first sheriff's deputy arrived he found Tommy squatted on his heels still holding his shotgun on what was left of the burglar. The guy was DRT, dead right there. The district attorney took the case to the grand jury and it took them only a short time to no-bill Tommy. The opinion of the panel was that the crook should have known better than to mess with Tommy Powell.

Over the next year, Tommy and I got to be good friends. Tommy really liked Highway Patrolmen, apparently because law enforcement types were the only people who paid any attention to him. I had noticed that Tommy had an old picture hanging in the station of a baby-faced young man in uniform and a campaign hat standing beside a mule. The picture had a round frame with bubble glass. It appeared to have been taken sometime during the early 1900's.

When I was working in the area, I would often stop by the station to get something to drink. Tommy would never let an officer pay for a soda. I usually stayed around the station for a while to talk to him. When Tommy got to know you well enough, he would take you back behind the station and show off his pet, Oscar—a six-foot rattlesnake that Tommy kept in an old well. From time to time he would drop something into the well for Oscar to eat. I don't like snakes. Tommy always got a charge out of messing with me about old Oscar.

Tommy also had a replica of old Fort Quitman, a nearby abandoned cavalry post, that he had built behind the station, and he would charge people to let them go through it. Basically, Tommy was just an old desert rat who made his own way in the world.

One day I finally got around to asking Tommy about the old photo. He told me that was a picture of him when he was sixteen. He had ridden with General "Black Jack" Pershing's soldiers when they went into Mexico after Pancho Villa in 1916. Tommy also told me he had smuggled guns south of the river during the Mexican Revolution. I had always been interested in the Mexican Revolution, so I liked to talk with Tommy about it.

During this time I was still carrying a Smith & Wesson .38 Special that I had bought when I got out of the academy. Tommy told me I really should get me another gun. He went into the back part of the station and came out with a bundled-up old red rag. He unwrapped the rag and handed me an early Government Model Colt .45. Tommy told me to take the old Colt and pay him when I could. He said I could give him sixty bucks for the Colt in payments. That was the first Colt .45 semiautomatic I ever bought. I carried the old gun until I decided to buy a new one. I sold it to a friend I had gone to high school with who was a deputy in Sierra Blanca. That's one gun I would give anything if I had kept.

Several months later I was contacted by the Hudspeth County Sheriff's Office and advised that Tommy had cornered another guy who had been trying to break into his station. I got into my unit and drove to Tommy's Town as fast as I could. When I rolled up I saw Tommy squatting and rocking back and forth with his 12-gauge pointed at someone on the ground.

Thinking Tommy had killed another crook, as I got out of the car I remembered what Mike had told me and yelled at Tommy to make sure he knew it was me. I got no response. Tommy was just rocking back and forth with that 12-gauge on the guy. It was dark, and I yelled again at Tommy to try to get his attention. Tommy finally looked up, and I pointed my flashlight at him so he could tell it was me. The old horse soldier was really stirred up, and it took me a while to get him calmed down. I finally went over to check on the guy. For once Tommy had not shot someone, so I cuffed him and put him in my patrol car.

I told Tommy I was going to take the suspect to jail. As we left, Tommy told the guy he had better not come back, or he wouldn't have to worry about where he was going next time. I drove the intruder to Sierra Blanca and put him in the county jail. I told him that he didn't realize how lucky he had been in his encounter with Tommy. I doubt that he ever understood how close he had come to meeting his maker that night at a lonely gas station in far West Texas.

Over the two years that I worked out of Fort Hancock, I continued to stop every time I went by Tommy's Town just to visit a while. I enjoyed hearing his stories.

I eventually got transferred to El Paso. I never really thought about it until I started writing this book, but I don't think I ever said good-bye to Tommy. I stayed in El Paso a couple of years and I transferred again.

Several years had gone by when I asked a friend who still lived in the area about Tommy and Marie. He told me they both had died. When Marie passed away Tommy never seemed to be the same. He started having heart trouble, and one of his friends took him to the hospital in El Paso. Tommy stayed there a few days, and then called his friend to come pick him up.

When the friend arrived, he found that against doctor's orders, Tommy had just decided to "discharge" himself from the hospital. Tommy asked him to take him home. Before they left El Paso, he had the friend stop at a store so Tommy could buy himself a new suit. The friend then took him back to Fort Hancock. Tommy just sat down in his old chair and died that night. He left a note asking that one of the area Highway Patrolmen preach at his funeral. When they had his service a few days later, I'm told it was hard to believe the number of troopers and other officers who showed up to pay their respects.

I wish I could have been there at the end. That old man had gone out of his way to be my friend, and I will always remember him like he was the last time that I saw him. I don't think they make men like him anymore.

Murder and Manhunt

While I was working out of Fort Hancock, Ranger McKinney handled a case where someone had tied up an old man working as a watchman and killed him. The Ranger developed a suspect who he later learned had been taken into custody in California. The suspect, Edsel Heslip, had been transported back to Hudspeth County and booked into the county jail in Sierra Blanca.

Clayton and Sheriff Cowboy Stubbs had decided they needed more security at the jail so arrangements were made for the area Highway Patrolmen to help out. For the next several days we took turns working around the jail. The sheriff then made arrangements for Heslip to be transferred to Pecos where they had a new jail and better security.

Soon after, Heslip escaped. Just about every officer in West Texas was looking for him. It was common knowledge that he would kill anyone that got in his way.

I was assigned to a roadblock between Van Horn and Sierra Blanca on Interstate 10. For the next day or two we checked every westbound vehicle. We then received word that Heslip had broken into an older couple's home and cut the old man's throat and attempted to rape the older woman, nearly beating her to death. He had stolen the family car and had headed east on the interstate. A Highway Patrolman had gotten into a chase with him near Abilene, and shot the car out from under him. Heslip was taken into custody and again brought back to West Texas.

Over the next few months Heslip was tried for the murder of the older man in Pecos and sent to state prison. He was brought back to El Paso on a change of venue to stand trial for the Hudspeth County murder. During his time in the El Paso County lockup he escaped again, this time with two other inmates. They were apprehended a short time later but Heslip remained on the run. I, along with every Highway Patrolman west of the Pecos River, was set up on a roadblock in an effort to apprehend the escaped killer. He finally showed up at one of the roadblocks on Interstate 10 with a hostage. One of the Highway Patrolmen in my sergeant area shot and killed him, saving the hostage. This happened October 29, 1974.

It was during this case that I first started working around Ranger McKinney. We became good friends over the next few years. Clayton was the best storyteller I was ever around. I think I became a better officer by just being around him and Sheriff Upchurch.

Our Highway Patrol sergeant's office was in the Culberson County Sheriff's Office, and I got to be around Sheriff Upchurch a lot. In those days a lot of the old time county lawmen didn't much like the FBI. Richard always thought the FBI must have been affiliated with the American Civil Liberties Union, and he did all he could to stay away from them.

The sheriff and Ranger McKinney were close friends and worked together a lot. When they arrested people, I often got a chance to watch them interview the suspects. They were really good at that. I saw them get more confessions out of crooks than I can remember. I was impressed that they always treated the defendants with respect. They would spend a lot of time getting to know them before they ever started trying to get the guys to own up to their crime. Clayton and Richard were the best talkers I was ever around.

After watching Clayton conduct interviews, I became really interested in trying to find new and better ways to get

43

suspects to talk with me. Clearly, one of the most important things a Ranger has to be able to do is talk to people.

One time just after I went to work for the department Clayton and I were talking about interviewing people. The Ranger told me about a case in which a man had knocked on the front door of another man's house and got invited inside. While the resident was sitting on his sofa, the visitor walked over and shot him in the head, killing him. The gunman then fled.

Clayton asked me what I thought about the case. I told him the law should hammer the guy. Charge him with murder and send him to prison for the rest of his life. Clayton told me that he had looked for the guy a long time before finally apprehending him. When he asked the man why he had shot the guy in cold blood, the suspect replied that the man had just raped his twelve-year-old daughter.

My expression changed. I thought about it for a while and told Clayton that if I had been in the guy's place I might have done the same thing. I have thought about that conversation a lot over the years. The Ranger had made his point: Work the case as it comes. Don't make your mind up about something until you have all the information. One little statement can make all the difference, and someone's freedom hangs in the balance.

The laws of the State of Texas are made in Austin and are written down in books—but people have to enforce those laws. You can never really take the human part out of the system. If you want to learn about that side of the criminal justice system, at your sentencing tell a state district judge to kiss your ass. I can tell you for sure that you are going to get a very good example. Maybe several additional years of example.

Over the years, these early lessons from Clayton and other older Rangers helped me solve a lot of cases. I wish those men knew how much they did for me by just letting me be around them.

Girly Gun or Colt 1911

When I got out of the academy I went down Lamar Boulevard to McBride's gun shop in Austin and bought me a Smith & Wesson .38 Special to carry off-duty. Over the next few months I began to notice that I was the only one carrying that type of gun. Finally one of the guys asked me when I was going to stop carrying that girly gun and get me a Colt .45 or a Browning Hi Power 9mm. Most of the officers I was around carried a Colt .45 semiautomatic. I bought my first one in 1973 from Tommy Powell at Fort Hancock and have carried one ever since. I asked Ranger McKinney back in those days why he carried a .45 and he told me because they didn't make a .46.

Clayton went out of his way to teach me how the gun worked and the best way to handle it. He always carried a lightweight Commander with what he called Mexican General grips. The grips were Mexican silver with gold designs on them.

All the Highway Patrolmen were required to carry a .357 Magnum revolver on duty, but to a man, the officers I worked with all carried a .45 semiauto under their car seat or off-duty. It was the gun that all others were judged by. For those who wanted a lot of bullets there was the Hi Power. In those days there were not that many sidearms to choose from, but those were the guns I started with. I would either carry the Colt .45 or the Browning Hi Power, depending on what we were doing. The Colt had a lot of knockdown power and the Browning Hi Power held a lot of ammo. Clayton always told me that you should fit the gun you carried to the type of job you were going to be doing. That made a lot of sense to me, and I still do that.

Most all the officers I was around carried the Colt in either the Commander or Government model length. I personally liked the Government model due to the length of the slide. I could stick it in my belt and it would stay put throughout the day. It was flat and easy to hide under clothing.

When I started carrying the gun there wasn't a lot of different ammunition like there is now. When you went to the store you just told them you wanted a box of .45 auto. What you got was 230-grain hardball ammo. I shot a lot of the hardball over the years and I still like to carry it. I have seen several people shot with a .45 and the hardball seems to get the job done. The only thing better than the .45 is some type of large-caliber rifle.

Engraved Colt 1911 .45 Auto

The down side of the Colt 1911 is that you have to spend a lot of time with the gun and get to know it really well. It will bite you if you don't pay attention to details. I have known four officers who accidentally shot themselves with a 1911. One did it twice in six months. Another shot himself through the butt. The round hit the floorboard of the car and bounced in and out of his leg—one bullet, four holes. He took a lot of heat from the other guys for that one.

The Fort Hancock school superintendent and Clayton were good friends, and met two or three times a week at a local café for coffee. During these sessions, Clayton and the superintendent constantly messed with each other. The superintendent always kidded Clayton about carrying his pistol cocked. In response, Clayton would go through the entire safety procedure of carrying a Government model. Still, the superintendent continued to rag on the Ranger about toting a cocked .45.

One day after coffee and yet another argument about the safety issue, when they got in Clayton's car, he drew his .45 and clicked the safety off. The Ranger was in the process of explaining to his friend that you could pull the trigger and the grip safety would still keep the gun from firing when the gun went off. The superintendent yelled at Clayton: "What in the hell are you doing?" Clayton turned, looked at his friend and very calmly said, "It's my car. If I want to shoot a hole in the son-of-a-bitch, I will."

Clayton drove the superintendent back to his school and returned to the café where Mike Greer and I were waiting. He had a neat .45 caliber hole in the front windshield of his car. Later Clayton told us that when he reported the accidental discharge to his supervisor, Captain Jim Riddles just told him to go get a new windshield. In those days, something like that was not a big deal. If you did something like that today, you'd be doing paperwork for the next week.

Loss of a Fellow Officer

During the first summer that I worked the road, my wife and I had gone to San Angelo to visit her family. While there, I was contacted by a patrolman friend who told me that Monroe Scott, one of the guys we had gone to the academy with, had been shot and killed in Houston. We had only been out of school a few months.

I later learned Scott had been working security off-duty at an apartment complex in Houston. At that time the apartment complexes in the Houston area would give officers a break on the rent if they agreed to help with security. Scott was leaving his apartment with his gun when he was confronted by Houston Police narcotic agents. When they saw the gun, the officers shot and killed him.

Scott, who was to have been married in a few days, was the first law enforcement friend I lost since going to work for the DPS and I felt that we had a lot in common. I had a hard time sleeping the night I found out that he had been killed. It was hard for me to understand how someone so young, with so much still ahead of him, could lose his life in such a senseless way. I tried to talk to my wife about it, but I could tell she didn't understand the bond that officers feel for each other even if they don't know one another. It makes you stop and think of how many times you have done the same thing that the officer was doing when he got killed. It made me try to be that much more careful in the way that I did my business.

Highway Patrol Manhunt

As a Highway Patrolman in Fort Hancock I was constantly called out to work after hours. In those days, DPS officers were expected to work their regular shift and remain on call to work whatever came up, twenty-four hours a day. Most of the time we were called out to work wrecks, but sometimes the calls were related to criminal activity in and around the area that we worked. Fort Hancock had only one sheriff's deputy and he was about seventy. The local Highway Patrolman was expected to answer any kind of call that came in.

About 2 a.m. one morning, I was contacted by the DPS radio operator and advised that a van full of marijuana had been running from the Border Patrol when the fleeing vehicle missed a curve and rolled, killing the driver. There were about fifteen hundred pounds of marijuana lying around the wreck scene. Everyone was stirred up about the fact that the dead driver was wearing a shoulder holster and had been armed with a pistol. His partner had crawled from the wrecked van and had fled on foot.

In those days, when someone ran from a load of dope, everyone got after him. The Border Patrol and the local deputy showed up along with Ranger McKinney, and we started to look for the suspect. The Border Patrolmen picked up his trail and started following him through the brush. The wreck had happened about one mile south of Interstate 10 and we knew that the suspect might see the lights from the highway and try

49

and catch a ride. I had a good friend who was a rookie game warden and he had come out to help with the manhunt. Game Warden Royce Wells and I got into the car together and drove up and down the interstate trying to keep the suspect from catching a ride until daylight. We thought that when it got light we would have a lot better chance of catching him.

While Royce and I were riding around we could hear on the radio that the suspect's tracks had crossed the interstate and were now on the north side of the highway. There was a large electrical highline that ran alongside the highway about a hundred yards north of the main road. The Border Patrol was on his trail, but the guy had at least an hour's head start. The Border Patrol finally called us on the radio and told us that it appeared that the suspect had hit a dirt road under the highline and was walking and running west toward El Paso. We continued to hunt him for the next several hours.

Every time the Border Patrol would radio us they would report the suspect still headed west under the highline. Royce and I decided we would drive out in front of the manhunt and cut for sign until we knew that we were ahead of the suspect. We drove down the road, and every mile or so we would stop and Royce would check for tracks under the highline. Every time he'd come back and say he'd seen tracks, so we knew the suspect was still ahead of us, heading west. One of the times Royce got out to check for tracks, he and the suspect walked right into each other.

The suspect had a gun in his hand, but when Royce yelled at him in the darkness, he gave up. We loaded him up and took him back to Fort Hancock. Royce and I were really glad that we had figured out a way to catch him. Royce had done most of the work but it's something that I have never forgotten. That was the first time I personally had anything to do with a manhunt for an armed suspect. I also learned that it made a hell of a lot of difference in the way that you did business when you knew the person you were looking for was armed.

Clayton had a talk with me later and told me that I should never have let Royce walk out to the highline by himself. He said that while in this case everything had turned out well, things could have taken a bad turn if Royce and the guy had gotten into a gun battle while I waited in the car. The Ranger told me that we had done a good job, but next time to make sure we never assigned an officer a job where he might have to confront an armed suspect by himself. This is another one of the lessons Clayton taught me. Officer safety must be taken into consideration all the time. Like Clayton always said, "We want to be the ones who go home at the end of the day."

Hudspeth County Drug Deal

One morning just after we went to work, my partner Mike Greer and I were contacted by Ranger Clayton McKinney and advised that someone had stolen Sheriff "Cowboy" Stubbs' pickup from his residence. "Cowboy" lived out in the country south of Interstate 10 near the Rio Grande. His house sat on a big hill that overlooked the area. You could see for miles from the sheriff's place.

Mike and I drove down the road to meet with Clayton so we could talk with the sheriff about his stolen pickup. As we got near his house we noticed that the sheriff's vehicle was stuck in the mud on the side of the road behind another pickup with a camper shell. At about this time Clayton arrived. As we were looking at the vehicles trying to figure out what had happened we discovered large bags of marijuana under every bush. There appeared to be at least 1,500 pounds of dope hidden in the brush near the pickup.

We decided that the drug smugglers had gotten their pickup stuck in the mud and had gone up the hill and stolen the sheriff's truck to try to push their vehicle out. The dopers had no idea that the vehicle they had stolen belonged to a law enforcement officer, a sheriff at that. They had then gotten the sheriff's truck stuck. Finally realizing they weren't going to free either vehicle, they had hidden the load of dope in the brush.

Clayton thought the dopers would most likely come back for the dope. We decided to hide our own cars in the brush and

52

watch the two trucks in an effort to catch the smugglers if they came back.

The older guys decided that deputy Mike Dutton and I would lie in wait west of the truck and would block the road after the dopers loaded the drugs. Well, we sat on the load for the rest of the day and most of the night. About 11 p.m. we noticed that a vehicle kept driving by checking to see if there appeared to be any heat on the load. A short time later the car drove up and let a guy out near the load. It took them about twenty minutes to load up the marijuana, and Dutton and I were about to go crazy wanting to jump them.

Clayton and Mike finally called us and told us that the dopers were headed our way. Dutton and I pulled our car across the highway so they would have to stop and we could throw down on them and arrest them. As they got closer, they realized what was going on and sped up. It looked like they intended to run over us. Dutton was carrying a Smith & Wesson .44 Magnum and I had my .45 Colt 1911. As they came toward us, both of us opened up on the front of the pickup, hoping to disable it. The dopers swerved into the ditch and flew past us as fast as they could go.

The deputy and I had fired several shots each at the motor of the vehicle, but it went by so fast that we could not tell how many people were inside. Clayton and Mike were right behind them. By the time Dutton and I got into our car, they were gone. I reached down on my belt to get a fresh clip for my pistol and I could not find one. As we started to try to catch up with the chase, I realized I only had a few rounds in my gun. We drove about a mile down the road, and there was the doper's truck, blowing steam out of the radiator.

All the suspects had fled into the brush. I think we caught one or two of them, but I really don't remember the details. One thing I do remember is that when I went back to where the shooting had taken place I found an empty .45 clip lying in the middle of the road. I had shot my pistol dry and changed clips, and didn't even remember doing it. From that day until today, I always have several loaded magazines around my vehicle and in my pockets. One officer asked me once why I always carried so many clips and I told him: "Because I ran out one time." That seemed to satisfy him.

Those days it was really no big deal to shoot a car off the road. If the people ran from you and you thought that they were putting other people's lives in danger, then you did what it took to get the vehicle stopped. It seems to me that we used better judgment in those days. Nowadays, after an incident like that, you'll either get sued or you'll end up with numbers on your chest in the federal penitentiary. At the time we felt that we were standing up for the good people in Texas and we didn't really care what the crooks thought. We told our sergeant about the whole deal and I don't think that he ever even reported it to the lieutenant or captain.

Clayton McKinney and some of the dope seized during investigation of Sheriff's stolen pickup.

54

Fully Automatic Weapons

Back in the day, most of the officers I worked with always had some type of fully automatic weapon to carry as what we called a car gun. Trooper Sugarbear Wohlking had a World War II-surplus M-3 grease gun. Randal Messick carried a .30 caliber M2 carbine with a folding stock. Mike Greer and I carried a .45 caliber Mac-10 and an AR-15. Burley Locklar had an M-16 with a lot of extra magazines. Clayton McKinney had a trunk full of stuff. Most of the time when we got on a manhunt or roadblock, he carried a .45 caliber Thompson submachine gun that belonged to one of the sheriff's offices. Clayton just liked the .45. In those days the DPS issued Highway Patrolmen Winchester Model 94 .30-30's, the same weapon old-time Rangers carried on the border during the Mexican Revolution. The guys I worked with were not satisfied with the lever-action Winchesters, so they came up with whatever they could to get a little more firepower.

The bosses knew we were all carrying the fully automatic weapons, but they never said anything about it. They knew the kind of incidents we got involved in from time to time, and I think they agreed that we needed them. In those days we didn't have a lawyer behind every bush waiting to sue someone, so we got away with it. Most of the automatic weapons were registered through the local sheriff's office where the patrolman was stationed. The officers usually bought them for themselves, but the weapons were registered through the federal Bureau of Alcohol, Tobacco and Firearms (ATF) as belonging to the sheriff's office. No one seemed to mind, and it gave us a lot more firepower in the event that we needed it. The area around Fort Hancock and Sierra Blanca was open desert, and it just made good sense to carry something that would shoot at a distance.

Van Horn Shootout

When I was working as a Highway Patrolman at Fort Hancock we roamed about seventy-five miles in each direction from town. We had a small sergeant area, and were expected to work in every direction to take up the slack for some of the other patrolmen.

Mike Greer and Randal Messick taught me from the very start to hunt fugitives and stolen cars at every opportunity. Most people think that DPS instructs its troopers to write a certain number of tickets. That's not true. I was never told how many tickets I should write. It was like Mike said: "They let us write all we want."

We would always go out and try to make a few contacts (tickets) at the start of the shift. Then the fun began. We started looking for stolen cars or wanted people. All of the guys took great pride in the number of stolen cars they found and the apprehensions they made. Finding a stolen car abandoned on the side of the road didn't count. You had to catch someone in it if you wanted to get credit from your peers for the apprehension.

Interstate 10 is one of the major routes across the southern United States. People who committed crimes in other parts of the nation often traveled that long highway, which stretches from Jacksonville, Florida to Santa Monica, California. They were either going east or west, and they had to drive by us. We were always hearing radio broadcasts from DPS communications to be on the lookout for vehicles and suspects in incidents that happened in other parts of the state. We would note the time and figure how many hours it would take until they could drive to our area. When it got close to that time, the units that were working would get out on the highway and start looking for that particular vehicle. You would not believe how many people we caught using that method. The Highway Patrolmen in my sergeant area always led the state in stolen car apprehensions. They did that because they worked at it, and when new guys like me came on they passed that work ethic on to the rookies. From what I hear it's still that way out there.

One day I was working alone and Sergeant Jack Straley decided he would do a ride-along to see how I was progressing. The sergeant and I were working around Sierra Blanca on Interstate 10 when we overheard a lookout on two black males who had kidnapped a service station attendant in Central Texas. The best that I can remember they were driving a blue two-door Chevrolet.

The sergeant and I both looked at our watch. We determined that if the kidnappers were heading in our direction it would take them six hours to get to our area. We made a mental note of the time, knowing that we needed to start looking for them one hour earlier than that because it might have taken the reporting agency that long to get the word out. Then we went on with our shift.

When the time came we started to look for the kidnappers. We looked for the crooks for the next two hours but finally decided they hadn't headed for our area. We drove to a café in downtown Van Horn where we met with two or three DPS officers and several sheriff's deputies. We hung around the café for a while and the sergeant finally told me to take him back to his car in Sierra Blanca.

He and I had made it only about 10 miles west of Van Horn when we heard one of the Highway Patrolman we had just been drinking coffee with radio for assistance. We didn't know it at the time, but as he and his partner left the café they had seen two black males in a two-door Chevrolet facing them at the one red light in Van Horn. When they turned on the Chevrolet, the chase was on.

During the pursuit one of the suspects pointed a handgun at the DPS unit. As the chase continued, the sergeant and I could hear gunfire whenever they keyed their radio. The gunfire sounded fully automatic. The sergeant and I were driving as fast as we could and were starting to close with the chase. They were headed directly toward us.

We did not know at the time that the two patrolmen had chased the suspects all over Van Horn before they got back on the highway. Now everyone was trying to get to them to help them out. Just as we reached the scene we heard that the unit involved in the chase had been in a major wreck with the suspect's car.

When I got out of my patrol unit and looked at the other DPS vehicle I would have believed it if someone had told me that patrol car had just been dropped out of an airplane. The front of the unit had severe damage. The hood had come off and torn the red lights off the top of the car. The sergeant ran up and found that no one was hurt and that the two Patrolmen had both suspects in custody. Soon a crowd started to grow. Everyone in town wanted to see what all the shooting had been about.

I could tell that the sergeant was upset about something so I stayed out of his way. I finally got one of the troopers off to the side and he told me that the suspects had pointed a gun at him and he had opened up on them with his M16, firing a lot of rounds.

At about this time one of the citizens from town walked up and told me that the troopers had shot his car full of holes back in town. I didn't want to provide that kind of information to the sergeant, so I pointed out the guy with the funny little things on his sleeves. I told the young man to go and tell his story to him. I just sat back and waited to see the sergeant's reaction when he got that piece of information.

Well, it looked like the sergeant had been hit with a thousand volts of electricity. He started looking around to find someone and found me. He told me to drive the young man back into town and ascertain if there were indeed bullet holes in his car. I loaded the citizen into my patrol car and back into town I went.

When we got to Van Horn he directed me to his car, which was parked at a truck stop. The vehicle looked like it had been strafed by a jet fighter. The bullet holes started at the back and went all the way to the front.

While still at the truck stop, several other people approached me about bullet holes in their cars or places of business. Again, I decided that I didn't want to be the one to give that kind of detailed information to the sergeant, so I contacted him on the radio and told him that he should come to my location. He asked me if there were any holes in the car, and I told him that the car looked like it had been in a dogfight with the Red Baron. I stayed there until the sergeant arrived and he told me to go back to the accident scene. We finally got all of the information and I was allowed to go home.

A few days later, the captain came out with a new policy that we were no longer allowed to carry fully automatic rifles in our patrol cars. I think to this day people still kid the two troopers who shot up Van Horn.

Sergeant Straley had transferred from Houston to the Van Horn area because he thought nothing ever happened there. The first three months he was there, six of his troopers were involved in shooting incidents. He found out a little late that he had relocated to one of the most active areas in West Texas. There was always something going on. Despite his desire for peace and quiet, Straley was a really good guy to work for. He took good care of his men and he faded a lot of heat for us with the upper supervisors. I learned a lot working that area.

Fudd's Patrol

I worked with Mike Greer a little more than a year before he transferred to El Paso. My new partner was Scott Warren, a guy I had gone to the academy with. Scott and I worked around Fort Hancock for the next year until I finally transferred to El Paso just to get out of Fort Hancock.

Shortly after I got to my new station, another guy who'd gone through the academy with me moved to El Paso and we became partners. He was a really good to work with, though we did a lot of things that some people might find a little strange.

This guy could do a great imitation of the cartoon character Elmer Fudd. He could carry on a regular conversation in Fudd's distinctive "w"-heavy voice.

In police work, the officer doing the driving decides who gets stopped and whether to write the driver a ticket. We always referred to that person as being the lead. My partner and I always had a good time working together, and when he was the lead he always made me laugh.

From time to time, he would make a traffic stop and proceed with the whole violator contact talking in his Elmer Fudd voice. He would start off with: "Hewwoo! He, he, he, Texas Highway Patwol, he, he! I need to see your dwiver's wicense. De weason dat I stopped wou was that wou were dwiving tooo damn fast."

I was expected to show no facial expression while this was going on. As he wrote the warning ticket he would continue to talk like the guy who liked hunting that wascally wabbit, Bugs Bunny. Meanwhile, the violator would sit there and look at me in disbelief. My partner would finish the traffic stop and we would try to leave before we broke out laughing.

The warning was always written by E. Fudd. Occasionally some crazy citizen would call our sergeant and complain that the Highway Patrol in the area had stopped him and had talked to him like Elmer Fudd. When asked, my partner and I never had any idea who that strange trooper could be.

Hunting Dove and Stolen Cars

During dove season my partner and I would carry our shotguns and bird bags in the trunk of the patrol car. You can usually find dove around water, and there was this really good stock tank that we could go to late in the afternoon. We would normally take off our pistol belts and uniform shirts and lay them on the hood of the car while we knocked down a few birds. We would turn on our outside radio speaker so we could hear if we had any calls.

One afternoon we were really busting a lot of caps when we heard the captain call our unit number. In those days you could tell by the sound on the radio if a unit was close, and the captain's call was really close. The captain asked for our location. Thinking quickly, I asked him for his. He again asked for my location and I again asked him for his. The captain finally told me he was near Fort Hancock and he wanted to meet with us. My partner and I ran for our car and grabbed our shirts and gun belts. We put the dove and the shotguns in the trunk and away we went to meet with the captain.

We met him at the café in Fort Hancock. We were sitting at the table talking with our big boss when I happened to look at my partner, who was sitting just across from me. To my horror, I saw that the nametag on his uniform shirt said HOLDRIDGE. I didn't know what to do. I was sitting there thinking of all the things that the captain might imagine if he noticed my partner and I were wearing each other's nameplates. I got a chance when the captain wasn't looking to catch my partner's attention and discretely point at my nameplate. My partner looked at it and it was like you had shot him in the butt. Fortunately, the captain never noticed. He finally left and both of us changed shirts and had a good laugh about the whole deal. I don't think that the captain would have thought it was very funny if he had noticed.

My partner loved ice cream as much as dove hunting. One night we pulled into a "Stop-and-Rob" just off of Interstate 10 and he had got out to buy some ice cream. While he was making his purchase I observed some bad-looking guys walk out of the store and get into a nearly new car. The car did not fit the guys, so I ran a stolen check on the vehicle. The guys left the parking lot and started toward El Paso. Just as my partner was getting back into the car the DPS radio operator advised that the car was stolen. I pulled out on the interstate and started to try to catch up to it. When I finally caught up, I reached down to turn on the red lights. But my partner would not let me stop the car until he had finished his ice cream. By the time we made the stop we had driven nearly all the way to El Paso, but he did get to finish his ice cream.

As a police officer you have to find a way to deal with the stress and all the bad things you see as part of your job. My partner kept things light, and you never knew what he would pull next. On the other hand, he was a balls-to-the-wall partner and you knew when you were working with him that he would be there if you needed him. He retired as a captain, and the last I heard from him, he's living somewhere in West Texas.

I stayed around the El Paso area for the next few years and continued to work in the Highway Patrol. During this time my first son, Justin, was born.

While working in West Texas I got to be around a lot of really good old-school Rangers. Rangers like Tol Dawson, Pete Montemayor, Joe Coleman, and Captain Riddles. I learned a lot from those guys. Working with them and seeing how they did business did a lot for me later in my career.

During this time I made a lot of friends in the area and from time to time we would all get together and go deer hunting. On one trip Larry Benningfield, Mike Greer, a Border Patrolman named Jim Mann, and I were hunting when our Jeep's brakes went out. Three of us were able to jump out of the vehicle but Jim was killed in the accident. He was a good friend and I enjoyed his company. He knew the border well and I learned a lot from him. He was the second close law enforcement friend that I lost while working for the DPS.

John Oldham

It was about this time that Sergeant Jimmy Nail ordered me to go to the Walls Unit of the Texas Department of Corrections in Huntsville to pick up an inmate being released from prison. The sergeant told me there were warrants pending on the inmate in El Paso County and I was to transport him back to the El Paso County jail.

I left El Paso on July 7, 1974 and was nearly to Austin when I heard a DPS radio broadcast that Highway Patrolman John Oldham had been struck and killed while making a traffic stop on Interstate 20. The report further related that John's partner had seen the whole thing happen and had died at the scene of a heart attack. I could not believe it.

John and I had gone through the DPS Academy together and he had been one of my best friends while we were in training. John was from Brady, and I would always swing by and pick him up on the way to Austin for school. We had lived and traveled together for eighteen weeks and had become very close. I called my sergeant and told him that John had been killed and requested permission to go to the funeral. The sergeant told me to go pick up the inmate and then go by Dallas on my way back to attend the funeral.

When I got there, John's family asked me to be a pallbearer. It was one of the hardest things I'd ever had to do at that point in my life. We buried John with full DPS honors and I transported the inmate back to El Paso as I had been ordered. It was about this time that I began to realize that people, good people, sometimes get killed doing the job that I had chosen to do. I started trying to be even more careful when I was working and to pay close attention to the older officers so that I could learn the do's and don'ts of the job. It's like Dad always said, "Everybody wants to see Jesus but nobody wants to die."

Sammy Long's Death

In 1976 I decided to transfer back into the interior of the state and filled a vacancy in Colorado City. I had a really good partner there, Marvin Keenen, but I did not like the area. I was used to working the border where something was always going on. Nothing ever seemed to happen in Colorado City. All I did was work wrecks and write speeding tickets.

Marvin and I got along fine. He was a good old country boy and he and I liked a lot of the same things. There were four troopers stationed in Colorado City. Most of the time one unit worked days and the other worked nights.

On the night of November 21 I had been working alone and had gone to the Highway Patrol office to do some reports when I received a telephone call from one of the DPS radio operators at El Paso. She said she had just heard that Highway Patrolman Sammy C. Long had been shot and killed just west of my hometown of Rankin.

I could not believe it. I called everyone I knew to try and find out what had happened. I finally ended up going to Rankin the following day to find out for myself.

I learned that two deer hunters had been returning from a hunting trip from West Texas when they noticed a vehicle being driven erratically. From time to time the car would slow down and the hunters would pass it. The hunters would drive along for a while and then the car would blow past them and slow down. This had gone on for a long time. While the vehicle was passing the hunters east of Rankin it attracted the attention of Patrolman Sammy Long, who stopped the car. The two hunters were concerned enough that they pulled into a roadside park to make sure everything was okay.

During the traffic stop the suspect shot Sammy down with a .38 Special. The suspect then took Sammy's .357 Magnum and shot him six more times in the back. All the time the two hunters were across the road trying to get their guns out so they could help Sammy. Just as the suspect finished shooting, one of the hunters shot him down. The suspect died just after he arrived at the hospital in Rankin.

I cannot say how much this affected me. I had known Sammy Long for most of my life, and I could not believe he was dead. This was a really big deal in our part of the world.

The Rangers conducted the investigation and the DPS ended up giving the hunters an award for trying to save Sammy's life. The department never publicized the names of the hunters. I was able to find out through my contacts in the area, but I have never told a single person, and I never will.

I went to the funeral at McCamey. Nearly everyone in the county, as well as officers from all over the state, attended the service. It took me a long time to get over losing Sammy. I knew in my heart that if it had not been for Sammy giving me so many breaks when I was young that I would never have gotten hired by the DPS. Sammy had gone to bat for me during my background investigation, and when I was in training he had come by to see me several times. The last time I talked to him he had told me that he hoped that I was as good in enforcing the laws as I had been in breaking them. Sammy had laughed and slapped me on the back and told me it would be my ass if I did not finish the training. That's the last time I saw him alive.

Moving to Laredo

In late 1976 the DPS got federal funding to beef up its personnel along the border from Del Rio to the Lower Rio Grande Valley. Several hundred Highway Patrolmen put in for the positions. I was lucky enough to be one of twenty selected to work the South Texas area. The department decided to put ten Highway Patrolmen, two Narcotics agents, and a Ranger in Laredo and McAllen to work nothing but stolen cars and drugs. We had two sergeants assigned to supervise us. I moved to Laredo in January 1977.

Laredo was a Highway Patrolman's dream come true. We were allowed to work anywhere we wanted in the Laredo, Zapata, and Hebbronville areas. A lot of people were smuggling drugs through that part of the state and we were expected to catch as many as we could. The first year we seized more than 100,000 pounds of marijuana and recovered eighty-eight stolen vehicles. We had a great time!

I started working with Art Gonzalez. He had been in the Del Rio area and he and I hit it off from the start. We busted a lot of loads of dope together. Art also tried to teach me about South Texas culture. The better you understand the ways of the people in the area, the better the job you could do for the state.

One day Art and his partner along with my partner and I were working Highway 16 north of Hebbronville in an effort to catch a large load of marijuana. In those days, we would just pull over on the side of the road and set up what we called a DL checkpoint.

70

We would check driver's licenses, and if some probable cause came up, we would also look for crooks and dope. Art and I were talking to a guy we had pulled over when another car pulled up behind the first one. Art hollered at the driver and told him that we would be with him in a few seconds. The guy yelled "F--- you!" and sped off. Art and I ran for the car and started to chase him. When we got close to him, the suspect turned his car and crashed it through the fence and drove into the heavy brush. He knew we would not take our patrol car after him. By the time we got to the car the driver was long gone. The vehicle had about five hundred pounds of marijuana in it, but we lost the driver. We called out a DPS chopper but after an extensive search by troopers and the Border Patrol we finally gave up. When we got back to Laredo our sergeant reamed us out and told us that we had better not let anyone else get away. He said that he wanted people arrested, not just drugs with no live body.

A large seizure of marijuana made in Jim Hogg County while working Task Force operations in 1977.

71

A few days later, Art and I were working the night shift on Highway 83 south of Laredo. We saw a large car pull onto the pavement from the river area. The car appeared to be heavily loaded. When we turned around to follow it, the driver of the suspicious vehicle started to run. We chased the car all the way back into town until the road we were on dead-ended. We pulled up, blocked the car, and got out of our unit. The driver then turned around and appeared to be attempting to run over us, so we unloaded on the car's tires. We were not going to take another ass-eating from the sergeant by letting another suspect get away from us. When the car finally stopped, all four doors flew open.

There must have been twelve to fifteen people in the car! We tried to catch them, but illegal aliens can run really fast, especially when you just shot a car out from under them. When we got to the car we opened the trunk and all we found was three more illegal aliens. At least we had something to show the sergeant, right?

Another drug seizure made during operations in Jim Hogg County in 1977.

When the sergeant got there he was really upset that we had shot the car off the road, until we reminded him that we hadn't let this one get away. DPS did an investigation into the shooting and found we were justified in what we did. I learned a lot from this incident. A person could really get into trouble doing this job if he did not use good judgment. Experience is not making the same mistake twice. Just because something looks like a duck doesn't mean it's a duck. We assumed that the car was carrying a big load of dope and it turned out to be illegal aliens trying to get into the United States to work. As far as the law and DPS policy, we had done nothing wrong, but I personally felt that I had put peoples' lives in jeopardy. I never made that mistake again.

River Surveillance

While we were working around Laredo we were sent to Starr County several times to assist in running raids and search warrants related to criminal investigations being handled by our Narcotics agents. In 1977 most of the drugs brought into South Texas came through Starr County. Those of us on the Task Force referred to Starr County as "Occupied Texas." There were a lot of good people there, but also a lot of dope dealers, and everyone knew it.

My partner and I worked a lot in the northern part of Starr County. There were people in the area who lived in $300,000 to $400,000 homes, and yet they seemed to be unemployed. You could tell who was involved in moving drugs. They drove brand-new pickups and always had fancy anteater or ostrich cowboy boots. They also wore a lot of heavy gold jewelry.

We always joked that the dealers seemed to have put on their outfits to say "STOP ME." They really stood out from the normal folks. When we first began stopping the drug dealers, most of them carried pistols. They carried either a Browning Hi Power or a Colt type automatic. Just like us. We put a lot of those guys in jail for carrying handguns.

After a while the crooks wised up and started carrying AR-15's because they knew it was not a violation of the law in Texas to carry a rifle around. The only way that we could keep them from carrying a rifle was if they were a convicted felon. In that case they ended up in the county jail.

At the time we had ten troopers assigned to Laredo and ten

to McAllen. On Saturday nights, we would start at the Starr County line and head south. The McAllen troopers would also start at the county line and head north.

We raided every bar in Starr County just to keep the drug dealers on their toes. We entered the bars in groups and searched everyone. We always found pistols and drugs on the floor under the tables of the bars. We also arrested a lot of people for carrying weapons and drugs. That's the way it was done in those days. We had been sent to South Texas to try to stop the flow of drugs into the state and we did everything that was legal to try to get the job done.

Each of the Task Force offices had a Narcotics sergeant and a Highway Patrol sergeant. The troopers worked for both. The Narcotics sergeant in Laredo was Dennis Vickery, a long time DPS officer. We all referred to him as the Imperial Wizard. Sergeant Vickery was a hard-core guy. He had worked the streets for a long time and knew what he was doing.

About six months after we arrived in Laredo, Sergeant Vickery contacted me and said he had developed an informant in Starr County. He told me that the informant worked on several ranches on the river and knew where the drug dealers were crossing the loads of marijuana. The sergeant said he wanted a cowboy type guy, meaning me, to go into Starr County in plain clothes. He wanted me to go around with the guy and map out the area so we could put teams on the crossings to intercept the dealers.

The assignment sounded good to me. I got in touch with the informant—I'll call him Butch—and made arrangements to meet with him in Starr County. We hit it off from the start. At one point the drug dealers had shot up his house so he'd stay out of their business. Butch liked the Colt .45 auto as much as I did. He carried one all the time. Truth be told, he carried two all the time. He had one on his belt, and one on his saddle.

Over the next five or six weeks Butch and I walked and rode the river looking for drug crossings. They were not hard to find. As we moved along the river, we would find areas where you could tell that a boat had been pulled up on the bank. We could always find drag marks in the mud where the sacks of marijuana had been pulled up on the bank on the Texas side of the river. At times, we would find marijuana plants around the crossings growing eight to ten feet tall.

There were always a lot of footprints around the area, especially on the trails leading up and away from the river. The dealers used those trails to walk the dope up to a waiting vehicle, house, or barn. The drugs were then moved out of the area.

A lot of brush grew near the river where we were working, but as you moved inland, most of the area had open fields that the local farmers used to grow their crops. There were always houses near the fields. We knew that the only way to work the area was to put in a team and leave them in there for several days.

The drug dealers had one hell of an intelligence network. They were always on the lookout to see who was going into their territory. They never wanted to be surprised, but no one realized what we were up to. Butch and I created maps of the area that we intended to work. We numbered the crossings and planned how we could get in without the dopers knowing that we were there. We knew that we might have to walk miles to get into the area without being seen. Butch told me that he would start checking the crossings, and when he developed a pattern he would contact me in Laredo so we could move in a surveillance team.

I was amazed at the number of crossings we found. I finally felt that it was time for us to make our move. I again met with Sergeant Vickery and told him about the plan we had developed. He said that he would request that volunteers be selected for the surveillance team. Troopers Glen Deason and Rex Akins said they wanted to be part of the team. Both were the kind of guys you wanted around. They were probably better at this kind of thing than I was. Both of them worked out all the time and tried to stay in shape.

Trooper Rex Akins and Doyle in 1977 during surveillance along the Rio Grande in Starr County. In those days we would stay on the river for days.

We contacted U.S. Customs to let them know that we were going to be on the river, and they assigned officer Bill Matthews—a former DPS officer—to assist us with the surveillance. We contacted the Army National Guard in Laredo, and they agreed to loan us some night vision equipment and military P-Sets. A P-Set is a ground sensor that you can set up next to a trail, and it will send a signal to a headset letting you know when there is movement in the area.

Sergeant Vickery informed us that the first surveillance would last five days. We were to be dropped off in the area where Butch had detected recent activity. All we had to do now was wait for his call. It didn't take long. Butch soon told us that two of the trails we had found were being used at least twice a week. We quickly got everything ready. We had to carry enough food and water to last us five days. We all wore camouflage, packs with food, water, and our weapons. We had decided to maintain radio silence and would only check in on the radio twice a day. The rest of the time we would leave the radio turned off.

I don't want to go into the way that we got into the area. I'll just say that the dopers would never have expected us to have used that method. When we arrived in the area of operation, we were actually within two hundred yards of the drug dealers' homes. At night we could hear them talking, and we could hear their dogs barking.

We entered the area in the middle of the night. We moved out near the river and placed the motion sensors next to the trails we intended to watch. We then crossed the open fields, brushing away our tracks, and found a good spot about two hundred yards from the river to hide out. We could move around a little at night, but when daylight came, we could not even stand up. We had taken several paperback books to read during the day to help us pass the time. The bugs and the heat nearly ran us crazy.

The first three days passed without incident. On the afternoon of the fourth day, we noticed someone walking around the fields as if he was chopping brush on the fence line. But we could tell by the way he moved around that he wasn't really working. It appeared that he was checking for heat, seeing if there was anyone in the area. We watched the guy for several hours until it got dark.

As darkness came, we began to monitor the motion

sensors to try to detect any movement at the crossings. Then it happened. The sensors began to sound the alarm. We knew the trails that the sensors were on, and we only had to move a short distance to set up an ambush. The four of us moved as quietly as we could to the two trails to see if we could intercept anyone.

Before long, I was sitting next to the trail in total darkness. With night vision on, I was watching the trail to make sure that I would see the dopers coming. I had been sitting there for what seemed to be a long time when I got this strange feeling that I needed to look behind me. Glancing over my right shoulder, I nearly fainted.

At least ten guys carrying bags of marijuana were walking down the trail within two feet of me. I couldn't move because I knew that they would hear me. At about this time Customs Officer Matthews stood up and yelled "U.S. Customs!" The next thing I knew, it looked like there were ten sacks of marijuana hanging in the air.

Trooper Deason and I started chasing one of the guys, and we tackled him and placed him under arrest. We got the guy handcuffed and started to walk him back up the trail. We sat the guy down next to the bags of marijuana. It appeared that we had busted somewhere around six hundred pounds. We made radio contact with DPS Communications and arranged for our pickup. While we waited for them to arrive, we got to talking about the fact that there might be a boat down on the river. We decided that we would leave officer Matthews with the suspect, and the other three of us would walk down the trail to see if we could find the boat that had crossed the dope.

Troopers Deason, Akins, and I started working our way down the trail toward the Rio Grande, trying to be careful because we knew that there were still a lot of suspects in the area. Just as we came into a right hand turn in the trail, we walked face to face in the dark with another group of at least ten guys carrying bags of marijuana on their shoulders. I had the night vision goggles on and I could see that one of the guys had a pistol in his right hand. As I yelled "GUN," the guy with the pistol brought it up and pointed it directly at me, Deason, and Akins.

I raised my Browning 12-gauge shotgun, pushed the safety off and started the trigger pull. The next thing I knew, there were another ten bags of dope floating in the air and everyone was running in every direction. Deason, Akins, and I chased the guy with the gun, and I saw him throw it down. We tackled him and took him into custody. I walked back to where I saw him throw the gun. I found that what I had thought to be a gun was a gourd. The gourd looked amazingly like a handgun. I have no idea why he was carrying the gourd, or why he had pointed it at us when we ran into each other.

To this day I don't know why the shotgun didn't go off. It all happened in an instant. I had my sight picture, started my trigger pull, and then he was gone. I knew if I had fired at that range I would have killed the guy. I would have had to explain why I had shot someone for pointing a gourd at me. We ended up making two arrests and seizing somewhere around 1,500 pounds of marijuana.

Those river surveillances were really hard on officers. But in those days, that's the way we did business. No one ever thought about overtime, comp time or working for days in a row without going home. That's just the way we worked.

Our Task Force troopers worked a lot of similar operations over the next two years. Most of the time when we went to the river, we busted dope. Butch worked with us over the next two years. He was taking such a risk because he cared about his community and he was trying to do what he could about the drugs being smuggled into Texas and the United States.

Butch no longer lives in Starr County. I still see him from time to time, and I have known him now for more than thirty years. I wish we had more people like him. Sergeant Vickery helped us buy him a brand new Colt Gold Cup .45

semiautomatic. From time to time I still see him carrying that old Colt. I know that he wouldn't take for it. He earned it the hard way. He gambled with his life to help us. I have never forgotten that.

Doyle, Glen Deason and Rex Akins as Highway Patrolmen with approximately 1,000 pounds of marijuana seized in Starr County. Seizure took place in 1977 during DPS Task Force operation along the Rio Grande.

Rio Grande Shootout

A new mall had just opened in Laredo, and I had gone with five or six other troopers to have lunch at the new cafeteria. We had all just finished eating when I received a call from DPS Communications. A gun battle was taking place about two hundred yards east of the new International Bridge in downtown Laredo. All the troopers ran to their cars. When we arrived at the scene, almost every officer in Laredo was on the riverbank

When I say on the riverbank I mean in the brush, along side the river. I approached a group of Border Patrolmen to try to find out what was going on. They told me that a senior Border Patrolman had taken two rookies to the river to show them the Rio Grande. While the senior agent was instructing the new hires, he noticed a boatload of people headed toward the U.S. side of the river.

The three Border Patrolmen hid in the brush and waited for the people to arrive on our side. Just as the boat reached the riverbank, the Border Patrolmen stepped out and identified themselves. The man seated in the front of the boat rose up with a M1 carbine and opened fire on the three federal agents.

That's when everything went to hell in a hand basket. The boat turned around and headed back toward Mexico. By this time the Mexican police got in on the fun and started to shoot at the boatload of people. The boat nosed into a small island in the middle of the river and all of the illegal aliens ran for the brush. This was about the time that we arrived.

The guy with the carbine would shoot at the officers on our side for a while, and then he would shoot at the Mexican officers. The problem was that the Mexican police tended to shoot back, if for no other reason than to hear their guns go off. The shooting finally came to an end when the guy on the island ran out of ammunition. The Mexican authorities got a boat out to the island and took the guys into custody. Amazingly, despite all the shooting, no one was injured.

I still have the newspaper clippings of the front-page photo, showing a group of troopers in the brush during the incident. When it was over, we told Sergeant Vickery (the Imperial Wizard) about the incident. He told us to get back out on the road and go to work. I don't think we even wrote a report, since we had not actually been involved in the fight. It's like I've said for years, when you work the river, any place else is boring.

Over the next several months, I worked with several partners and we busted a lot of stolen cars and loads of dope. I stayed on the Task Force for two years, and then we started hearing that the operation was going to end. I had gotten to work around a lot of DPS Narcotics agents and Rangers and I knew that I did not want to go back to West Texas and have to start writing tickets and working wrecks again.

I realized that I was more interested in investigations. With my accumulated time in service with DPS, I was eligible to test for possible promotion to the DPS Narcotics Service, and that's what I decided to do. I studied for the next few months and took the test for DPS Narcotics agent. I made Narcotics and was assigned to El Paso. I moved there from Laredo January 1979.

Narcotics

At this point in my life, I had a wife and two sons. My second son Jared was born in 1978 while I was stationed in Laredo. A promotion in DPS usually meant that you had to move your family to a new duty station. Sometimes it would be in the same area, but most of the time it was all the way across the state. This was always hard on the officers' families.

An officer would have to take his kids out of school and if his wife had a job, she would have to quit. Then there was the trouble of selling the home you had, and trying to come up with the money to purchase a new one. I have seen numerous officers who attempted to go to their new duty station without their family end up divorced. It was one of the things that you knew: If you wanted to promote, you did it the DPS way.

When we arrived in El Paso we set up our new homestead and I started to work. I was assigned to work undercover and attempt to buy dope and develop information on area drug-dealing operations. There were four agents and a sergeant in the office I worked from. Going back in El Paso was like coming home. I had worked the first few years of my career there, and I still had a lot of friends in the area. I knew the sheriffs and deputies in the area and a lot of the guys that worked for the police department.

Narcotics agent Ronnie Stinnett and I were good friends and had both worked the El Paso area as troopers. Now Ronnie was longhaired and looked like a younger Willie Nelson. My sergeant assigned me to work with him and learn the ropes.

Ronnie was one of the best undercover guys I ever worked with. When he was in character he really did look and act like a crook. He was also well known within DPS circles as being a major pack rat. He would pick up anything that he found on the side of the road. I cannot count the times he would find something and say, "I need this in my business." No one ever could figure out what his business was or where he kept all the junk that he picked up. He just thought he needed it.

Over the next few years Ronnie and I bought a lot of dope together. We also put a lot of people in prison. I thought it was funny that Ronnie always carried his buy-money rolled up with rubber bands around it. He would keep the roll of money in his sock. He'd always say: "Just because you are paranoid doesn't mean that they are not creeping up on you."

Though we had fun working dope deals, the stress and strain that it put on the family really took its toll. With only four agents assigned to the area, and it seemed that we worked day and night.

Dope dealers never do anything on time. If they tell you that they will meet you at 2 p.m., then you are lucky if they show up at 5 p.m. Actually, you're lucky if they show up the same day.

Informants are a whole other thing. Some are trying to work off a charge to get out of a legal bind, and others are just trying to take out the competition. Our job was to use the information they gave us without getting them killed while doing it, and to make good arrests and seize a lot of dope. Simple, right?

The reporting system was a major complication. When you made an arrest it would take days to write the reports and get everything ready to turn in to the district attorney. You would also have to appear in court to testify against the people you had arrested.

In the case of the El Paso duty station, we always had police agencies from all over the United States requesting our assistance in their investigation so they could put their case together, since the dope they seized was coming from our area. We worked almost continuously. Our area of responsibility was from the Pecos River west to El Paso. If you don't think that's a lot of area, look at a map of Texas.

Ronnie, Clete Buckaloo and I did a lot of undercover work together. Clete was the kind of guy you wanted around when it was time to run a search warrant or do a buy-bust. He would later become a Ranger Captain and I would work for him the last few months that I was a Ranger.

Doyle and future Ranger Captain Clete Buckaloo working together in 1979. Photo shows a large amount of cocaine seized by Doyle and Clete while working undercover in El Paso County while both were DPS Narcotics agents.

Clete, Ronnie, and I were always messing with the new guys that came into the office. When a rookie DPS agent would show up in our office, we would tell him that one of the other guys in the office was gay. We would take great joy in telling him that he should really watch out for the guy who happened to be this month's "gay" guy. We would run the scam out over several days and tell him to be really careful when he was alone on surveillance with him.

It was fun sitting back and watching how the rookies would act for the next few days while they were around the victim we had singled out. At the time our sergeant didn't know what was going on, but after we had done this several times, he caught on. He was a good sport about the whole thing, but we knew not to push our luck.

There was one particular heroin dealer that Ronnie, Clete, and I had been after a long time. He lived in a two-story house, and the bottom of the house was built like a fort. All the doors and windows were steel, and it always took us a long time to get into the house when we ran a search warrant.

We worked on a lot of heroin dealers and had a lot of informants who told us he was the main supplier in the area where he lived. Nearly every agency in town had taken a run at him but had been unable to catch him actually holding dope. The strange thing about his house was that the kitchen was upstairs. While we were breaking into the door we could see the guy standing by the window washing his drugs down the sink. He always got rid of them before we could get in.

Well, we came up with a plan. When we ran out of something to do we would gather up some officers near the noted house. All of us would then drive up to the house, slide to a stop, tires screeching, and run toward the house yelling "POLICE!" We would then stop just short of the front door, turn around, and get back into our cars and drive off.

It was our way of jacking with the guy. If we could not actually catch him, we wanted him to know that we were around. What was the guy going to do, call and complain that we were causing him to destroy his heroin when he thought that we were going to run a search warrant on his house? The guy never said a word. We did this quite a few times.

Heroin Cases

Ronnie Stinnett and I worked so many drug cases together that it got to the point that one of us knew what the other was thinking while we were working undercover. During the time we were partners we bought nearly every kind of dope that was for sale. We became really good friends, and we risked our lives together numerous times. I cannot count how many times Ronnie saved my ass while we were running with the dopers. He was a stand-up guy and I knew that I could count on him if things got bad. He was a mean-looking dude and he could really spook the guys we were trying to buy dope from.

When I first went to work in Narcotics, Ronnie and I started buying a lot of heroin from street-level dealers in El Paso. I was young-looking and had short hair. Ronnie and I decided to make it appear that I was in the Army, so that's the story that we put down. We had two good friends who were El Paso Police detectives. Eddie Estrada and Armando Nava were two of the best street officers I ever worked with. They knew most of the street dealers all over El Paso by name. Eddie was about thirty and Armando was near fifty. They both helped Ronnie and me with intelligence information on the people that we were trying to purchase drugs from.

We knew that a lot of the heroin dealers sold their product around the Methadone clinic, so we decided that I would start hanging around the area so the dopers would get used to seeing me. Just about every day, Detectives Nava and Estrada would run through the clinic parking lot and roust the dopers just to let them know they were in the area. Most of the time the heroin dealers had their heroin hidden close by, but they moved their stash daily.

The two detectives knew most of the guys that hung around the area by name or at the very least their street name. When you are buying drugs on the street, one of the hardest things to do is identify who sold you the dope. No one uses their real name, and it's nearly impossible to identify them or find out where they live because they really don't want you to know.

We came up with the idea that I would attempt to buy heroin from some of them, and when I did I would get a good physical description of the dealer and the clothing he was wearing. Detectives Nava and Estrada would wait about an hour after I had made the drug purchase and they would go through the parking lot and roust the group of dealers as usual. I would have already given them the description of the guy I bought from and they would just mess with the guys until they figured out who I had purchased the drugs from. Nava and Estrada would then go to their department's identification section, obtain a mug shot of the guy and bring it to me several hours later. I would look at the mug shot, make the identification, and we would then have a good solid case for delivery of heroin.

Ronnie would drive me to the clinic area, provide surveillance for my safety and pick me up after the drug buy was made. The four of us made a lot of drug buys over a three-month time span. Toward the last part of the operation, the dealers got really suspicious of me and at one point they tried to pen me up in an area. Fortunately, I was able to get out to the street and Ronnie picked me up.

During the time Ronnie and I were working the clinic the dopers killed one of the guys who hung out in the area. It finally got to the point that we decided to bust out and we brought the investigation to a close. We had all of the DPS

Narcotics agents, along with several El Paso police officers assist with the bust-out. By the time we finished, we had made more than twenty defendants for delivery of heroin. We made a lot of good informants out of some of the defendants. This was my first taste of working undercover.

My supervisor at the time was Sergeant Johnny Koonce and he really liked to work heroin dealers. Johnny always said that you could catch a guy with a hundred pounds of marijuana and most of the time he would get probation, but if you had one good buy where a guy was dealing heroin, in those days he was going to go to the penitentiary. We put a lot of guys in the joint.

While working at the clinic I learned that the heroin addicts would get their free methadone—which was supposed to wean them of smack—and then buy heroin to boost the methadone hit. The addicts would then spend the rest of the day stealing everything they could get their hands on to get enough money to buy more heroin.

I could not believe how much damage the addicts did to normal working people in society. When I showed up they always had something they had stolen that they tried to sell me. They stole everything—water hoses, lawn mowers, TVs, radios, jewelry, even kid's toys. They would go to the malls in groups. They would park their car at one end and walk through a mall stealing anything they could, put it in the car, and then start another run through the mall. If they had put that much effort into a straight job they could have made a good living. I learned to hate drug dealers with a passion. I wish John Doe citizen knew the damage drugs do to our society.

After I got my first taste of undercover work I was hooked. I really liked to get next to the drug dealers and see the expression on their faces when we took them into custody. I felt like I was making things right for what they had been doing, especially after I had actually watched one heroin dealer feed canned dog food to his children so he could have enough

91

money for his habit. I just felt that maybe I could make a difference and I got satisfaction from that. A lot of people told me that what I was doing was really dangerous, but I personally felt that a trooper on the road was in more danger just walking up on a car that he had stopped in the middle of the night. At least I knew what I was dealing with when I was buying dope. A trooper never knows what he's walking up on. It never really bothered me to work undercover.

What did bother me was being placed under suspicion for doing something I hadn't done.

By this point in my career, Floyd Hacker—the same Floyd Hacker who had scared me to death over that accidental hot check to the DPS for dry cleaning back when I was in the academy—had been promoted to chief of the Criminal Law Enforcement Division. Chief Hacker, Ranger Captain Jack Dean and Director James B. Adams all stood up for me when no one else would and saved my career. I had been accused of doing something that I hadn't done related to some funds seized in a narcotic raid. If it were not for Hacker I would never have been cleared by an internal affairs investigation or had a career with DPS beyond that point. (Though the DPS investigation showed that I had nothing to do with the incident, another Narcotics Service agent not only lost his job, he went to prison over the matter.) Chief Hacker has long since retired from the agency, but I hope Chief Hacker knows how much I respect him for what he did. He's another one of those men you run across in life who teaches you how to handle your business by his own example. He helped set my foundation in law enforcement.

The Mexican Connection

About two years after I started working undercover, Ronnie Stinnett and I were contacted by California State Police narcotics authorities and advised that they had some agents coming to El Paso with an informant to pick up ten pounds of heroin and twenty pounds of cocaine. They said the informant was terminally ill and had decided to try to get right with God before he died. Apparently the snitch had been a big drug dealer in California. He was to pick up the drugs in El Paso, board a commercial airliner at the El Paso International Airport and fly back to California.

The California authorities were requesting that we assist them with the surveillance of the informant while he was in El Paso and then follow him back to the airport to make sure he got on the plane with the drugs. They said that they would be sending several agents to El Paso with him, and they wanted to pair them up with us so they would know their way around.

Sergeant Johnny Koonce told our supervisors in Austin of the plan and everything was set to go. Ronnie and I, along with every agent in the office, met the airliner when it landed at the airport. We greeted the California agents and worked out who would be with whom. Then the informant got into a rental car and we began to follow him. He would stop from time to time to use a pay phone. In those days there weren't any cell phones. We had to be really careful during the surveillance because we knew that most likely there was going to be counter-surveillance.

Ronnie and I were really excited about this case. Normally we would work months to get to the point where we were buying ounces from a guy. In this case we were talking about thirty pounds of hard drugs. Cocaine sold on the street for $3,000 an ounce. Heroin sold for thirty to forty bucks a shot. This was big.

The plan was that after the California authorities had made apprehensions on their end, we would take down the stash house on our end. Ronnie and I wanted to do that in a big way. We had been busting our ass to purchase ounces of this stuff and here was a chance we could bust multiple pounds.

As we followed the informant, we watched him drive to the international bridge and cross into Juarez. We could not follow him into Mexico, so we stopped at the border and watched him disappear into the Juarez traffic. The California agents had no idea that he would be going across the river.

We all went back to the DPS Narcotics office to figure out what to do. We lost contact with the informant until the next day. He finally called and told us that he was in the process of completing the drug deal and that he would cross back into the United States the following day. But he refused to tell us where he was going to cross. Back in Texas, he finally contacted us and we made arrangements to follow him as he boarded the plane for California. Ronnie and I, along with the California narcotics officers, maintained surveillance on the guy until he boarded the plane.

I could not believe that he could walk thirty pounds of hard drugs through the middle of the International Airport and nobody even checked him. Two California agents boarded the plane with him and flew back to the West Coast. As far as we were concerned our part of the investigation was over. We went back to taking care of our own business.

A few days later the California authorities told us they had done a controlled delivery and had busted a lot of people, seizing cars and several houses related to the investigation.

Toward the end of the conversation they told us that they were going to send us the informant because he had been in a house in Juarez that was full of cocaine and heroin.

This guy was telling them that the heroin and cocaine was stacked all over the stash house. He was willing to cross back into Mexico with us and show us the location of the residence so we could get the Mexican authorities to hit the house and seize the drugs. This was the chance of a lifetime, they said.

The chance to get that much dope off the streets really excited Ronnie and me. We thought we could talk the Mexican authorities into letting us go with them when they raided the residence. The California authorities gave us the flight and time that the informant would arrive back in El Paso. Ronnie and I intended to be at the airport so we could get started on the case. We wanted this case really bad.

As soon as he got off the plane, we loaded him up with the intention of taking him to the DPS Narcotics office so we could debrief him. But the guy told us he wanted to take us to the house right then. Ronnie and I thought about it for a while and decided, "Why Not?"

We got rid of our guns and away to Juarez we went. The informant took us directly to the house. We could tell when we drove by the place that something illegal was going on because they had guards standing around. When we drove by we were able to get the address. We then returned to El Paso.

We put the informant in a hotel room for the night and contacted Sergeant Koonce to tell him we had located the house. We suggested that we contact authorities in Mexico City rather than the local Juarez authorities, but the sergeant said he knew some of the *comandantes* across the river. He said we would cross into Juarez the next day and meet with them to tell them about the house.

I was so excited about the deal I had a hard time sleeping that night. In the morning we all met at the office. Sergeant Koonce made contact with the *comandante* of the *Judiciales* (the Mexican state police) and told him we wanted to meet with him. The *comandante* told us to come on across. The sergeant wrote the address of the drug stash house on a slip of paper and put it in his pocket. Ronnie, Koonce, and I drove into Mexico went directly to the State Police headquarters in Juarez.

Attending a meeting with a *comandante* is a big deal in Mexico. They always make you wait for a while because the *comandante* is such an important person. When we finally got in to see him we had to go through the small talk, but finally Sergeant Koonce got to the point. Present in the room was Ronnie, the sergeant and me. The *comandante* had two or three of his people standing behind us against the wall. Sergeant Koonce told him that after a lengthy investigation we had developed information that a certain residence in Juarez contained pounds and pounds of cocaine and heroin. We went on to describe the area where the house was located. The sergeant then handed the *comandante* the piece of paper with the address.

A funny expression came over the *comandante*'s face. I could tell he knew a lot more than he was going to talk with us about. He said he would have to get things ready and that we should follow the officers who had been standing behind us all this time. The *Judiciales* then led us to the basement and sat us in a room. The officers got us something to drink, but several of them stood around the door. In effect, they had us under arrest. They kept the three of us in that room for more than three hours.

We were then taken back to the *comandante*'s office to meet with him about the raid. The Mexican commander appeared to be under a lot of stress. He said his men had raided the residence but found nothing. He said he wanted us to go to the house so we could see for ourselves that there was nothing there. The three of us looked at each other and we knew what had just happened. We told the *comandante* it was his country, not ours, and we were going back to Texas. We got into our car and the *Judiciales* followed us until we crossed back into Texas.

It was obvious what had occurred. The *comandante* had kept us in the basement of the police station until the drugs could be moved out of the house that we had been watching. Our informant had provided the California authorities with more than thirty pounds of heroin and cocaine and was trying to do his best to put the Mexican drug stash house out of business. At the time I was very young and did not have experience dealing with Mexican police. The whole thing made us sick. All it would have taken was a little help from the Mexican authorities and we could have made a hell of a seizure. I would not learn for years how things are done in Mexico. At that point in my career I believed that a policeman was a policeman no matter which side of the river they were on.

This case really opened my eyes. I learned that you could not trust the police in Mexico, and you had better keep that in mind, because that's the way it was. If you forgot it, it could cost your life. Money is what makes the world go around in Mexico. Any time you are dealing with Mexican authorities you have to keep that in mind in making decisions related to an investigation. You have to think not only about the case, but who the case is going to affect. You must consider the relationships that you may be causing problems with, and the people around the investigation. It's hard to get everything lined up in a Mexican investigation, but it can be done. You just have to remember who you are dealing with. Most of the time, those people have really good reasons not to want to help you, and you can bet it's somehow tied to money.

Last Case

Ronnie and I had been buying ounces of cocaine from a guy who had introduced us to his source from Juarez. We had made arrangements to purchase a kilo of cocaine from the men from Mexico. We brought in about $125,000 from Austin to use as flash money to show the drug dealers. I had called fellow Narcotics agent Clete Buckaloo and asked him to assist us because we had the deal set to go first thing the following morning. Clete came into El Paso and was going to spend the night at my house so we could do the deal the next day. Just after dark I was contacted by an informant and told there was another man in the northern part of El Paso who had a kilo of cocaine hidden in his house. The informant had been in the house and had seen the drugs.

Clete and I decided that we had time to do the deal before we had to make the buy the following morning. We called Ronnie and a few other officers and we got a team together to hit the house. I drafted a search warrant, found a judge, and got the warrant signed. We hit the house with five agents. When we got inside we found seven people, all of them were armed. We soon found the kilo of cocaine we were looking for. It was located right where the informant had told us it would be.

We still needed to search the entire house so we decided to have Clete and another agent take the suspects to the DPS office so they could be processed while we continued searching the residence. We normally did not work like this, but we only had five agents to get the job done.

After we loaded up the suspect, three of us stayed behind to finish searching the house. About thirty minutes later we received word that the main suspect had escaped. We finished up at the house and headed to the office to see what we could do.

When we got to the office my informant called and told me that the suspect that had escaped had called him and told him that he was going to go to his house to hide out.

We decided that we were going to set up on the house to try to get the doper back into custody. Ronnie, Clete, and I set up surveillance on the house and the next thing we knew, we saw the informant's car leave the apartment. Just after the car left, I received word from the informant that it was the escapee driving the informant's Firebird. We called the El Paso Police Department and asked that they make a traffic stop on the Firebird so we could get the guy back into custody.

Then everything fell apart. When the police tried to make a traffic stop on the suspect, he started to run. We had a high-speed chase with the suspect and ended up with two wrecked El Paso police cars. We finally got the guy back into custody, but by the time we got the deal done it was nearly time for us to meet the other drug dealers to purchase the kilo of cocaine.

We got ready to do the other deal and we again met with El Paso detectives and their SWAT Team. Clete, Ronnie, and I were going to do the undercover part of the deal. We began by setting up on a motel room where the drug dealers had told us that they would be. The three of us had about $125,000 in cash to show the drug dealers when they showed us the dope.

It really gets dangerous when you get the drugs and the money together. When we pulled up to the motel room I got out of the car and left Ronnie and Clete to cover the money. We had planned for me to go into the room, see the dope, and then return to the car to give the bust signal so the SWAT team could take the guys down and arrest them. When I went into the room I saw two guys, both carrying Colt semiautomatics in their belt. They said the drugs were nearby, but they refused to show me the dope until they saw the money.

I returned to the car and got the bag containing the money. The drug dealers didn't know it, but there had to be at least thirty officers waiting to take them down. I walked back into the room with the money. While I was standing near the door, one of the dealers walked over to the door of the restroom. He was trying to get an angle on me and I didn't like it. I pitched the bag of money to the guy sitting on the bed. When he opened the bag and saw the money, he gave the sign to his partner to get the dope. He then pitched me a bag containing the cocaine.

I walked out the door and gave the bust signal, and all hell broke lose. Ronnie and Clete had been backing me up outside in front of the room. As the other officers came running up, the two guys slammed the door. The SWAT team beat the windows out of the motel room, and the two guys figured that it was best that they give up. We arrested them and recovered the money that I had left in the room. Then we went back to the DPS Narcotics office to do the paperwork. We had not been to bed in over thirty-six hours. Ronnie, Clete, and I were exhausted. That was one of the last deals that I did while I was in Narcotics.

Becoming a Texas Ranger

I knew by this point in my career that what I really wanted to be was a Texas Ranger. I had worked around a lot of Rangers and saw they really had it together. I watched them handle a lot of interesting cases and most of the time they got them solved. In those days they did not have DNA profiling and computers. They solved the cases the old way: They followed leads and obtained confessions from the suspects. Rangers back then were not high-tech, but they had a lot of common sense and they knew how to get the job done.

Occasionally our narcotics cases would relate to a Ranger case and I would get to see how they did business. I had enough time with DPS as well as the age to be eligible to take the Ranger test. When the test date was getting near, I started studying to do well enough to make the Ranger interview board. I knew a lot of officers wanted the job just as badly as I did. You had to make a really high score on the written test because the competition was so stiff. I studied for about two months and then took the test.

Afterward I did not feel that I had done well, and had to wait several days until the list came out to see if I had made the cut. I knew that they were going to take the thirty highest test scores, and I was hoping I had made it into that group. But when the test results came out, I found that I had scored 32nd in the state, two below the level I needed. I took it really hard. I had never been a book-learning type guy, but I knew that if I put my mind to it, I could do it. I had let myself down. I was so mad at myself that I didn't know what to do. I would have to wait another year just to take the written test again.

Several weeks passed, and I told myself that this was never going to happen again. I might not make Ranger, but it would not be because I was not smart enough to pass the damn test. The Ranger test in those days was usually given in September or October. I told myself that I was going to start studying on January 1, and that's what I did. I studied two or three hours a day until spring. Then I started studying six to eight hours a day, seven days a week. I read everything I could get my hands on. I called people who were testing for other services to find anything I could about what new things were being put on the test. I talked with a college professor and he told me that I should record all of the study material on cassette tapes so that I could listen to them while I was working. I bought a tape player and recorded all of the study material that I had. For the next six or eight months I sat around the house listening to the material. I also made flash cards and used them to study. I did everything possible to study everything so I would not let myself down again.

I took the written test for the second time in September 1982. I had to drive from El Paso to Midland to do so. I was a nervous wreck, but somehow I got through it. After taking the test, I had to wait several days to find out if I had scored high enough. About a week later, I found that this time I had made it to the interview board.

I really don't remember how long I waited to go to the board, but I finally went to Austin and made my appearance. I again had to wait for another week until all of the candidates had been seen before a decision was made. The eligibility list finally came out, and I was notified that I was number one. If I had known studying made that much difference, I would have tried it in high school and college!

The first thing I did was call Dad. I do not have words to explain how I felt, being able to tell him that I would soon be a

Texas Ranger. I knew what he thought of the Rangers and I knew what it meant to both of us at the time. There was nothing I could have done to make him more proud.

Over the next few days, I was given the choice of being stationed in the Dallas area, the Waco area, or Brady. I chose Brady. The next day I was notified that Stan Guffey, the Ranger in Laredo, had chosen to transfer to Brady. My choices were now Dallas, Waco, or Laredo. I knew that I had a lot of experience working the Mexican border. I knew the people, their ways, and the types of crimes that occurred on the border. At this point in my career I had been with the DPS for ten years, and more than nine of those years were on the border. I chose Laredo. It was during this time that I found out that my wife wanted out of our marriage. When I moved to Laredo as a new Ranger, I moved alone.

Texas Ranger

I got promoted to Texas Ranger on October 1, 1982. At thirty, I was the youngest Ranger in the state. I went to the ceremony in Austin and met my new captain, Jack Dean. Captain Dean ordered me to drive to San Antonio and meet with him at Company D Headquarters. When I showed up at his office, he told me what he expected from me, and said I would be working in the San Antonio area for the next few weeks.

He told me that he wanted me to work around some of the older Rangers to get an idea how they conducted their business. I was told to watch how they did things, and after working with several Rangers, pick out the way that suited me best. The captain took a lot of interest in me and supported me while I was going through the divorce. I never thought that he liked me much, but I respected the way that he ran the company. At the time I was really hurting for money, and he allowed me to work in San Antonio and claim per diem from the state since my official duty station was Laredo. Without his help, I don't know what I would have done.

I stayed in San Antonio for about two months before Captain Dean told me to get to Laredo. When I got there, I met with Ranger Guffey, who was going to transfer to Brady. I had worked with Stan when we were both on the drug Task Force back in the 1970's. He took me around the counties where I was now assigned and introduced me to a lot of people to get me off and running. I would be working La Salle, Webb,

Zapata, and Jim Hogg counties.

I quickly found that when a new Ranger took over an area, the people the previous Ranger got along with were not necessarily the same ones the new man would get along with. Captain Dean had told me when I first started that he expected me to get along with the sheriff's departments and the area police departments. He also expected me to work closely with the district attorney's office in my area. He said that if all three of those were happy, he would be happy. He told me when I was in Narcotics they paid me to be in bars. He said, "I pay you to stay out of bars."

From some of the older Rangers I learned that Captain Dean was the one who ran Company D. If I needed something, it was the captain who would make any decisions. That's the way it was the whole time I worked for him. There was never any doubt as to who was in charge.

I found that I had several friends from my Highway Patrol days who were still around Laredo. One of the guys who really helped me get started was O. J. Hale. He was the district attorney's chief investigator and knew everyone in town. For the next several months Hale was the one who got me into most of my investigations. He would call and request my help; I would work the cases and then submit the reports to the DA's office.

During this time, I was introduced to another DA investigator, Louie Zapata. Louie and I became close friends and have remained so. He loved to hunt and we hit it off from the start. At one point, Louie and I investigated three separate murders in five days and got confessions from all of the suspects.

Hale and Zapata always had something for me to do. For one thing, they got me into a lot of white-collar crimes. I would work on day-to-day offenses until something major happened, which I usually learned about when one of the sheriff's or DA's offices would call, and I would do whatever they needed.

105

Working in this way kept me busy most of the time.

During the first year after I made Ranger, Captain Dean made sure that I was sent to as many training schools as possible. I think it was meant to teach me to keep my mouth closed at in-service school, but really, the end result was that it made me a better officer. For the first few months, I spent more time in Austin attending schools than I spent in Laredo.

In the early part of 1983 a friend of mine, Wayo Ruiz, made arrangements for me to have a blind date with a young lady originally from Nuevo Laredo, Mexico. Wayo told me she had green eyes and liked to eat pizza. He said if I asked her out for pizza, I might have a chance of getting her to say yes. Her name was Leticia Zamora.

A pharmacist, Lety had been married before and had two young sons, Polo and Carlos. Coincidentally, Polo was Justin's age and Carlos was Jared's age. The older boys were eight and the younger ones, five.

Lety and I dated over the next year, and the boys got to know each other over the summer vacation and the holidays. We got married on May 25, 1984. She is most likely the best thing that has ever happened to me. We are now working on our 25th year together and she has put up with all the many things a Ranger's wife has to put up with. After years of getting called out at all hours of the day and night, the missed days off and vacations, and the constant telephone calls, I have never heard her say a bad word about my work.

In fact, without the help and support of my wife I would never have been able to do the things that I was able to do as a Ranger. She acted as my translator more times than I can remember. I cannot remember all the times we had been out together and I either had to leave her at the function alone or find someone to take her home.

All the time that I was a Ranger I spent driving from one place to the other. I practically lived in my car. On my days off I didn't want to go anywhere because I had been driving all week. I wanted to sit on my ass and watch TV or relax around the house. My wife accepted the fact that she didn't get to go many places because I had been going all week, and I wanted to sit on something that wasn't going down the highway.

Engraved Colt Commander .38 Super given to me
by my wife Lety as a wedding present.

During the week, it seemed that I was always going in and out of the house in the middle of the night. Each and every time she told me to be careful when I left, or she met me at the door after I had been up for days working on some case. The wife of a police officer lives with the fact that when her husband walks out the door she may never see him alive again.

On one occasion when I was out working, Trooper Ray Garner went by my house to pick up something. Ray was in a marked DPS unit and in full battle dress. He didn't give much thought to the fact that he was showing up at my house uninvited and my wife was not expecting him.

Ray went up to the door, and when my wife opened it he

realized by the expression on her face what she thought. I had always told Lety that if something ever happened to me, DPS would send an officer to our home to notify her in person that I was dead, or they would bring her to the hospital where I had been taken. Ray told her quickly that nothing had happened to me, but he could tell she was still really upset. As soon as Ray could get to a phone, he called me and told me what had happened.

I've always thought that the wives of police officers should be given credit for supporting their men in what they have chosen to do. Each and every day that we do our job, they live with the knowledge that at any given time they may be widowed. Whenever you see an officer out on the street, remember that there is someone at home praying that he gets to come home that night. I have known and been friends with seven officers who didn't make it back to their family.

One of the many things that I liked about the Rangers was that they always tried to stay ahead of the game. When something new came up, within a few months we received training in how to do whatever it was. The Rangers always took good care of their men and we always had the best weapons, body armor, and investigative equipment that money could buy. Senior Ranger Captain Maurice Cook was the one who seemed to get us started in buying good equipment. He always spent a lot of money on his men and I always thought well of him for that.

As a Ranger, it was always in the back of your mind that there were a lot of Rangers who had gone before you. The history of the Rangers traces back to 1823. You knew that you had a lot to live up to. You knew what was expected of you and you knew that the tradition, reputation, and honor of the Rangers depended on the way you did your job and conducted yourself both on and off duty. That fact was never far from your mind. You never wanted to be the one Ranger who let everyone else down.

I knew that I had to get to know the sheriffs in my area, and one way to do that was help them as much as possible. I made up my mind that there was no case too small for me to work. If someone called I tried to help them in any way that I could. Before long this attitude started paying off. Several of the sheriff's offices in my area started calling me on a regular basis. I always thought that if they called on the small cases, they would surely call when something major happened.

At about this time I began to understand how important it was to know how to interview witnesses and suspects. One of the things that Ranger Al Cuellar had told me just after I had gone to work was that it would take me around five years to understand how a Ranger fits into the system. I was lucky enough to work with Al and to watch how he conducted his interviews. He would sit and talk with a guy a long time to find out what made him tick before he ever started the process of trying to get the suspect to confess to an offense. Watching Al I learned to be patient during an interview and not push so hard that the suspect would close down. I would always remember the way Clayton McKinney and Sheriff Richard Upchurch had conducted their interviews. They gave me the foundation to build on when it came to interviewing suspects.

I interviewed a lot of people and began to develop my own system. I always wanted a small room, no pictures on the wall, and no telephone. When you are talking with someone trying to sell them the fact that they need to tell you the truth about something that you are investigating, you sure don't need to be interrupted. It's like I always say, if you are working on ten cases, your community expects you as a Ranger to solve all ten of them. They pay baseball players hundreds of thousands of dollars if they bat .300. That's three out of ten, but Rangers are expected to bat 1000. So when you go into an interview, you've got to have it in you mind that you are going to do just that.

You have to be ready to sit in that room for hours. If the

guy keeps talking, then you stay with him until he gives it up. I always wished it worked like it did on TV crime shows. In real life it's not that way. Each time I interviewed someone and found something that worked, I would include that technique in my interview system. If something didn't work or caused problems, then I never used it again. I did that over an extended period of time and I finally came up with a system that worked for me more often than not.

One day I was at the La Salle County Sheriff's Office in Cotulla when Sheriff Darwin Avant asked me to go to Carrizo Springs to interview an inmate about a burglary of a habitation that had occurred in Cotulla. The inmate had been identified as a suspect in the Cotulla offense, but he had been arrested for something else in Carrizo Springs. The sheriff told me he really did not have any evidence on the guy, but that he had heard on the street that he had done the burglary.

I drove to the county jail in Carrizo Springs. I talked with the Dimmit County sheriff and told him I needed to interview one of his inmates about an offense that had occurred in Cotulla. I went into a small room with the inmate and began my dog-and-pony show. I told him I knew that he had committed the burglary and why he should tell me the truth.

I talked for a long time, and when I finally stopped, the guy just sat there and looked at me. He sat there for what seemed five minutes and finally said, "That's exactly the same thing you told me the last time I talked with you, and when I confessed the last time, I got three years in the penitentiary." I swear I could not remember that I had ever seen this guy before in my life. Well, while I was trying to figure out where to go next, the guy went ahead and made a full confession, including where he had hidden the stolen property.

I took a written statement from him, and a few months later he went back to the penitentiary. I thought about it on the way home and figured that either I must have come up with a system that worked, or I was really lucky. For the life of me I could not figure why the guy would make the same mistake by talking with me when he knew what was going to happen.

In conducting hundreds and hundreds of interviews over the years, I found that the better you treated people, the more information you obtained. If another officer was involved in the interrogation, I would always try to do the interview with someone I had worked with before. The more two officers work together, the better they are as a team. It gets to the point that both of you know what the other is going to say before he says it. When you can get to that point, it makes things work a lot better.

I have seen a lot of officers go into an interview and get very aggressive with a suspect. Most of the time, in my experience, this always caused the suspect to shut down. No one wants to talk with someone who is yelling and threatening them. This system works most of the time with normal people. Then you have the hard-core crooks. I always tried to size up those people and just let the interview flow and see where it led. There was always the good cop, bad cop routine to fall back on if all else failed. Above all else, the most important thing that a Ranger has to be able to do is talk to and interview people. The better he is at conducting interviews the more cases that he will solve.

Most people never really think about what it takes to solve a crime. When an offense occurs there may be no witnesses. Or there may be several witnesses to the crime, and all of them need to be interviewed and their statements taken. On the other hand, there may be a victim who has to be interviewed, and his statement needs to be taken. If you do get to a suspect, that's when the real work starts. You have to interview the suspect and attempt to get a written statement that can be introduced into court at his trial. There is nothing more satisfying in the world than walking into a room with a crook, and several hours later coming out with a written confession. So you can see that, depending on the offense, a Ranger may take numerous statements during the investigation that will allow him to get a conviction when the case is taken to court.

I worked with several sheriffs in La Salle County the first few years that I was a Ranger. I had been raised in a small town and I knew how a small town worked. From the very start I liked the people and made a lot of friends in the area. I felt comfortable working there. I'm sure, however, that there were probably a lot of people who wished I hadn't.

I began to work with Sheriff Avant right after he took office. Over the years, we handled a lot of offenses together and put a lot of people in prison. He and I got along really well from the start. Darwin was a working sheriff. When something major happened, he would stay with me for days, not going home until I did. I have spent many a night working all night long with him. I always seemed to have something working in the Cotulla area.

Darwin had his mind on two things most of the time. He was either working or hunting. Both of us loved to hunt whitetail deer, and South Texas has the best deer hunting in the world. Raised in Cotulla, the sheriff had been hunting most of his life.

During deer season, we would work on some type of offense until about 4 p.m., and then we would find some place to ride around and look at deer. When it got dark, we would continue with whatever investigation we were working on. Over the twelve years that I worked with Darwin, I cannot count the number of big bucks that he cost me. He would wait till I got ready to shoot, and then say something that would break my concentration. The next thing I would see was the buck's butt running through the brush. He got a big kick out of that, and I fell for it every time.

If you asked Darwin, he would most likely tell you that the reason the DPS had Rangers was to open ranch gates for the sheriff. I opened thousands of gates for him. For some reason, he always wanted to drive, and I have just now begun to realize that it may have had something to do with the fact that the passenger always had to open the gates.

A death scene in La Salle County.

Avant and I became good friends. In fact, my wife Lety and I often took vacations with him and his wife, Betty. One time we had all gone to Las Vegas to the National Finals Rodeo. The first night we had taken a shuttle bus to the arena. It took us ninety minutes to get back to the hotel when the rodeo was over.

We decided the next night that we would either find a ride or take a taxi so we'd get back to the hotel faster. After the second night's performance, when I left to go to the restroom Darwin told me he was going to find us a ride. Just as I walked out of the restroom, Lety ran up and told me that Darwin had us a ride and to hurry up. I followed her and found Darwin standing next to a Rolls-Royce limousine. We loaded into the limo. About halfway back to the hotel Darwin leaned over and told me very quietly to be sure and not tell the driver that he was not Mr. Jones. I'm sure that the real Mr. Jones looked for his limo for a long time. We got back to the hotel in record time.

I was in Laredo one day when Darwin called me to tell me that someone had started a fire in a man's carport, and it had nearly burned the victim's house down. He asked if I could come up and help him look into the case. I drove to Cotulla and met with him as requested.

Darwin related that he had developed two suspects who lived near the victim's house. The two suspects were a man and woman who had some problems with the victim. We went to the scene and looked for any physical evidence that might help us identify the people who had committed the offense.

When we got there we found that the house had indeed nearly burned down, and it was apparent that it was some type of arson. Darwin and I walked around the back of the house, and I found a yellow plastic antifreeze bottle lying on the ground about fifty yards behind the house. I picked up the jug, twisted off the lid, and found that at one time the jug had contained gasoline. It appeared to us that the suspects had brought the gas that was used to start the fire in the antifreeze jug and had thrown the jug away after they had started the fire. We were not able to find any more physical evidence, so we returned to the La Salle County Sheriff's Office with the plastic jug.

Darwin wanted to bring in the two suspects so we could interview them and get a feeling as to their involvement. I told him that I wanted to make an effort to fingerprint the jug and see if I could get some prints to help in identifying the culprits. He sent a couple of his deputies out to pick up the suspects while I was printing the antifreeze jug.

I worked on that jug and was not able to lift *any* latent prints. It was obviously a dead end. So I reached over, grabbed the jug, and put *my* fingerprints on it. I dusted the jug again, and sure enough, I got some of the best prints I had ever seen.

When I walked out of the office, the deputies were coming in with the two suspects. I saw the reaction on the faces of the suspects when they saw I had the antifreeze jug. It was priceless.

I never interview two people at the same time, but I did in this case. We walked into the sheriff's office and I set the jug down on his desk. Darwin and I never told them that the prints were theirs. For the next hour or so we talked to both of the suspects, and neither one of them could take their eyes off the jug with my prints on it. Finally, I told them that I was going to send the jug to Austin and have the prints compared to their prints to see if they were the ones who left the jug at the scene of the fire.

Both of the suspects then admitted that they had started the fire, and gave Darwin and me a full written confession as to how they had committed the offense. We put both of them in the county jail, and we had a really good laugh about solving a crime based on a Ranger's fingerprints.

On another occasion, Darwin called me and told me that he had received information that some people were going to conduct an illegal chicken fight on a ranch about ten miles north of Cotulla. He asked if I could come up and assist him with the investigation. I told him that I would be there in about two hours. I had just been issued a new black Chevrolet Caprice that everyone referred to as a Shamu because of its shape.

I drove to Cotulla and met with the sheriff at the courthouse. He told me to park my car and ride with him in his personal pickup. We then drove to the ranch and located the area where the suspects had been holding chicken fights. We took photos of the fighting rings, but found no one in the area. We drove back to the courthouse, and I put my camera back into the car.

While I was at my car I noticed Darwin's son, Scott, standing by his pickup across the parking lot. Scott yelled at me and when I looked up, his brother, Dale, took my picture. I really didn't think much about it at the time. I got back into Darwin's pickup, and we drove off to get some lunch. When we finished eating, Darwin took me back to my car, and I headed back to Laredo.

A few weeks later I got an envelope in the mail that appeared to be a Sea World ad. When I opened it, I found a photograph of me standing by my state car, but that's not what caught my eye. Someone—I quickly realized it had been Darwin—had made a cutout of a killer whale using butcher paper. The sheriff's son had taped it on my car door while we were investigating the chicken fights. The cutout really made the car look like Shamu, and there I was standing behind it looking like an idiot. Darwin mailed the photo to everyone I knew and told them that this was a photo of the Shamu Ranger who worked his area. I almost didn't live that one down.

Darwin played a good joke on me putting this paper design on the other side of my state car. The sheriff sent the photo to area sheriffs and Ranger headquarters.

It wasn't long after this incident that I decided to clean out the inside of my state car. Rangers spend a lot of time in their cars. It was nothing for me to jump in the car and run to Austin, submit some evidence related to a crime, and return the same day. That's over five hundred miles. You wouldn't believe the mess in the car after working out of it for a few weeks. Well, anyway, I was cleaning out the inside when I reached down under the front seat and pulled out a humongous brassiere. I had no idea where it had come from. The only person I recalled being with me was Sheriff Avant. I made up my mind that this time I was not going to let him get away with it. I waited a few days, and I drove all the way to the courthouse in Cotulla to find his county car. Darwin had a bumper hitch on the back of the vehicle. I got up under the car and tied the brassiere so that it would hang down under the car when it was parked. When he drove the car, it would look like twin parachutes.

I waited for a day or two expecting to hear something. A few days later, Ranger Joaquin Jackson called me from Uvalde and asked me if I had found anything under my car seat. Clearly, Joaquin had been the one who planted the bra. About an hour later, Darwin called all pissed off that some kids had tied a bra under his car. Some of the people in town told him they had noticed it and really got a good laugh seeing his drag chutes. I didn't have the heart to tell him at the time, but I told him a few days later after he'd had a chance to calm down. We both had a good laugh about it. We never did get to pay Joaquin back on the deal.

Joaquin, on the other hand, was always messing not only with me, but with the other Company D Rangers as well. On one occasion, we both went to firearms training with the rest of the guys in the company. From time to time, I would go back to my car to get something, and after a while I began to notice that my hands were really stinky. I would go and wash them, but it seemed to do no good. Every time I went back to the car, they would start stinking again.

117

The next day I found that Joaquin had put coyote dope under the door handles of my car, and every time that I opened the car, it would get on my hands again. For those who do not know what coyote dope is, it's the most revolting-smelling stuff that you can imagine. It smells like urine, feces, and skunk all in one. A lot of the government trappers use it to put on their traps to snare coyotes. My wife would not sleep with me for several days. My hands stunk so bad that I could not put them near my face when I went to sleep. I was a relatively new Ranger compared to Joaquin, but I decided to retaliate anyway. A few weeks later, I found his car and filled his hubcaps full of catfish stink bait. I don't know to this day if he ever figured out it was payback from me.

Sporting Goods Store Burglary

When I first moved to Laredo after making Ranger I moved into an apartment next door to a good friend of mine by the name of Roque Hines. After living alone for several weeks I began to notice that food did not magically appear on my table and socks and underwear did not wash themselves and run and jump into the bottom drawer of the dresser. I most likely would have starved to death if it were not for Roque and his wife Laurin. They asked me to eat with them so many times that I am sure that they thought they had somehow accidentally adopted me.

Roque owned Border Sporting Goods, the best gun store in town. Besides having a great stock, Roque let his friends buy and payout guns over a few months. Truth be told, I have owed Roque money since 1977. Every time I get a gun paid for, I charge another one and the circle continues. Anyway, Roque took good care of me over the years and when it came time to get married again he was the best man at my wedding. He is one of the best friends a guy could have.

Roque was always having trouble with people breaking into his store. I had worked several of these burglaries on other occasions and I had recovered some of the stolen guns and arrested several people. Roque finally decided that he was going to go high tech and had a really good alarm system installed.

One night I was at the house watching TV when the telephone rang and it was Roque. He told me that he had just been notified by the alarm company that someone had broken into his store. I lived closer to the store than he did so he asked me to go there. He would meet me there as soon as he could. I grabbed one of my .38 Super's, stuck it in my belt and ran to the car. Sure enough I was the first person to get to the store. Roque got there just after I did. A short time later the Police Department arrived.

We all knew that Roque had a lot of guns and ammo at the store and were concerned that the burglars might have gotten weapons and loaded them. With that in mind, we went into the store with our guns out. We found that the thieves had piled up a lot of guns they intended to take, but apparently had been scared off when we arrived. They had gotten into the store through the roof, but the alarm had worked. The police officers told us they would make a report about the incident for Roque's insurance company and after they got all the information they needed, they left.

Roque and I stayed and decided to walk around the store again just to make sure nothing had been stolen. There was a long three-foot-wide hallway in the back of the store that dead-ended at the hot water heater. For some reason I walked down the hall to look behind the hot water heater. It was kind of dark in the hallway and I couldn't see very well. I walked up to the hot water heater and stuck my head around the side to make sure that no one was there. When I did I found myself eyeball-to-eyeball and nose-to-nose with one of the crooks. We both jumped straight up and the next thing I knew I had the guy by the hair and was dragging him down the hall. I'm sure it looked like a scene out of one of the Roadrunner cartoons. Roque came running over and we both got control of the guy. We called the Police Department and officers showed back up to take the burglar into custody.

Roque and I had a good laugh about the whole thing but we realized that if the guy had wanted to, he could have hurt us. Both of us learned something from the deal: A man needs to stay on his toes all the time. Never let your guard down. You just never know what's going to happen.

Roque and I have known each other for more than thirty years now. He's one of those guys who you come across in life that you know that you can depend on. I'm lucky to have him as a friend.

Cattle Rustling

When I think back on all the cases I worked over the years, a few have stuck in my mind because of the reasons that people committed the offense. They didn't commit the offense for personal gain, they did it just to get by in life. I've always thought that if I were in the same position as they were at the time, I might have done the same thing.

A few weeks after I made Ranger I was contacted by telephone by a man who wanted to provide information on a cattle theft case. The man refused to give his name, but he related that a man from Dilley had borrowed his rifle and had gone east of town and killed a yearling steer. The man on the phone said that the suspect had butchered the steer and had the meat in his icebox at his home in Dilley.

I drove to Pearsall and met with the Frio County sheriff. I identified the suspect and after a few hours' work was able to find that he lived in a trailer house east of town.

I drove by his house and I noticed that there appeared to be blood in the back of his pickup and on the back bumper. I returned to the courthouse and over the next several hours obtained a search warrant for the suspect's trailer home. I went back to the trailer and knocked on the door with the warrant in my hand. A woman with a baby answered. She apparently had been having a baby every ten or twelve months for the past six years. There were six kids in the house.

The home had no running water or electricity. I could tell by the way the house looked that the people were just getting by. I opened the cabinets and found that there wasn't any food in the house. When I opened the refrigerator I found that the people had put a bag of ice on the steer meat that sat unfrozen in the back of the freezer compartment. At about this time the man I had been looking for walked up into the yard with a .22 caliber rifle.

I told him to put the gun down and he did as I instructed. He told me that he had been out hunting rabbits so he and his family would have something different to eat. I arrested the guy and drove him to the Frio County Sheriff's Office. As we drove along he told me that he had been working in the oilfield and that he had lost his job a few months back. He said that he normally didn't steal or kill other people's cattle, but that it had gotten to the point that he and his family didn't have anything to eat.

He told me that he had shot the steer several times but the steer wouldn't go down, so he hit it on the head with the .22 rifle that he had been using. The rifle had broken in half. He said that he had borrowed the rifle from a friend of his, and when he later told the friend that he had broken his rifle, the friend told him that he was going to call the law. Now it was obvious who had made the call to me about the stolen cattle. I took the man before the judge and told him the whole story about what had happened and the conditions of the man and his family.

The judge called a local church and made arrangements to get some help for the family. We let the man go after he agreed to pay the victim for the steer when he got back to work. I later found the owner of the steer and related the story of the family to him. The rancher told me to forget the whole thing and that he no longer wanted to file the case. I wrote a report on the case but never submitted it to the DA's office.

Over the next several months I checked on the man and his family and learned that the people in the community had helped him get a job, and he had gotten back on his feet. I always thought that there had been more justice in this case than any other case that I had worked. I know in my heart that if I had been in the same position, I would have done anything to take care of my family. In a way you had to respect the guy.

Company Meetings

The reason that Rangers work so well as a group is that the Rangers in each company spend a lot of time together. Each Ranger personally knows all the guys in the company, and so when he needs something, it's like calling a friend for help. I always enjoyed the company meetings that we had every few months. You never knew what to expect when we all got together.

At one meeting at the YO Ranch near Mountain Home, one of the Rangers stole Joaquin Jackson's pants and ran them up the flagpole. At another meeting, someone threw a smoke grenade into one of the motel rooms. And then there was the time that Joaquin threw a six-foot long black snake in bed with me. When I looked up, I saw the snake's head come up over my right shoulder. I actually hurt my back trying to put as much distance between me and the snake as I could. When I got a hold of myself I was about a hundred yards down the road. Rangers are like sharks, you can't let them know your weaknesses because they will drive two hundred miles to play a prank on you.

On another occasion, Joaquin was around several Rangers when he walked out into the brush to handle some personal business. While he was answering the call of nature, one of the Rangers took a photo of Joaquin from the back. The photo didn't really show anything, but you could tell what he was doing. The Ranger never said a word to Joaquin and the meeting continued. Several weeks later, Joaquin was sure surprised when he walked into one of the sheriff's offices and saw the new twenty by thirty-inch calendar featuring the photograph hanging on the wall. The caption on the bottom of the photo read "IT TAKES TWO HANDS TO HOLD A WHOPPER." The Ranger had made several calendars and had sent them to all the sheriff's offices that Joaquin worked.

At another meeting that we were attending at a local ranch, we were standing around having a beverage. Our host had set up two spinning metal targets. One was about the size of a coffee can and the other about two inches in diameter. The two metal targets were about ten inches apart. Joaquin pulled out his .45, took aim, and shot the bigger target. The target spun around and Joaquin looked at everyone and grinned.

I pulled out my .45, shot, and hit the little target. I watched it spin several times, and then put my gun back in the holster. Joaquin tried several times to hit the little one but he couldn't do it. I never told Joaquin that when I had fired the shot, I had been aiming at the bigger target but missed and hit the little one. I was not about to admit that to Joaquin or the other guys.

Missing

On Sunday, June 14, 1987, I was contacted by Sheriff Avant about a missing person reported to the La Salle County Sheriff's Office. Darwin asked if I would drive up to Cotulla and meet with him about the case.

When I got to Cotulla, the sheriff told me that he had been contacted four days earlier by the family of Dolores Garcia, who reported her missing. Darwin and his deputies had started working on the case and had learned that Dolores had last been seen with a local man identified as Carlos Ayala. The sheriff asked me to start an investigation from the beginning.

We went to meet with the family and found that Dolores had not been seen since she had gone out with a friend the previous Wednesday. The family told us that Dolores had a young daughter and that she would not have gone out of town without letting her family know.

After the interview with the family, the sheriff told me that Ayala had previously been convicted of aggravated rape. We began to interview witnesses and learned that Dolores and one of her friends had gone to a local bar and met with two local men, one of them Ayala. Another woman who had been with Dolores left when her boyfriend came to the bar, leaving the two other men with Dolores. Ayala had been driving an old van and the three of them had driven out to Billy Goat Hill just east of town.

That's where the story fell apart. As Darwin and I worked on the case over the next few days, we developed Ayala as the

127

main suspect. Every time we followed a lead, it led back to him. Ayala, on the other hand, told us that Dolores had gotten out of his van and walked back to town.

We asked him to submit to a polygraph test at Walker Security in Laredo. Ayala took the test and passed it. This killed our investigation. I could not figure out how he passed the test.

Darwin and I interviewed Ayala numerous times but it was like trying to get information out of a rock. We both knew that he had something to do with Dolores's disappearance, but we were unable to come up with any evidence that would allow us to take him into custody. The main thing that was holding us back was the fact that we had not found Dolores's body. In Texas, it is nearly impossible to obtain a conviction for murder if you do not have a body.

A lot of the women in Cotulla were very concerned that Dolores was still missing and that the main suspect was running around town acting as if nothing had happened. Over the first few months of the investigation, Darwin and I tried everything we could think of to develop evidence that Ayala committed the offense. We even wired up some of his friends in an effort to try to get him to talk about it. During this time, Ayala was arrested several times for other offenses and each time Darwin and I interviewed him hoping to get him to talk about the disappearance, which we believed involved Dolores' murder.

At one point, we had DPS Polygraph operator Pat O'Burke again run him on the polygraph in an effort to develop additional information. Ayala failed the test three times, but refused to change his story. It had gotten to the point that Darwin and I were taking this case personally. We told each other that we were not going to give up until we put the case together. But we had no real evidence, not to mention having no body.

Still, we continued to work on it for more than two years. I cannot remember how many times we interviewed Ayala about the disappearance. Sometimes our interviews would last as long as six hours, but no new information was developed. It seemed there was nothing more that we could do.

And then the thing that we had been waiting for happened. The sheriff was contacted by some local bird hunters and advised that they had found a skull and bones southwest of Cotulla. Darwin called and told me that some female clothing lay around the bones. I drove to Cotulla, met up with him, and went to the scene to process the area for physical evidence. Photos were taken and the items were recovered.

I then took the bones to the Bexar County Medical Examiner's Office in San Antonio and the clothing to the DPS laboratory in Austin. The sheriff and I contacted the victim's family and asked what kind of pants Dolores had been wearing the day she disappeared. The family said she had been wearing Braxton jeans, size 9. That was the brand and size of the pants we had found at the scene.

A few days later, the DPS laboratory reported that they had inspected the jeans and had found that the pants had been taken up in the middle of the back and the inside each leg. Darwin and I contacted the family again and they were able to find another pair of jeans belonging to Dolores. When we inspected the jeans, we found that they had been altered the same way, with the same color thread. We knew that the remains were those of Dolores.

We presented this information to a La Salle County district judge so he could rule Dolores dead. Once this was done, Darwin and I met with the district attorney in an effort to obtain a murder warrant for Carlos Ayala.

The meeting with the DA did not go as planned. Darwin and I, along with the DA, knew that we could not prove cause of death to Dolores. We had to be able to prove that Dolores had died as a direct result of Ayala's actions. We could prove that Dolores was dead, but we could not prove that she hadn't died of a heart attack or some other natural cause. The DA agreed to give us a murder warrant, but if we did not get a written statement from Ayala, he would have to dismiss the case before we went to trial.

Meanwhile, Ayala had moved to Crookston, Minnesota. I contacted the Minnesota State Police and requested that they arrest him for the murder of Dolores Garcia. I provided them with copies of the warrants and mug shots of Ayala. A few days later we received news that he had been arrested by Minnesota authorities. Over the next few weeks, Captain Dean made arrangements for the sheriff and me to fly to Minnesota to pick up Ayala in a DPS aircraft.

Darwin and I decided that when we picked him up all we were going to tell him was: "We got you now, we found Dolores's body." We flew to Minnesota, picked Ayala up and put him on the plane for the flight back to Texas. As we got in the plane I told him, "We've got you now." Ayala wanted to talk to us, but we told him that we did not need to talk to him anymore since we had found Dolores's body. During the ten hours it took to get back to Cotulla, Darwin and I never said another word to him. When we got back, we put Ayala in a cell and I told him that if he wanted to say anything about the death of Dolores, he had fifteen minutes to call the office. Darwin and I drove to the courthouse and found that Ayala had called and said he wanted to talk.

I knew that he realized he could go to the penitentiary for a long time if he admitted killing Dolores. When Darwin and I interviewed him, he told us he had made a pass at Dolores while they were at Billy Goat Hill. He said Dolores became angry, got out of his van and started to walk back to town. He said he picked her back up, but she had gotten scared and jumped out of the vehicle while it was moving. Ayala said that Dolores had died as a result of the fall from the van. He told us that as a convicted sex offender, he knew that no one would believe his story, so he decided to hide Dolores's body. He said that he put her in the van and took her to the location where the body was later found.

Darwin and I obtained a written statement outlining all that. Based on what Ayala had told us, the DA changed the charge against him to involuntary manslaughter. Of course, we knew that Ayala was not telling the truth. He had nearly three years to make up the story. The problem we had was that we could not prove cause of death. As a result, Ayala went to the penitentiary for the manslaughter charge.

I take a lot of pride in this case because the sheriff and I had kept pushing, finally getting the victim's family some closure. I worked harder on this case than any other. My offense report contained more than 500 numbered details in addition to reports from a forensic anthropologist we consulted in an effort to establish cause of death. I know in my heart that Ayala killed Dolores and that he should have been charged with murder, but sometimes you have to take what you can get with a case.

Embezzling from a Title Company

Not every case a Ranger works involves a homicide. On one occasion the owner of Laredo's largest title company contacted me about a possible theft case. He told me that his company had been audited and that a lot of money appeared to be missing. He said he had not been able to find out how the money had been taken out of his company.

I had used a title company on two or three occasions, but I really had no idea how that kind of business worked. I started working on the case, and over the next several months tried to learn as much as I could about how the company functioned. I had met with Webb County DA investigator O. J. Hale, and he and I worked on the investigation almost exclusively for a long time. I thought at times that it was really funny that I was working with subpoenaed bank records by the box-load when I had trouble balancing my own checkbook.

The woman we suspected in the thefts was well known and respected in the community. She had worked for the title company more than twenty years. Complicating the case was the fact that she was married to the Webb County sheriff's chief deputy. Still, it made no difference at all to me whose wife she was. My job was to find out if she had stolen any money from the title company, and if so, how much. After a lot of hard work, we found that there was more than a million dollars missing from the company.

Over the next few months, I assisted the Webb County District Attorney's Office in conducting a full criminal

132

investigation into the theft. This included working with the owner of the title company and his auditing agency. We finally determined that the theft had been accomplished by floating money through an escrow account. The woman was such a trusted employee that there were no checks and balances in place to prevent something like that from happening

We worked with a grand jury and subpoenaed a lot of witnesses until we finally got a theft indictment naming the woman. She and her lawyer did everything they could to make it appear that she had not stolen the money from her employer, but a jury saw through her. She was convicted of the theft and placed on probation. The owner of the title company also recovered some of his money.

I really learned a lot from working on this investigation. I don't think I made a lot of friends at the sheriff's office, but the way I looked at it was, that was what the state paid me to do. I sure wasn't there to get voted homecoming king.

The owner of the company and I became friends and I still see him from time to time around town. He never fails to mention the case and all the work that we did together trying to make things right those many years ago.

Backpacking Poacher

When you live in South Texas you cannot get away from the fact that people pay a lot of attention to deer season every fall. People come from all over the United States to hunt deer in the brush country along the border. It's nearly impossible to find a lease anywhere around any of the counties that I worked as a Ranger. People will pay as much as $20,000 for a trophy whitetail buck. A lot of the ranchers in the area depend on the income from the hunting leases to make their ranches profitable. A regular hunting lease will cost at least $5,000 and will allow the hunter to kill only one buck.

I have been a hunter all of my adult life, but as a Ranger I always had a lot of problems in my counties during deer season. There were booze-fueled assaults, people shooting at each other and every kind of offense you could dream of. When men go hunting they let their hair down and a lot of times it ends in major problems, even death.

While I was working my assigned area, I began to become aware of an outlaw hunter with a bad reputation. Ranger Stan Guffey and several other officers had arrested a man named Ronnie Carroll for illegal hunting on the Robert East Ranch before I had been stationed in Laredo. Carroll was the worst kind of illegal hunter who ranchers had to deal with, a "back packer." He would have a friend drop him off at night near a really good ranch and he would walk into that ranch and hunt for several days.

Carroll would only carry food, water, a sleeping bag, and a

134

rifle. He always made a cold camp, meaning no fire. He was a hard-core poacher only after the horns. He would carry a small saw, and when he killed a deer, he would just cut off the horns and continue to hunt for days. Carroll could do a lot of damage to a rancher when he was killing deer that the landowner could sell for $5,000 a hunt. The ranch owners in this part of the world hate "back packers."

While most crooks try to keep a low profile, Carroll was proud he was an outlaw hunter. He had even given an interview to an outdoor writer with one of the newspapers in Houston, and they had done a big story on his exploits in South Texas. Most of the ranchers with large spreads had heard of Carroll and they hated everything he stood for. He and others like him were taking money out of their pocket each time they sneaked on a piece of property. But for Carroll, it was like a game. He would keep doing his illegal hunting and we had to catch him if we could. All of the game wardens in the area knew him well and they would have given anything to catch him.

I normally did not get into the game wardens' business so I had not been paying much attention to Carroll when I got word that he had been hired as foreman on the Galvan Ranch, about fifty miles north of Laredo. At the time the ranch was in an estate and had been leased to a man from Cotulla. The ranch was located across the highway from country singer George Strait's ranch and next to the Piloncillo Ranch, in one of the best areas for deer hunting.

I had talked with Strait and the foreman of the Piloncillo and they were not happy that Carroll was in their area, much less their neighbor. I had talked with Strait's foreman, Ted Moffett, and asked him to keep an eye on Carroll and let me know if it appeared that he was up to no good.

I drove out to the ranch and had a long talk with Carroll and told him that I knew what he had been doing and that he was not going to pull that crap in my area. Carroll was real friendly and told me that he had changed his ways. All he wanted to do was make a living working on the ranch. I didn't really believe him, but there wasn't much I could do about it but let him know that I knew that he was in the area. Most of the ranchers in this part of the world take good care of their deer and spend thousands of dollars a year on feed and supplements for them.

One day after deer season started, I was contacted by DPS Communications and advised that Carroll wanted to talk to me as soon as possible. I got in touch with him and made arrangements for him to meet me near the ranch on Highway 44 outside Encinal. Carroll told me that some guys from Austin had leased a pasture for hunting but he didn't think they were interested in game.

He asked me if I remembered that a few weeks earlier an airplane had crash-landed in a field near the Rio Grande just north of Nuevo Laredo. Carroll told me that the airplane had been loaded with about 1,500 pounds of marijuana and the pilot had gotten away by swimming the river into the United States. I was very much aware of what he was talking about. The information was all over Laredo. It had happened just like Carroll had said.

Carroll said that he had been around the ranch house when the hunters from Austin drove up and asked him to go into Laredo with them. He said he had ridden into town with them, and they had picked up the pilot in question, an Anglo. They had gone back to the ranch and taken the pilot with them. The men got drunk at the ranch and later asked him if they could use the ranch's airstrip to fly in a load of marijuana. Carroll said he really didn't know what to tell them, but he had been thinking about it and he didn't want anyone to believe he was involved.

I asked Carroll if he had given them an answer and he said they were going to call him back for his decision. I asked if he was willing to work with me on the deal and he said he was. I told him to call the guys back and tell them that they could land a plane on the ranch for $15,000.

A few days later Carroll made his pitch to the dopers and they flew in the money he had asked for. Now they were making arrangements to fly in the marijuana. I then called DPS Narcotics Sergeant Ken Maxwell and told him about the deal I was setting up. I met with Ken and we agreed that we should put an undercover Narcotics agent at the ranch with Carroll so we would know what was going on.

Doyle and friend Rene Barrientos with two South Texas bucks killed in November 2008 north of Webb County. With bucks like these on your ranch it's easy to see why area ranchers hate poachers.

We got in touch with agent John Whitley and made arrangements for him to meet with Carroll so he could act as a ranch employee while the drug deal was being set up by the Austin guys. Over the next few weeks agent Whitley worked at the ranch and watched as the drug smugglers set up their operation. The drug dealers then flew the plane to the ranch to make the final arrangements to smuggle the load.

The smugglers took out the seats of the plane and installed a rubber bladder in the floor of the aircraft. They planed to fill the bladder with fuel and fly into Mexico. When they arrived in Mexico, the bladder would be empty. They would then load the marijuana into the plane and fly back to the ranch using the fuel in the aircraft's built-in tanks.

Sergeant Maxwell brought in additional personnel for the operation. I had asked DPS Motor Vehicle Theft investigator Frank Malinak (he later became a Ranger) to help with any surveillance that we might need.

We knew that the marijuana was going to be taken to Austin, so we decided to take the load down while it was en route, on the chance that the dealers might decide to use the airstrip again. I contacted Sheriff Avant in Cotulla and he made arrangements for all the officers involved in the investigation to stay at a ranch just outside Cotulla. Agent Whitley notified us when the plane left for Mexico, and when it returned to the ranch loaded with marijuana.

Sergeant Maxwell had stationed two additional DPS Narcotics agents near the airstrip to assist Whitley if something went wrong. Those agents had taken photos of the ground crew as they unloaded the bags of marijuana from the plane. The smugglers then stacked the marijuana in a pickup and placed sacks of cattle feed on top to hide the load. They then drove out of the ranch to Interstate 35 and started north toward Austin. We had Highway Patrol Trooper Bob Loza stop the pickup just north of Cotulla to "discover" the load of marijuana during his traffic stop.

The load was around three-quarters of a ton. We had done the deal without the smugglers ever knowing that we knew about the ranch operation. I talked with Carroll and told him to try to do the same thing again. Agent Whitley had done the undercover work and Sergeant Maxwell had helped in putting the whole deal together. It had worked out great, but I really never thought that the smugglers would want to do the same thing again.

Trooper Raul Garcia and Doyle with the load of marijuana seized during the Ronnie Carroll air-smuggling investigation in Webb and Dimmit County.

But a few days later we were again contacted by Carroll and told that the smugglers wanted to do another deal. They thought it had just been a fluke that the trooper had stopped them. Sergeant Maxwell came up with the idea that the next time we should follow the load to Austin and try to find out where they were going to deliver it. That was fine with me.

A week or so later we did the same thing all over again and we successfully followed the marijuana to Austin. Sergeant Maxwell had requested assistance from several DPS Narcotics agents in Austin and we made several arrests and seized another 1,500 pounds of marijuana. I could never have done the investigation without Sergeant Maxwell and agent Whitley. Both of these officers had worked with me for years and we were close friends.

A few months after the drug deal, I was contacted in the middle of the night by La Salle County Justice of the Peace Lee Schooley. The judge told me that I had better get to his house in a hurry. Carroll's wife was standing in front of the judge's house with a .30-.30 Winchester with the hammer back stuck in a guy's belly. The judge said he had tried to talk to her but she appeared intoxicated and kept saying she had made a citizen's arrest. I got in my unit and drove the thirty-eight miles to the judge's house.

When I pulled up it was just like the judge had described. I walked over to the girl and told her that I would take it from here. She put the gun down and walked away. The guy told me he was a plumber and had been sent to repair a water line in one of the hunting cabins on the ranch Carroll managed. Carroll's wife had assumed that he had broken into the cabin and proceeded with making her citizen's arrest.

I contacted Carroll and had him come to the judge's house to pick up his wife. I knew that there was something wrong with her but I figured that the easiest way out of the deal was to let Carroll take care of the wife. The plumber said he didn't want to file any charges on her. When I drove back to Laredo, I dropped him off at the bus station. He said he was going to have someone else pick up his truck. He had done all the ranch work that he wanted.

Carroll called me a few days later and told me that his wife had been drunk and everything was fine now. I told him that it might be a good idea to keep his guns away from his wife unless he wanted to be looking at the business end of one of them someday. He laughed and said that he would take care of it. That's the last time I ever talked with him.

Despite his game-poaching past, Carroll had been a stand-up guy during the whole drug investigation. He had done the right thing and had placed himself in considerable jeopardy in double-crossing the drug dealers. Over the next few years Carroll continued working in the area and never had any trouble with the drug dealers that I knew about. Several years later I got word that he had killed himself in front of some of his friends during a hunting trip. I never did get the facts of the case. As far as I was concerned, in giving us the information that helped us make a major drug case, Carroll had gone a long way toward redeeming himself for his earlier offences.

Snakes and Stolen Cars

During my association with Sheriff Darwin Avant, he unfortunately learned that I was really afraid of snakes. Big snakes, little snakes, poisonous, non-poisonous, I was afraid of them all.

On one occasion when Darwin and I were out hunting, I had gotten out of the car to use a fence post as a rest for my field glasses. I was standing on a cattle guard looking through my binoculars when I kept feeling something rubbing my boot. At the time I thought it was a stick or brush sticking out of the cattle guard. Darwin was sitting in the car waiting for me to tell him if there were any bucks in the clearing.

I happened to look down and saw a large, black snake with the toe of my boot in its mouth. I screamed like a little girl and tried to run three different directions at the same time. I ran about fifty yards down the road before I got myself under control. For the rest of the day, Darwin had trouble driving because he kept laughing at me. One thing I learned from this is that you should never let someone like Avant know that you are afraid of snakes.

A few months later, I was assisting Motor Vehicle Theft agent Frank Malinak on an investigation. Frank had developed a good informant connected to an auto theft ring out of Nuevo Laredo. Every once in a while, the informant would call Frank and tell him they were going to San Antonio to steal cars and pickups. The group always stole Ford Crown Victorias and Chevrolet SUV's.

Frank and I would drive to Cotulla and meet with Avant. The suspects would run scouts ahead of the stolen vehicles to warn them if there were any Highway Patrol cars in the area, so we set unmarked units on the side of Interstate 35 to watch for possible stolen vehicles. When a Suburban or Crown Vic came by, we would call a marked unit to make the stop. We always had several on standby. The Highway Patrol unit would appear out of nowhere, undetected by the scouts. We recovered a lot of stolen cars that way.

The theft ring members knew that if they worked the movie theaters and shopping malls they most likely could have the vehicles across the river in Mexico before they were reported stolen and entered in our database.

One night, busy as we were with one of those interception operations, I could tell that Avant was up to something. I got so suspicious of him that I got back in my car and locked the door. At one point, he walked up to the window and asked me if he could borrow my flashlight.

I reached down to pull out my flashlight and felt something that did not feel like a light. I switched on the dome light and looked down. I had picked up a five-foot rattlesnake! I had my seatbelt on but that didn't stop me from trying to get out of the car. I finally got out of the car and I was mad as hell. There were five or six officers practically rolling on the ground with laughter. They stayed on me the rest of the night. I swore that I would get even with Avant for that one. He had killed the snake earlier in the day and had saved it for when Frank and I would be working with him that night. We ended up getting three or four stolen cars, but it still bothers me to think about picking up that snake.

Horse Thieves

One day during my first few years as a Ranger I was at the DPS office in Laredo when I was told by someone at the front desk that there was an old man who wanted to talk to me. I escorted the man back to my office. He was a Mexican-American who must have been more than 80. I could tell that he was very poor. He said he had taken a bus to the office so he could talk to me in person.

He was almost embarrassingly respectful in the way he talked to me. The man could not speak English, so I had to get one of the other officers to assist me with the interview. The old man told me that he had a white horse on a small piece of land at the southern edge of town. That horse was the one thing in the world that he owned that he took a lot of pride in. He said he had gotten too old to ride the horse, but that he took a lot of joy in going out each day to take care of the animal.

Several weeks before, he continued, some young men started trespassing on his little ranch. They drank beer and made a mess of his property. He said he had gone to his place one day and found the young men on his property. They had run him off his own land and told him they were going to take his horse. Too frail to confront them, he left. When he went back to his place a few days later, his beloved white horse was gone. He told me the group hung out in a feed store in the southern part of Laredo. He said he was afraid of the men and thought they would hurt him if he complained about the horse being stolen. Even so, he said he had gone to the police

144

department and sheriff's office and that neither agency had done anything about the horse theft.

I asked if he knew what time of day the young men could be found at the feed store. He told me that they normally got to the store about 6 p.m. after they got off work. I told him I would check into the situation and get back with him in a day or two.

Late that same afternoon, I drove by the feed store and observed a group of six or eight Hispanic males sitting around outside drinking beer. I drove right up into the middle of them and got out of the car. I told them who I was and that I was looking for a stolen white horse. They all said that they had nothing to do with the stolen horse. I told them I was going to make it my life's mission to mess with them any way I could if the horse didn't show back up at the old man's place. I told them they had better have good insurance on their trucks, their driver's licenses better be current, and that they better have a designated driver when they left the feed store because I was going to check on all those things every day until the horse came back. Then I got back in my car and left.

The next day I was in my office when one of the secretaries in the front told me that a man wanted to see me. It was the old man again. He told me that he had gone back to his little ranch that morning and found that the horse was back in his pen. He'd gotten word that the young men he suspected had brought the horse back during the night and had promised not to bother him anymore.

He then asked me how much he owed me for the return of the horse. I told him he did not owe me a thing and that I was glad to help him anyway that I could. He said that he had lived on the border his whole life and had always heard that the Rangers treated Hispanics in a bad way. He told me that he knew now that was wrong. He said that I had been the only officer to go out of his way to help him and he would never forget it. He left the office and I never saw him again.

A few months later, when it got close to Christmas, I came into the office and the secretaries told me that an old man had brought me a bag of oranges. They said he hadn't wanted to leave his name but I knew who it had been.

Murder by Fire

Sheriff Avant called me one day and said a man had burned to death in a fire in Encinal. He said he didn't think the fire had been intentionally set but he had picked up a witness he wanted me to talk with to see what I thought about his story. I drove to Cotulla and met with the sheriff as requested.

The guy Avant wanted me to interview was about sixty, a next-door neighbor and drinking buddy of the man who had died in the fire. (The victim's wife had survived the fire.) When the two men drank, they always drank too much, the sheriff said.

I went to the county jail, where I ran into Highway Patrol Trooper Miguel Rodriguez. I asked him to sit in on the interview in case I needed his Spanish. I started talking with the neighbor and found that his story didn't add up. He said that he had been drinking with his friend, and that the man had dropped a lit cigarette into a glass of gasoline. Once the fire started, he was unable to save his friend.

I told him he was lying. You could put out a lit cigarette in a cup of gasoline, I said. Gasoline couldn't be ignited that way. Of course, I didn't know if he knew that was nuts, but I decided to give it a try. Trooper Rodriguez had a strange expression on his face but didn't say anything.

I put a little pressure on the suspect, and he finally admitted that he had waited until his friend had passed out from drinking and then set the house on fire. The suspect said he had fallen in love with his friend's wife and wanted her for

147

himself. That was the reason he killed his friend. I took a written confession and put him in jail.

When we walked out I told Rodriquez never to try putting out a lit cigarette in gasoline. We both laughed and I took the confession to the sheriff.

Suicide or Murder?

One night I was just getting ready to go to bed when I received a telephone call from Company D Ranger Kasey King. Kasey was a good friend and I trusted him and his judgment. I had worked with him for years, and I can tell you that he was the best pistol shot I have seen in more than thirty-six years in law enforcement.

Kasey told me he had been contacted by the sheriff in one of the counties in his area about the death of the sheriff's son in Laredo. He said Sheriff Eddie Reeves wanted me to call him about it. He went on to tell me that the sheriff's son reportedly had committed suicide earlier that day.

I had worked a lot of suicides and knew it is always hard for the victim's family to accept that their relative had killed himself. I told Kasey I would call Sheriff Reeves as soon as we got off the phone. As soon as I got off of the phone with Kasey, I called the sheriff. He told me he had been contacted by the Webb County Sheriff's Office and advised that his son had committed suicide. He said deputies were still at the scene. He asked that I go to the scene and look it over to make sure that it was a suicide. I said I would do that and call him as soon as I got through.

"I know you hear this all the time, but my son did not kill himself," he said. I assured him I would call him back as soon as I had additional information. I then contacted the Webb County Sheriff's Office to get the sheriff's son's address. They said he had worked in the oil field and lived at the company yard just east of Laredo on Highway 359.

I drove to that location and met with the deputies on the scene. They told me that the sheriff's son had apparently shot himself in the side of the head while lying in bed. The body had already been removed but I walked through the residence and noticed a large pool of blood on the sheet where the young man had been lying. I could not find anything that looked out of place.

I spoke to the wife, Sharon Reeves. She said she had been in the other room and had heard a gunshot. When she ran into the room, she found her husband shot in the side of the head. She seemed very upset.

I went back to the bedroom to take another look. One of the Webb County deputies had the weapon. I asked to look at it and saw that it was a cheap .22 caliber, 9-shot revolver. I opened the cylinder and noticed that the weapon was fully loaded, with one fired round in the cylinder.

Nothing in the bedroom looked out of order. I decided that I had seen all I needed to see and I started to leave the room. As I walked by their TV I noticed a pistol box on top of the set. I picked up the box and opened it. The box was for the pistol found on the bed when the first officers arrived. I opened it and saw a sales receipt for the pistol. Sharon Reeves had purchased the pistol earlier that day at a gun store in Laredo. Located in the box was one small box of .22 caliber ammunition, the same brand as the pistol was loaded with.

I started hearing bells and whistles. I thought it really strange that the wife had purchased the weapon the same day her husband decided to kill himself with it. I walked out of the room to find the new widow to talk with her about the purchase of the gun. I asked her how she had come to buy the gun that very day. She told me that she had bought the revolver to give to her husband for Father's Day. But she never thought he would do anything like this to himself.

I knew that most of the time, when you are dealing with

.22 caliber, a gunshot residue test will not work, but I decided to ask her if she would submit to a test just to see what kind of reaction I would get. I told the young woman it was normal in this type of situation to have everyone in the house submit to a gunshot residue test to rule them out as a suspect, just a formality to help confirm that the person had actually killed themselves.

When I mentioned the gunshot residue test Sharon got a strange look on her face and appeared to get really nervous. After thinking about it for a while she told me she had no problem with the test. I left her alone and went back to the bedroom to take another look at the scene. A short time later, Sharon approached me and said she needed to talk with me. She told me that she had just remembered that she and her husband had shot the gun earlier in the day, just in case the test came back positive.

I asked Sharon how she had come to shoot the pistol, and she said that her husband wanted her to know how to use the gun. I asked her how many times she shot the gun, and she said she had shot it out in the back yard one time. I asked her to show me what she had shot at and she said she had pointed the gun straight up and had fired one time. I then asked her if she had bought the .22 caliber ammunition that was in the box at the same time she had purchased the weapon. Sharon related that she bought the gun and cartridges at the same time.

At this point I knew that something was really wrong with Sharon's story. I went back to the bedroom and got the pistol box and the ammunition. I walked back to the area where I had parked and got into my car. I opened the pistol box and took out the box of .22's. I counted the number of rounds in the box and found that there were forty-one rounds in the box. I knew that there were nine rounds in the gun, eight unfired and one fired. That was a total of fifty, the number of cartridges that came per box. I must have counted the cartridges ten times.

Where was the one round that she had fired into the air? I

knew that I had her. She had killed her husband and tried to make it look like a suicide. I did not arrest Sharon right away. I went to the Webb County DA's office and met with Assistant DA Angel Moreno. I related everything that I knew about the case, and Moreno agreed with me on what really happened.

We took the case to a Webb County grand jury and they indicted Sharon Reeves for murder. We had the trial in Laredo's old courthouse, and Moreno did a really good job presenting the case to the jury. The fact that Sharon Reeves bought the gun and ammunition on the same day that her husband was killed and the missing .22 round sank her story.

Sharon never admitted that she committed the murder. The trial took a week, and the jury found her guilty and sent her to the penitentiary. I really don't remember how much time she got, but I remember thinking that it was not enough. After the trial was over, I told Sheriff Eddie Reeves that he knew what he was talking about when he told me that his son did not kill himself. He couldn't have been more right.

James Cluiss

I worked on one guy in the Laredo area for most of the time I was a Ranger: James Cluiss. He lived in eastern Webb County and was always up to something. Sometime during his life he had worked in the oilfield, and he had a good working knowledge of the business. I had worked in the oilfield myself during high school and college, so I had an idea how expensive some of the equipment was.

Cluiss made a living hauling off anything that wasn't tied down. He drove a large truck equipped with a winch, and he would latch on to anything he thought he could sell to make a little money. The area scrap metal dealers knew him well.

Most oilfield equipment is made for a specific purpose, and unless you actually know what it is used for, it's really hard to put a value on it. Cluiss had a yard near his residence, and if he couldn't sell the stolen piece of equipment to someone, he would cut it up and sell it for scrap iron.

A local oilfield company representative came into my office one day to report the theft of sixteen frac tanks. He told me that the tanks had been in a yard on the south side of Laredo, and that when the owners had gone back to the yard, the tanks were gone. Oilfield frac tanks are the size of truck trailers and weigh thousands of pounds. I knew that whoever had stolen the tanks had to have known what they were used for, and I knew the first person that I was going to talk with.

I started looking for Cluiss but realized he was giving it his best shot not to be found. I kept leaving business cards in his

153

mailbox. I knew that he had to have gotten the cards, but he was really going out of his way not to be located. I started checking the scrap metal companies to see if they knew where I could find him.

When I walked around the back of a scrap metal company on the south side of Laredo, I noticed Cluiss' truck parked on the company scales, loaded with junk iron. As I looked up, I walked right into Cluiss coming out the office door. I asked if he had a bill of sale for all of the old equipment he was in the process of selling. He told me that it was just some old junk that he had picked up from his yard.

I then asked him what he had done with all the frac tanks he had taken from the yard in south Laredo. Cluiss got this really concerned look on his face, paused for a few seconds, and said, "I sold all of them to some guys in California."

I have no idea why Cluiss decided to give me that little piece of information. I had worked on him on close to fifteen cases, and he never admitted to something unless I had an airtight case on him. I asked him how in the world he had gotten those frac tanks to California, and he just said, "On a train." I told him to follow me to the DPS office so we could try to get the mess straightened out.

At the office, Cluiss told me that he had noticed that someone had parked the frac tanks on a lot in south Laredo. Over the next several months, he never saw anyone check on the tanks, so he came to the conclusion that no one wanted them any more. He told me that since no one wanted them, he thought he could sell the junk and make a little money.

Cluiss said he contacted a company in California and made arrangements for the tanks to be transported to them by rail. At the time, I thought Cluiss was really coming up in the world. He was using the rail system to move his stolen property. I ended up putting him in jail for the theft of the tanks. I arranged for the victim oil company and the company that purchased the tanks to get together, and they worked it out between themselves as to the payment for the stolen tanks.

Stealing the frac tanks didn't net him much jail time, but Cluiss soon paid a much higher price for his criminal lifestyle. It wasn't long after this case that I heard he had been murdered in the Houston area. I don't think that they ever found who killed him. I always thought it had to have been someone he had crossed in one of his business ventures. He just couldn't leave well enough alone.

KKK

As a Ranger, I was periodically assigned to go to Ku Klux Klan rallies. From time to time the KKK would schedule a demonstration at the Capitol in Austin hoping to get a lot of people stirred up. Thousands would show up for those gatherings. The DPS called a lot of troopers and Rangers into Austin to provide security for state property and to keep the crowds from beating the crap out of the Klan members.

Most of the time, in addition to Austin Police Department personnel and Travis County deputies, there were several hundred troopers and forty or fifty Rangers called in to provide security. When they made up the teams I always liked to get paired with Ranger Coy Smith of Uvalde because he always got into something and it was always interesting to see what it would be.

On one occasion Coy caught one guy throwing eggs at the Klan and dragged him out of the crowd by the hair. We got the guy cuffed and loaded, and I sincerely doubt he ever did that again.

We could not believe the kind of people who would show up at the rallies. It would run from the rainbow-hair types to grown men wearing thongs. It was like someone had gone all over Texas and picked up every village idiot that they could find and brought them to the capital. Add the cast from *Deliverance*—hillbilly, snaggle-toothed Klan members—and you can see what we were dealing with. Throw in two or three hundred state police officers and it got interesting, to say the least.

One rally turned really bad. The Klan tried to leave after insulting the crowd for several hours, and the crowd started to riot. I had been assigned to the east doors of the Capitol and was told that no one was to enter the building. I was working with Ranger Kasey King of Kingsville, along with several other Rangers, and we were trying to keep the people out of the building. The rioters had surged from the south side of the Capitol, where the Klan members had been putting on their show, to the east side of the building.

We were pushing and shoving people off the Capitol steps, keeping them from getting inside. Kasey was a Vietnam vet and had been an officer. He and I were standing shoulder to shoulder shoving the crowd back when both of us saw a brick thrown from the crowd, coming at us like a mortar round.

Kasey never missed a beat. He just turned, looked me in the eye and yelled "INCOMING!" For some reason that struck me as really funny at the time. Here I was in the middle of a riot and both Kasey and I were busting a gut at the fact that he had said that!

The brick ended up hitting a trooper in the head, which wasn't funny. The only thing that saved him from being hurt was his riot helmet. We never did find who threw the brick.

We finally got the riot under control, but the crowd did a lot of damage to several of the buildings around the Capitol. One thing I can say is that not a single person got inside.

Protecting the Governor

Not long after I made Ranger I found that my duties included providing security for the governor when he came to my area. The DPS has always provided gubernatorial security, the Criminal Intelligence Service and the Rangers alternating by month as to which service got the duty. If the governor came to the Laredo area on the months that the Rangers had the responsibility, then I had to assist the Governor's security detail in providing transportation to and from wherever he was going.

I had never been around the governor before, and I was a little nervous when it came my turn to pull that duty. When Governor Mark White came to Laredo I picked him up at the airport and took him to where he made a speech. Everything went well and I drove him back to the airport for his flight to Austin. While we were waiting for the plane Governor White came and started talking with me. At the time I was really surprised that he would take the time to visit. He seemed genuinely interested in the conversation and asked me how long I had been a Ranger. It was one of those times that I wanted to ask him, "Counting today?"

But I wasn't going to say that. I told him that I had just made Ranger and we continued to talk until his plane was ready. As he left he asked me my name. Over the next year or so he came to Laredo several times and he always called me by name. It impressed me that he could remember it, with all the people that he met being the governor.

Governor White was a pleasure to be around. A lot of times we had to take him to some function where a meal was served. He always made sure his security detail got the same meal he did. He took care of his people.

Over the next few years the governor came to Laredo with some regularity and I got to be around him quite a bit. He had a deer lease about thirty miles east of town and from time to time would fly in and I would drive him to the ranch. On one of those trips he showed me a Smith & Wesson 9mm pistol one of his friends had given him. He asked me to show him how it worked, and we shot it at an old tree next to the main house on the lease. I noticed that the 9mm rounds would not go through the tree. We tried my .45 Colt semiautomatic and it wouldn't go through the tree either. I walked over to my car and got a Colt .38 Super out of the trunk and the governor and I shot the old dead tree several times with that gun. We found the .38 Super went all the way through the tree and knocked a large chunk off the back side. The governor told me he was going to get a .38 Super when he got back to Austin. I don't know if he ever did, but it was fun shooting with him.

Over the next few months I messed around with the .38 Super and found that it was one of the best pistols a man could carry. I started shooting corner posts to see if it would go through them. I found that it would go through almost anything you shot with it. I did a little reading and found that the .38 Super was designed back in about 1929 for shooting through bullet-proof vests and cars. I started carrying the Super a lot and I fell in love with the gun. I now own more than twenty of them and still admire the way they shoot.

The only down side to working security for Governor White was that he loved to go to Nuevo Laredo. He would make up his mind that he was going across the river to Mexico and away we would go. I don't think that he had any idea how much trouble it was for me to take the Governor of Texas across the river. I would have to call one of the state police *comandantes* and have him send some of his *pistoleros* to help me with security while we were across. I never encountered any trouble, but I always carried several guns just in case.

In those days the Mexican authorities wanted to help us and the governor always treated the Mexican officers with a great deal of respect. He really had it together in the way he treated people. I always liked that about him.

When I decided to write some of the stories about things that happened while I was a Ranger, I didn't know if I should go into my reputation when it came to handling governor security. Well, I decided to tell my side of the story in dealing with Governor Ann Richards.

When Richards was governor, like Mark White, she came to Laredo fairly often. Over a period of time, I got to know her well and felt comfortable talking and joking with her. On one of her visits, I had picked her up and was taking her back to her plane for her return trip to Austin. As I drove she asked me what I thought of the proposed free trade agreement with Mexico. I asked her if she wanted the truth. She said yes, she wanted to know what I really thought since I had spent my career on the Texas-Mexico border.

I asked again if she was sure that she wanted to hear my opinion. She said yes, she did. This is where I made a really big mistake. I told her that in my opinion Mexico did not really like the state of Texas. I related that from what I had seen in my years on the border, Mexico was only interested in taking whatever it could get and had no regard for what was good for Texas. I told her that I thought that someday Mexico was going to sink into the ocean, just like Atlantis, from the sheer weight of all the stuff that its people had stolen in Texas and taken back to Mexico. I told her, as a joke, that we should do the same thing to Mexico that we had just got through doing to Iraq. She laughed, and we continued to talk all the way back to the airport. She got on her plane, and off she went back to Austin. All of this happened on a Saturday. I went home and

160

never thought much about our conversation.

On Monday at 8:01 a.m., I received a call from Captain Dean to be in San Antonio at 10 a.m. I drove to San Antonio knowing something was up, but I had no idea what. When I walked into his office the captain told me to close the door. When your boss tells you to close the door, it's not good. Captain Dean got right to the point with one question: Did I tell the governor that we should bomb Mexico? Now, how do you answer a question like that? Let me say that the captain and I came to an understanding as to how I was to act the next time I was around the governor. He did all of the talking. I returned to Laredo knowing that I was going to be more careful when I was around a governor.

A month or so later, the captain called and told me that I had to pick up Governor Richards on Saturday. I told the captain that I had gotten an invite to go on what promised to be a really good deer hunt that Saturday and asked if someone else could handle it. Captain Dean told me it was my area, and that I would do it. Well, I picked up the governor that Saturday and took her to her meeting. While standing around outside talking with one of her aides I casually mentioned that I had rather be hunting than doing this. We talked for a while longer and then the governor came out and I took her back to the airport.

The following Monday morning Captain Dean called to ask if I had told the governor that I would rather be hunting than guarding her. I said I had not told the governor that, but I had said that to one of her aides. The captain advised me again to keep my mouth shut when I was around the governor.

A month or so went by and Captain Dean again called and told me that Richards was coming to Laredo, and that I had better be on my best behavior. He said he was sending Ranger Smith from Uvalde to help with security because the governor was going to be in the annual George Washington's Birthday parade. Coy and I showed up at the airport and were waiting for the governor to arrive.

161

While we were standing there, a man neither Coy nor I had ever seen walked up and told us to move our cars and to do this and that. When the man walked away, Coy looked at me and said, "Who the hell was that?" I told him I had no idea. Both of us returned to reading the newspaper and continued to wait for the governor.

The governor arrived and we loaded her up and took her to the parade. When we got there, we parked near the area where they had the convertible the governor was supposed to ride in. The governor left to do whatever governors do, and Coy and I were standing near the car waiting to see what they wanted us to do next. One of the governor's aides walked up and asked if we wanted to drive the car in the parade. I looked at Coy and I told them that I did not want to, and Coy said that he didn't, either. Now, stop and think about what we were asked: "Do you want to drive the car in the parade?" It sounded like we had an option.

The governor rode in the parade, and we took her back to her plane. All of this happened on a Saturday. At 8:01 a.m. Monday, I received another one of those fun-filled calls from Captain Dean. He requested that I meet with him in San Antonio to talk about what had happened on Saturday. Again, he asked me just one question: "Did you refuse to drive the Governor of Texas in the parade?" Again, how do you answer a question like that? I related the facts as I knew them, and I was again reminded how I would act around the governor. The captain further related that Coy and I had refused to move our cars when the governor's aide had instructed us at the airport. That was the guy neither one of us knew!

It was at this point that I was informed that I would never be around Governor Ann Richards again. A few months later, she lost her reelection effort to George W. Bush. I was never around her again. I got a lot of ribbing from the other Rangers about all of this. Most of them thought it was really funny. I can see the humor in it now, but at the time it was not funny at all. The one thing I learned is that when a politician asks for your opinion, you should not assume they really want to hear it.

Webb County Jail Break

On February 3, 1986 my good friend Ranger Joaquin Jackson told me that he had to meet with a guy getting ready to make a movie about the Texas Rangers. He asked if I could drive up to Uvalde and talk with the man about the movie. I made arrangements to meet with him at about 4 p.m. I never asked who we were going to meet, but I figured it would be something different so I agreed to go. I never thought about the fact that I was going to be out of my area and I forgot to tell anyone I was going to be out of town.

I met Joaquin at a café on Main Street in Uvalde and we had a glass of tea while we waited for the man to arrive. When I saw a guy pull up outside and get out of his vehicle I thought he looked somewhat familiar. The man walked in and came over to our table and Joaquin introduced him as Nick Nolte. I had never met a movie star before and we started talking about Nolte's next movie. He was going to play a Texas Ranger and wanted to meet with Joaquin about his part. Nolte wanted to get as much information about the Rangers as he could so he could do the part right.

Over the next several hours we talked with Nolte and answered his questions about the Rangers. We finally ended up at Joaquin's house, still talking. About 9 p.m. the telephone rang and I heard Joaquin talking with Captain Dean. "He's right here," Joaquin said, handing me the phone. The captain told me there had been an attempted jail escape at the Webb County Jail in Laredo and that everyone in town was trying to find me. He said it might be a good idea to get my ass back to Laredo since three jailers had been shot and some of the inmates had taken over the jail and fired several shots out the window at officers. I told the captain I was on my way and drove the 130 miles back to Laredo in one hour and fifteen minutes.

When I arrived at the county jail I went straight to the command post that had been set up in the Sheriff's Office next to the jail. I met with Sheriff Mario Santos to get a better understanding of what was going on. The sheriff told me that he had asked the Laredo Police Department for its SWAT team and they were now in place around the jail. I was also advised that numerous other officers from most every law enforcement agency in Laredo was on the scene. Santos told me that we might have to assault the jail but that he did not have any gas masks. I said I could get gas masks out of Austin and have them flown to Laredo in the next few hours. The sheriff asked me to go ahead and make the call because he thought that Rogelio Hernandez, the apparent leader in the escape attempt, was not going to give up. I called the captain and told him what I needed. He said he would contact Austin and have the gas masks on the way as soon as possible.

Sheriff Santos told me that he had spent the last hour or so trying to get Hernandez to give up. Hernandez was a convicted murderer and everyone knew that the last man he killed was an off-duty U.S. Customs Inspector. We knew what kind of guy we were dealing with. It was believed that Hernandez was armed with two handguns and had several other inmates aiding him in his escape attempt.

For the next several hours, Santos continued to talk with Hernandez. He tried to negotiate but you could tell he really wasn't getting anywhere. Hernandez kept telling the sheriff he was going to start killing inmates if he didn't let him out. Laredo PD SWAT team members had been placed on the roofs of nearby buildings but they were unable to provide much information because the inmates had placed blankets over the jail windows. We already had three officers shot and we were trying to keep anyone else from getting hurt. There was no way that we were going to lose containment of the jail.

A DPS aircraft arrived in Laredo around 3 a.m. with about 150 gas masks. The masks were picked up by sheriff's deputies and brought to the county jail. At almost the same time Sheriff Santos called me into his office and said that he had just received word from the hospital that Webb County jailer Gerardo Herrera had died from the gunshot wound to the head he had sustained hours earlier.

The sheriff called a meeting with most of the heads of the agencies that had responded to his call for help so that a course of action could be developed. The Webb County jail is located downtown. We all knew that when morning came there would be a lot of people milling around and we would have a hard time securing the area. We now thought that we had at least four inmates with handguns and we could not allow them to start shooting out the windows of the jail.

Sheriff Santos asked most of the officers in the room their ideas as to what action should be taken. To a man we all said that we needed to retake the jail before daylight. At approximately 4:30 a.m. the sheriff made the decision to assault the jail.

The ten-man Laredo police SWAT team would make entry to the second floor of the jail and attempt to secure that area. A second team of forty officers from DPS, Laredo PD, the Border Patrol, the Sheriff's Department and the Webb County DA's Office would secure the ground floor and support the SWAT team. A third team of sixty officers from the same agencies would secure the outside of the building to make sure no one got out.

We executed the plan and were able to regain control of the jail in about twenty minutes without a shot being fired. After the jail had been secured Hernandez was taken into custody and brought to the holding area on the first floor. All of the remaining inmates were strip-searched and placed in Border Patrol buses while officers worked the crime scene. We found five handguns with the serial numbers ground off as well as ammunition during the search of the jail.

Over the next several weeks I did nothing but work on the investigation into how the guns got into the jail. We found that a Columbian by the name of Alberto Audemar had paid for the escape. He was facing a long prison sentence on Federal cocaine charges and had the weapons smuggled into the jail with the intent to escape. Audemar had made a deal with Hernandez to lead the escape.

I took the guns used in the escape attempt to the DPS laboratory in Austin and they were able to raise the serial numbers. Once we obtained the serial numbers we were able to identify the people who bought the weapons. We ended up arresting thirteen people inside and outside the jail who had been involved in the escape plot.

Hernandez was later convicted of capital murder and sentenced to death for killing the Webb County deputy. He died in prison before the State of Texas could kill him. Audemar got life in prison. He is still there for his part in the attempted escape. The two other jailers wounded in the incident recovered and went on with their career.

One thing I learned from this case: Always let someone know where you are going when you leave town. That's another one of those lessons that you never forget.

Zapata County Sheriff's Office

When I first went to work as a Ranger, I started going to Zapata to start building a relationship with the local sheriff's office. Zapata is on the border and has a lot of crime related to the illegal aliens who live and work in the area. I really don't know how much the other Rangers who had been stationed in Laredo had worked in Zapata, but I got the idea that the sheriff's department was not used to working with Rangers.

Over the next year or two I would go to Zapata for no other reason than to eat lunch with the local officers and get to know them. Over that period of time I became friends with Sheriff Romeo Ramirez. The sheriff seemed to be a good guy and didn't mind that I was working with his investigators. I also became good friends with deputy Lico Lopez and investigator Joaquin Solis. If you needed to find someone in Zapata, Solis was the go-to guy. He also had a lot of informants.

One night Sheriff Ramirez called me at home and told me he thought that someone in his department was stealing marijuana from the evidence storage area. I knew the storage room was located on the second floor of the courthouse inside the sheriff's office. We talked about the situation for a while and I made arrangements to meet with him the following day.

The next morning I drove to Zapata. Sheriff Ramirez told me that he thought that he was missing a lot of marijuana. He and some of his trusted people had re-weighed the seized marijuana and had found that in a lot of the cases, the weights were significantly less than they had been recorded initially. The sheriff then decided that we would look into the evidence room and see if we could figure out how the marijuana was being stolen from right under his nose.

When we went into the room, I noticed that the door had several deadbolts and the walls were solid. The sheriff said he had the only keys to the room. He and I then began to look at the ceiling, where we noticed that some of the tiles appeared to have been moved. He and I removed the tiles to see if anyone had been in the crawl space above.

We got a ladder and I removed one of the tiles and, sure enough, you could see where someone had crawled across the ceiling beams. I could see that the trail in the dust led to an area just above the men's restroom. I climbed into the attic and could see what appeared to be handprints on some white PVC pipe that ran the entire length of the room just above the evidence storage area.

The crawl space was only about three feet high and I had a hard time getting around. It was dark and had about twenty years of dust all over the area. I had taken a lot of prints before, and I knew that if I tried to lift the prints in the dust I would most likely mess them up. I had to figure out how I could preserve the prints so they could be lifted from the pipe.

I called the DPS lab in Austin and told them about the problem. They said they had a special spray—similar to hair spray—to protect prints. I told the sheriff that I had to go to the store and would be back in a little while. I went down the street and bought two cans of hair spray.

When I got back to the sheriff's office, I got my camera out and took photos of the prints with a micro-lens. That way I would have some kind of record of the prints in case I messed them up when I tried to lift them. I got back up into the attic and covered the prints with a mist from the hair spray. I let it dry for a while and then lifted the prints in the normal way with a feather duster and powder.

169

After I lifted the prints with tape, I put them on three-by-five cards so I could send them in for comparison if I ever got a suspect. In those days having a perpetrator's fingerprints really didn't do you that much good if you didn't have a suspect to compare them to.

When I got out of the attic, I had several prints I thought were good enough to identify whoever had stolen the dope. The sheriff and I then went to his office to talk about what we had just learned. We realized that the only people who normally used the second floor-restroom were sheriff's department employees.

I asked the sheriff how many people he had working for him, and he said there were twenty-five or twenty-six people, counting deputies and radio operators. I asked him if we could fingerprint all of his employees so we could eliminate everyone not involved in the case. He said if I would be at his office the following day, he would have every one of his employees present so they could be fingerprinted. I agreed to that and returned to Laredo.

When I got back to Laredo I ran into an FBI agent I knew and I told him about the case that I was working. He said that if I could get all of the prints together, he would send them to Washington to have the comparison done at the FBI laboratory and would have the results back to me within a week. I knew if I sent the prints to our lab in Austin it would take months to get the results back. I made arrangements to bring him the print cards as soon as I got everything together.

The following day I drove back to Zapata. Sure enough, the sheriff had every employee waiting to be printed and I printed all of them, with the sheriff, at his request, being the first one printed. I got everything together and drove back to Laredo to meet with the FBI agent and hand over the prints. He told me he didn't know how long it would take, but that he would let me know as soon as he got the results.

About a week later, the agent contacted me and said the

lab in Washington had identified two Zapata County deputies' prints as matching the prints from the PVC pipe that ran over the evidence storage area. I knew there was no legitimate reason for the officers' prints to be in that area. It wasn't like they had been working on the plumbing in the attic. I drove back to Zapata and told Sheriff Ramirez that we had identified the two deputies.

I knew that all we had to do now was interview them and get written statements. You would think a police officer would be the hardest guy to break during an interview. But in my experience they were the easiest. I always thought that they knew right from wrong and seemed to want to tell the truth.

I brought in the two deputies and interviewed them. Both admitted that they had been stealing marijuana from the room, and I took written confessions. They told me that they had been working with a sheriff's radio operator who had kept watch for them while they stole the dope.

We filed criminal charges on the three Zapata County sheriff's employees and I placed them in the same jail where they had been working. It never made me feel good to arrest a fellow officer, judge or prosecutor. I always got a sick feeling in my stomach but I knew it had to be done. I know that it looked bad for the sheriff but when I talked with him, he was glad we had solved his problem.

A few years after Sheriff Ramirez and I worked this case together, he was arrested for taking payoffs from an FBI informant who was allegedly going to cross loads of drugs on some land that the sheriff owned. The county lawman ended up doing time in the federal penitentiary. I later ran into him near the Zapata County Fair Grounds when I was there for a roping competition and he just bowed his head and walked on by. He knew what I thought of officers that went over to the dark side. He gave up his life, job, and reputation in the community for around $20,000. Such a waste.

Zapata County

Over the years I was stationed in Laredo, I continued working in Zapata County. I worked with Sheriff Gilberto Villarreal, who died in office, and Sheriff Sigi Gonzalez, who succeeded him. Sheriff Gonzalez and I had been friends since he had worked at the DPS as a communications operator. He has been in law enforcement for well over twenty-five years, having worked as a deputy and with the county attorney's office before being elected sheriff.

Someone else I always got along with was Chief Investigator Joaquin Solis. He's a good guy to be around, always doing something funny and generally keeping things interesting. He and I worked a lot of cases through the years, and we solved a lot of them because he knew the people and the area.

Deputy Lico Lopez is Soliz' sidekick, and he's as much fun as Soliz. He's one of the best drug interdiction officers in Texas. When he and Soliz are working together they take down a lot of loads of dope. I worked a lot with them the last six or eight months before I retired, and we busted over 10,000 pounds of marijuana in numerous seizures. Soliz and Lopez would call and tell me that they had something going on, and I would meet them in Zapata. We would either run a search warrant or do some kind of surveillance on a certain location. We almost always got a load of dope.

The drug dealers always find someone in need of money to drive their loads. They give the driver the keys to a car already loaded and tell him to deliver the vehicle to a given location. If the police attempt a traffic stop on the vehicle the driver is instructed to drive off the highway and through the fence, getting the car as far away from the highway as possible. The driver then abandons the vehicle and makes his way away from it until he can be picked up later.

The two Zapata County officers and I have gotten numerous loads of dope in this way. They were very good at what they did. When we had a major offense, such as a murder, they would call me and we would work the case together. We made a lot of good cases.

One case we worked involved a string of armed robberies that had occurred in the Zapata area. During this same time period, the Laredo Police Department had had several robberies there. It appeared to us that all of the hold ups were being done by the same people. Lopez and I thought we had developed a lead and had gone out to a ranch to interview several illegal aliens to see if they might be involved. We got permission from the ranch owner to search a trailer house for any handguns or masks that could have been used in the robbery.

Lopez started looking around one part of the trailer while I went into the bedroom to check it out. The trailer was very clean and the beds were all made. From past experience I had learned that a lot of people will place handguns under their pillows or between the mattresses. I walked over to the bed and started to run my hand under the pillow to see if there was a gun under it. Just as I started to put my hand under the pillow, something told me not to do it. I just picked up the pillow and looked under it. The first thing I saw was a large SNAKE. When I saw the snake, he darted under the sheets.

I tried to run in three directions at the same time, and all of the people ran into the bedroom to see what was going on with all the screaming and jumping. We ended up killing the snake with a stick. Lopez was really on me about the way I had acted when I saw the snake. Remember, I do not like snakes. Both of us then went to the barn to see what we could find.

The room we were searching in the barn was kind of dark but both of us saw what appeared to be a black bag. As Lopez went over to check it, the object moved, and Lopez screamed just as I had with the snake. Both of us were thinking, "snake" and we headed for the door. The "snake" turned out to be a black puppy that was curled up asleep. Lopez and I had a really good laugh about that. Two really big, bad, tough law enforcement officers being run out of a barn by a puppy. We had to tell the guys at the sheriff's office for self-preservation. If they found out any other way, we would not have lived it down. We ended up solving the armed robberies and making several arrests with the help of the Laredo Police Department.

On another occasion Sheriff Gonzalez called me and said he had a questionable death he wanted me to help them with. I drove to Zapata and met with the sheriff and deputies Jessie Chapa, Solis, and Lopez to help them work the investigation. When I arrived at the scene, I found the nude body of a female lying on her back in the middle of the kitchen. The woman's eyes were open.

The victim looked to have been burned over about seventy-five percent of her body. The fire appeared to have started near the front door of the residence. We had also been advised that the woman's husband had been transported to the hospital due to severe burns on his hands. We all worked the crime scene, but we could not explain how the female had gotten the burns all over her body. It took us all night to work the scene, and we still did not have a good idea how the woman had died.

The following day we learned that the husband had been transferred to the burn center in San Antonio. Several of the Zapata County officers and I drove to San Antonio to interview the husband. He told us that his wife had been dancing around and that she had gotten a piece of her clothing on fire from a candle. He said that he had burned his hands trying to put out the fire on his wife. The hospital was not the place to try to interview a suspect in detail, but we all left San Antonio thinking that the husband had something to do with the his wife's death.

We waited several weeks until he got out of the hospital, and then met with him to get some additional information. Deputy Chapa and I interviewed the suspect, and he finally admitted that he and his wife had been drinking and had gotten into an argument. During the argument the suspect had poured model airplane fuel on his wife and had set her on fire. Chapa and I got a written confession from him, and he later went to the penitentiary for seventy-five years.

The Zapata officers were a hard-working bunch, and yet they always managed to have fun. Soliz was telling me one day that one of the jail cooks had gone to him asking about some of the blue pills that he could take so he could keep his wife up all night. The deputy said he told the cook he was out of the blue pills, but he had some other pills he could use that were sure to keep his wife up all night. The cook agreed to give the "prescription" a try. Soliz gave him four pills and told him to take two and wait a little while and take two more.

The next morning the cook came to talk to Soliz. The guy looked really bad. The cook told him that he had the worst diarrhea that he had ever had in his life. Soliz just laughed and said, "I bet your wife didn't sleep at all last night, did she?"

One of the cases I worked involved Zapata County Attorney Arturo Figueroa. Though most county attorneys only handle misdemeanor cases, he helped the district attorney in getting felony cases ready for the grand jury. I had worked with Figueroa for years, and I knew he was in charge of the county forfeiture fund.

I began to get information that there was something wrong with the way he was handling the seized drug money. I had several friends who told me that a lot of money was missing from the fund, but I really didn't have anything to justify an investigation. I went to the U.S. district attorney's office in Laredo and told them what I had been hearing. I was told that was not a federal problem and that they could do nothing. Over the next few months I continued to get information that something was wrong at the county attorney's office. One morning I decided to go to Zapata and have a talk with Figueroa. I called him and said I would be in Zapata in about an hour and needed to talk with him.

I really didn't beat around the bush. I told him I knew something was up with the forfeiture fund, and I wanted to know if he had done something that he knew he shouldn't have.

Figueroa told me he had screwed up. I asked him how bad he had screwed up, and he told me about $193,000 bad. He asked if I would go and speak to the DA and relate that he was willing to plead guilty. I drove to Laredo and met with District Attorney Joe Rubio and advised him of the situation. A few days later Figueroa pled guilty to the theft of the money.

I had two separate federal agencies call me after the case was resolved to ask why I had not gone to them when it was time to file a complaint. I told them I had gone to the U.S. Attorney and that he told me there was nothing that they could do. I was a state officer and that left me only one place to file the case, the Webb County District Attorney's Office. I never really understood why the Feds showed no interest when I first brought the case to them.

Murder in Zapata

Zapata County Chief Investigator Joaquin Solis called one day to tell me they were working a murder that had occurred at a bar on the north side of town. The victim had been found in the restroom with his pants down.

I drove to Zapata and met with Soliz. He said that the night before, the victim had gone to the bar for a beer or two. Not to speak ill of the dead, but the victim had a criminal history. Several years before he had killed an area man. When he walked into the bar on what would be his last night on earth, he had not known that a relative of the man he had killed was also in the bar, and that he was hell-bent on getting even. One thing I'd always noticed about Zapata was that the people there lived by the feud. No matter how long it took, it always seemed important to them to get even.

After drinking beer for a while, the about-to-be victim walked into the restroom to relieve himself. While he was standing at the urinal, the suspect walked in and shot him numerous times in the back with a 9mm semiautomatic. Of course, once everything goes to hell in a bar, suddenly no one's thirsty anymore. By the time deputies got to the scene almost everyone had vacated the place. The deputies did get a physical description of the shooter, but no one wanted to get involved when it came to giving up a name.

It was one of the only bar shootings I ever worked where everyone didn't claim to have been in the bathroom when it happened. Soliz and I spent most of the day working and we

177

finally got a lead on the suspect. We picked him up and tried to interview him, but he refused to make a statement. One of the deputies told us he had been to the suspects' house in an effort to locate him earlier in the day and had noticed several 9mm shell casings on the ground just outside the back door.

Soliz and I both knew that it was a common thing in the area for local residents to fire weapons into the air during holiday celebrations. When the suspect had been arrested, officers had not been able to find the murder weapon. Soliz, Lopez and I went to the suspect's residence and picked up the 9mm casings so they could be compared to the brass recovered at the crime scene.

I drove to the DPS laboratory the following day, and submitted the two separate groups of shell casings for comparison. About two weeks later, I received word from the lab that both of the exhibits I submitted had been fired from the same gun. We could now tie the suspect to the bar. There was no way he could explain how the same casings found at his house were found next to the murder victim. Case solved.

A Zapata County grand jury indicted the suspect for murder. He later pled guilty and was sent to the penitentiary. As far as I know, he's still there. A lot of times as a criminal investigator, you don't have to be good—you just have to be lucky.

Mess with the Bull,
You Get the Horns

As a Ranger you are assigned to work from 8 a.m. to 5 p.m. five days a week, but you are on call twenty-four hours a day, seven days a week, three-hundred-sixty-five days a year. The only exception is if you have made special arrangements with the captain to be off-duty. You have to be willing to make that kind of sacrifice if you want to be a Texas Ranger. When the telephone rings at your house at a certain time of night, you know before you answer it that it's about work.

One night I was sitting around watching TV when I got one of those calls. The DPS communications operator told me that DPS Trooper John Reed was just north of Zapata in the middle of a gun battle and was calling for help. I grabbed my guns and badge, and headed for the car. When I got in my unit the police radio was going nuts. I started south through heavy traffic to get to the area as fast as I could to help Trooper Reed.

As I neared an intersection in south Laredo I looked both ways and proceeded through a red light. The next thing I knew my vehicle was spinning around, finally coming to rest facing the opposite direction. I was wearing my seat belt and was not hurt. Looking up, I saw a Laredo Fire Department ambulance sitting crossways in the road. The first thing I thought was, *How in the hell did they get here so fast?* Then I realized that I had hit the ambulance broadside, nearly totaling my unit. The two firemen in the ambulance also were uninjured. Luckily

179

there were no patients being transported at the time.

In a short time the Laredo Police Department arrived to work the accident. About the time the Laredo units began pulling up, Highway Patrol Sergeant Don Valdez arrived to make sure I was okay. I handed my driver's license to the Laredo PD officer and told Sergeant Valdez that we were going to Zapata County to work the shooting. We left the wrecked vehicles sitting in the middle of the road and headed south on Highway 83.

As I walked up to the scene I saw that Trooper Reed appeared uninjured but very upset. He had made a traffic stop and the driver of the vehicle had pulled a gun on him. John then shot and killed his assailant. Trooper Reed was a good, seasoned officer with years of training. I knew what he must be going through. No police officer ever wanted to have to take someone's life.

I examined the area between the DPS unit and the suspect's vehicle where the assailant had gone down. We recovered one small revolver from the ground in the area where the assailant fell and another revolver from the front seat of the dead man's car. I knew the assailant. He was a convicted felon. He had previously been involved in two murders and had just gotten out of the Texas penitentiary. In fact, he was committing two additional felonies by just being in possession of the two handguns.

I worked the crime scene for the next several hours with the assistance of the Zapata County Sheriff's Office. When I finished, I drove into Zapata to take a statement from Trooper Reed.

I could tell he was having a real problem, as anyone would, with the fact that he had killed the assailant. As I interviewed him, I found that he had made a traffic stop on the suspect because he thought that he may have been driving under the influence of alcohol. When Trooper Reed got the guy out of the car, he ran a check to ascertain if he had any outstanding warrants. Trooper Reed lived and worked in Zapata. He knew just about everyone in town, including the man he had stopped. Knowing the man had a long criminal record, John proceeded very carefully.

Shortly after making the stop, John walked back to his unit to answer the radio. When he got off the radio, as he got out of his car he saw the man walking toward him with a small handgun pointed directly at him. Trooper Reed pulled his DPS issue service weapon and shot the guy in self-defense just like he had been trained to do. A Zapata County deputy arrived just as the shooting ended.

I interviewed all of the officers involved, and to me it was an open and shut case. After taking a statement from John I concluded my investigation within two or three days. I learned that the suspect had been looking for another guy who he had a dispute with when he was stopped by the Highway Patrol Trooper.

The family of the dead man was upset and complained about the way that John handled the matter. I don't mean complaining a little, either. The family got to the point that they had an eighty-year-old grandmother in a wheelchair holding signs on the grass lawn in front of the federal courthouse in Laredo. The news media went nuts, pitting the dead man's family against the state police.

We took the case to the Zapata County grand jury, which no-billed Trooper Reed. In Texas this indicates that the Trooper had done nothing wrong and had followed the letter of the law. Despite that, things got worse. John started receiving death threats from some of the people in town. The dead suspect's family built a shrine on the side of the highway where the shooting took place. Each time I would go to Zapata I would notice that the shrine got bigger, with more flowers. DPS finally moved John to another duty station.

This shooting was the most justified officer-shooting I ever worked. In my opinion, if there was one guy on the planet who needed to be stopped, it was this guy. He had already been involved in numerous criminal offenses and was out committing several more when he tried to kill a state trooper. When you mess with the bull long enough, you're going to get the horns. From time to time when I traveled to Zapata I would personally stop at the shrine and water the flowers.

Carrizo Springs Murder

When Joaquin Jackson retired in 1993, I started working Dimmit County in addition to my other counties. I had known and been friends with Sheriff Ben "Doc" Murray for several years. I always liked to work around him because of the way he treated people. Murray worked like an old-time sheriff. He handled the street and even cooked a lot of the meals at the county jail.

I had been in Doc's office when some people down on their luck would come in and tell him that they needed money to buy something to eat. The sheriff would reach into his pocket and give them some money, knowing he would never see the money again. He was a World War II veteran and told me several times that the war broke him from hunting game. Doc was a lot older than me, but he could work just as hard as I could. We worked a lot of cases together, and I always had a lot of respect for him.

He called me one day and asked me to meet with him in Carrizo Springs to talk about a case that had occurred a few days before. I drove to Carrizo and met the sheriff at his office on the second floor of the courthouse. He told me that an old man who had been living in a school bus east of town had been found murdered. The sheriff said he didn't have a clue as to who had committed the offense.

He and I went to the crime scene to have a look. While we were at the scene we checked out everything as best as we could, but we came away with nothing more then we had when

183

we started. We drove back to the courthouse, and I asked Doc to let me see the crime scene photos so I could get a feeling for the amount of violence used in the murder.

They were the strangest crime scene images that I had ever seen. The victim appeared to have skeletal arms, but the rest of his body appeared to be fresh. I thought back to my homicide investigation training, but I could not come up with an answer. There was no way that I could explain it.

I finally asked Doc how long the guy had been dead, and he told me only a few days. When the sheriff told me that the victim had lived with several small dogs, it hit me. The dogs had been locked up with the body and had eaten the arms of the victim-owner as they got hungry. We worked on the case for the next several days, but never came up with a possible suspect.

About a week later the sheriff called and asked me to return to Carrizo. When I got there, Doc told me about a man living on the Nueces River east of town. The man was kind of strange. He just roamed up and down the river, sleeping wherever he happened to be when it got dark.

Doc said he had a gut feeling that the guy had something to do with the murder. The problem was trying to find the man. No one knew where he was. I told the sheriff to have his patrol deputies start looking for him, and when they got him located to give me a call so I could interview him.

About a week later, Doc called and said he had the guy at his office. I told him I would be there in an hour. I started that way, and for some reason I thought about calling Ranger Coy Smith to help with the interview. Coy and I had worked a lot of cases together. When we interviewed someone, one of us would take up the slack for the other. He agreed to meet me at Carrizo Springs and both of us got there about the same time.

Murray told us what little he knew about the suspect and we prepared to do the interview. As a police officer, this type of interview is the hardest. We had nothing to put on the guy and we could not dispute anything he said because we could not even place him near the scene.

From the start, the guy seemed really nervous. His body language told us he was not telling the truth. We interviewed him for about two hours, but got nothing. Just as we were about to leave, I asked him if he would be willing to take a polygraph test and he said he would be glad to. At this point, Coy and I were pretty much convinced he had nothing to do with the murder. When we got up to leave Coy tossed out that it was really a shame that the dogs had eaten the victim.

"What do you mean?" the suspect asked. Coy and I showed him the photo of the victim with the skeletal arms. We told him that the guy's dogs had eaten his arms off and that's all that was left.

The man appeared to get physically sick, his gag reflex taking over. After he regained his composure Coy and I started in on him again. Still nothing, but he did agree to take the polygraph test the following day. Despite his suspicious reaction to the crime scene photo, we had to let him go.

We met with the sheriff and told him we had the guy who had killed the old man. His reaction to the picture indicated to us that he was involved. Now all we had to do was build a case. I made arrangements for the suspect to be transported to Corpus Christi the following day by one of Doc's deputies so he could be run on a polygraph machine.

About 4 p.m. the next day, the polygraph operator telephoned me to report that the suspect had changed his mind, refusing to take the test. He said he wanted to talk to the Rangers again and was on his way back to Carrizo. I called Coy and told him what had happened, and we agreed to be waiting for the guy when he returned. I drove to Carrizo and again met with Coy. When the suspect was brought into the Sheriff's Office, we sat down and started another interview.

Within fifteen seconds the suspect told us he had killed the man because he intended to rob him. We took a written confession and put the suspect in the Dimmit County Jail. He got convicted and ended up going to the penitentiary. I kidded Coy that it was his charming personality that had made the guy want to throw up, not the crime scene picture. We had solved the case, but it had been Sheriff Murray's gut feeling that led us to the suspect.

Snakebit, or Shot?

One night I was contacted by DPS communications and advised that a kidnapping suspect was running north on Interstate 35 with a Laredo Police Department unit behind him. I grabbed my AR-15 and ran to my car to try to catch up with the rolling hostage situation. I soon caught up with the suspect's car, a large older model station wagon, about eighteen miles north of town. The police car and I followed the suspect's vehicle for several miles as it continued northbound.

As we headed north, several more DPS and Laredo police units joined us, and by radio we began to try to figure out how to get the vehicle stopped. While we worked on a plan, the station wagon pulled off the highway onto the east service road and stopped. We took that opportunity to block its path and surrounded the vehicle.

As I got out of my unit I noticed that the man in the station wagon held a small child in front of him as a shield. He was also yelling for us to stay away. All the officers got out of their units and took cover behind their cars. Over the next hour we found out that the suspect had gotten in a fight with his wife and had taken his son hostage. He told his wife he was going to hurt the child. The information we received indicated that the man had some type of handgun. He also had a history of having trouble with the police.

We set up a command post and started to formulate a plan aimed at getting the guy to give up. While waiting for the Laredo Police Department SWAT team, we continued to try to persuade the suspect to surrender. I had worked my way to within about twenty yards of the station wagon and crouched behind a car looking at the guy through the scope of my AR-15.

I could have killed him at any point, but we wanted to try to get him to give up if we could. I didn't really care if he got hurt, but we sure didn't want anything to happen to an innocent child. I was thinking at the time that it took a really sorry SOB to put his own son in danger.

While I was standing there with the rifle I caught a movement out of the corner of my eye. I looked down and saw a six-foot rattlesnake had crawled from under the car I was hiding behind. The snake was within one foot from me. I had to make a quick decision whether to risk getting snake bit or shot.

I jumped about five feet in the air and hit the ground running to get away from the snake. I was about twenty yards down the road before I got control of myself. Stopping, I looked around hoping no one saw me. Then I walked over to the command post and casually asked if anyone had come up with a plan yet.

I was standing with about six other officers beside one of the cars we were using for communication, when I again noticed movement on the ground. Another rattlesnake, this one a little five-footer, slithered from under the car. I yelled, "SNAKE!" and reverted to my standard save-your-ass-from-a-rattler routine. I don't think anyone cared if they got shot at that moment. It looked like a sandlot-rules football game with everyone running into each other trying to get away from the snake.

When I realized where I was, I found myself standing in the middle of the car hood, an easy target for our hostage-taker. One of the officers told us that the snake had gone into the brush, and we all got back to the business at hand. About this time the Laredo SWAT team showed up and deployed in the brush so they could sneak closer to the station wagon.

I could not tell exactly where the SWAT guys were because they were dressed in black and not using their flashlights. I walked over to the Laredo PD command lieutenant and asked him if they had thought to tell the men about the two snakes we had run across. The lieutenant got on the radio and related that small piece of information to his men.

I was standing on the side of the road looking out into the pasture when all of a sudden it looked like an international airport with all the flashlights that suddenly came on. Light beams were going everywhere! Despite the circumstances, that struck me as really funny, and Highway Patrol Sergeant Don Valdez and I had a good laugh.

We had decided to let the Laredo Police Department run the show since the problem had started in town, but the DPS would provide support if they needed it. One of the Laredo lieutenants decided it would be a good idea to bring the suspect's wife to the scene and let her try to talk him into giving up.

When the wife arrived, we put her on the loud speaker in the Highway Patrol sergeant's car. Hearing his wife over the PA system really got the guy stirred up. About this time he decided he no longer wanted to play, and was going to leave. I was behind the wheel of the Highway Patrol sergeant's car when he started to drive off. I hit the gas and rammed his car from the front to make sure he stayed put.

I injured my right knee in the impact. He somehow kept moving, wrecking three of our cars before he made it back on the interstate. Then he drove off as fast as he could. We chased him all the way back to Laredo, finally stopping him at the international bridge, just before he got into Mexico. Thirteen police cars got wrecked trying to get that guy corralled. We could have used a lot more aggressive measures during the chase, but we were concerned for the safety of the small child in the station wagon.

When we finally got the vehicle stopped, we rescued the

child and found that the father had not been armed. We filed every charge we could think of on the suspect and placed him in the Webb County Jail.

Despite all the damage to government property, no one had been hurt. Beyond that, I found that I wasn't the only law enforcement officer in South Texas who was afraid of rattlesnakes.

Sheriff Murray

In December 1991 my two sons, Justin and Jared, came to Laredo to spend the Christmas holidays with me. I always looked forward to their visits because my ex-wife had moved them to California after our divorce. I never liked that my sons lived in the Republic of California. I've never been there, but from what I have seen on TV and read in newspapers, at any given time the place is either on fire, flooding, or about to fall into the ocean. I won't even go into what I think about the kind of people who live there and the opinions many of them seem to have.

Anyway, my two stepsons, Polo and Carlos, were looking forward to my sons' visit. We spent Christmas together and did a lot of hunting. Just after the first of the year, I had taken two of the boys out early to go deer hunting with a good friend, Russell Deutsch. Russell and I had hunted together for years. He had a good place close to town. I had just met up with Russell when I got a telephone call from the DPS office in Laredo. I knew that if I was getting a phone call from communications at 7 a.m., it wasn't to wish me happy New Year.

They told me that my friend Sheriff "Doc" Murray had been found dead in his home in Carrizo Springs. The communications operator did not have any information as to how the sheriff had died, but said I needed to contact the Dimmit County Sheriff's Office as soon as possible. When I called the sheriff's office in Carrizo the radio operator could hardly talk. I was thinking that the sheriff, being an older man, had died of natural causes. The only thing I got from the radio operator was that there was blood all over the house and a large knife sticking out of the sheriff's chest.

I told Russell I had to leave and to please give my boys a ride back to our house when they finished their hunt. I drove to Carrizo Springs as fast as I could. I talked with Ranger Coy Smith on the way and made arrangements to meet him at the sheriff's residence.

When I got to the scene, I parked and entered the house through the back door. I don't think anyone can be prepared to see one of their friends in the condition that we found Sheriff Murray. I had worked a lot of murders by that point in my career and I thought I could take almost anything that came along, but when I walked into the room and found my friend butchered, it really hit me hard. It took me a little while to get my head on right, put aside my personal feelings, and get on with what we had to do to find out who had done this.

When I walked into the house the heat was overwhelming. It was cold outside and the gas heaters were on. I could smell the blood when I entered the room. I found a piece of Doc's ear lying just inside the room. I was really angry and wanted payback. Coy and I looked at each other, and we told each other almost at the same time that we were not going home until we got the people who did this. We would go after them with every thing we had and do whatever it took to bring them to justice.

Coy and I had worked together since he had made Ranger in late 1986. Ranger Joaquin Jackson had transferred to Alpine and when Smith made Ranger, he was stationed in Uvalde to replace Joaquin. For the first four or five years after that Coy and I worked a lot together. We had done a lot of interviews together and practically knew what the other one would say before he said it. Both of us were also close friends with La Salle County Sheriff Avant.

192

Since Coy and I had done a lot of work together, we knew each other's strong and weak points. He always said I was good for the first twenty-four hours of an investigation, and that I could really get things done on the street. He excelled at working crime scenes and getting the complicated things done. That's the way we decided to work Sheriff Murray's death. Coy would handle the detail work and I would turn over every rock for information. We both felt a lot of pressure. This was one of those cases that could not go unsolved. A county sheriff being murdered in his own home was just about as bad as it could get. Add the fact that the sheriff happened to be a close friend. We were going to do whatever it took to catch the guys that had killed our friend.

Sheriff Ben Murray and Doyle with a recovered stolen Chevrolet Corvette. Photo taken only a short time before the sheriff was found murdered in his home in Carrizo Springs.

Chief Deputy Raul Medina, Coy, and I made up our minds that we would take our time in working the crime scene to be

193

sure that we didn't miss anything. We wanted to make sure that we found all the evidence possible to help us identify the people that had killed our friend.

It appeared that the suspects had entered the residence through the back door. Sheriff Murray always parked his car in a carport in the back of the residence, and he would come in through the back door. After walking through the crime scene, we believed the fight had started at the back bedroom, progressed into the kitchen and finally into the living room where the sheriff's body was located. The sheriff was lying on his side, shot one time in the forehead with a large caliber weapon. He also had a large butcher knife sticking out the middle of his chest. Blood was everywhere.

When I walked out the back door to get something out of my car, I found almost everyone in town gathered around the house. I went back inside and told Coy it looked like the Dallas Cowboys were playing in the super bowl outside. We needed more officers to help us with crowd control.

Coy and I were in constant contact with Lieutenant C. J. Havrda at the Company D headquarters in San Antonio The lieutenant told us we could have whatever resources we needed on this case. We said we needed a DPS crime lab team to assist us in working the crime scene. He told us the team would arrive at our location just after lunch.

One thing that got us off on the wrong trail at the beginning of our investigation was the wallet we found in the kitchen. The billfold held the Texas driver's license of a man from Kingsville. It appeared that the wallet had been lost during the fight with the sheriff, which made us really want to find the guy who owned it.

At this point every law enforcement officer in South Texas was aware that someone had murdered the sheriff of Dimmit County. We had every kind of officer a person could think of show up in Carrizo Springs wanting to help with the investigation. Coy and I got some of the officers together and told them their assignment was to locate the guy from Kingsville. La Salle County Sheriff Avant came to the scene along with Webb County District Attorney Chief Investigator O.J. Hale. Both O. J. and Darwin had also been friends with Sheriff Murray.

Over the next several hours Coy and I worked the crime scene by making diagrams and taking photos of things we thought might relate to the offense. Chief Deputy Medina had been at the scene when I arrived, and he had a lot of helpful input as to the sheriff's home routine.

As we cataloged evidence, we realized the sheriff's handgun was missing. I knew he carried a chrome-plated Colt 1911 Government Model .45. I knew the pistol well, since I had given him the grips that were on the weapon. A Border Patrolman friend of mine made really nice grips, and I had gotten him to make a pair of custom grips for the sheriff's pistol.

Medina told us that most of the time when Sheriff Murray got in from work, he would take his gun out of the holster and lay it on the kitchen table. We found one live round of .45 ammunition on the living room floor and one .45 projectile that had been fired and bounced off the wall. But we could not find the gun. It appeared that the suspects had taken the weapon with them.

At about this time the officers showed up with the guy from Kingsville. I was disappointed to learn that the man had lost his wallet a week or two before in a bar in Carrizo Springs. He had been at work and could not have had anything to do with the death of the sheriff. We were back to square one.

We made arrangements for the sheriff's body to be transported to the Bexar County Medical Examiner's Office in San Antonio, where further tests and an autopsy would be conducted. We loaded the body of our friend and had a Highway Patrol unit escort it to San Antonio.

At about this time I asked all the local officers available to meet me at the courthouse. I had been raised in a small town and I knew how a small town works. The local officers would be a key factor in finding out who had killed the sheriff.

I told the officers it was apparent that a fight had taken place throughout Sheriff Murray's house. The fight was so violent that there were body-size holes in the walls of the living room. Whoever committed this offense, I continued, would show signs that they had been in a fight. I asked the officers to make a list of anyone they thought might be capable of doing something like this to the sheriff.

They came up with about fifteen names. We divided the officers into teams and I asked each group to take three or four names, find them and see if they appeared to have been in a fight. As the local officers left, I returned to the crime scene to continue to assist Coy in locating and preserving any evidence that might be important to the case.

When I drove up to the sheriff's house it really hit me that I was working the murder of one of my best friends. While I was busy I was fine, but when I would get away alone my mind would wander to some of the good times the sheriff and I had together. I really had to work hard to keep my mind off Doc and trick myself into thinking this was just another case I was working.

About 2 p.m. the DPS crime lab team arrived to lend their assistance. While I had been at the meeting at the courthouse, Coy had requested a dog team in an effort to trail the suspects from the sheriff's residence. The dogs followed a trail from the crime scene to the shack where Joe Briseno, one of our possible suspects, lived. Coy drafted a search warrant for the shack and recovered one live round of .45 ammunition. While we were there, I was advised that the local officers had located Briseno. When they saw he had deep cuts on his hands, they picked him up.

I immediately drove to the Dimmit County Sheriff's Office to interview Briseno. Ranger Johnny Allen had come in from Del Rio to help with the investigation, and I ran into him at the courthouse. I asked Johnny to assist with the interview. We went in and talked with Briseno for several hours. He could not explain how he had gotten the cuts on his hands, but he refused to admit that he had anything to do with the murder. Briseno's cuts appeared to be all the way to the bone. Any normal person with wounds that severe would have gone in for medical treatment.

Briseno was taken to the local hospital. In the meantime, Coy started drafting the required paperwork so we could take hair and blood samples from the suspect. It was at this point that we received word that another suspect had been apprehended in Crystal City. I was informed that Albert Gonzalez appeared to have a through-and-through gunshot wound to the wrist, and he could not explain how he had gotten the injury. I drove to Crystal City and met with local officers at the police department. I then interviewed Gonzalez about how and where he had gotten the wound.

Gonzalez said he had fallen, sticking a nail through his wrist. I continued the interview for about an hour, and it became obvious that Gonzalez was not telling the truth. He said he had nothing to do with the death of the sheriff. I told Gonzalez that I was going to take him to the hospital for medical treatment and while he was there I was going to take hair and blood samples so I could place him at the crime scene. He got very quiet, and I loaded him in my car and started to Carrizo Springs. On the way I continued to talk with him. Just as we pulled up to the Dimmit County Courthouse he told me that he did not kill the sheriff, but Joe Briseno did.

About this time Coy walked up to the car. I gave him the high sign and he turned and walked away without saying a word. I took Gonzalez into an office and he made a full confession.

Gonzalez related that he and Briseno did not like Ben Murray. He said that on the morning before his death, the sheriff had stopped by their house and had asked if they knew anything about a large amount of jewelry that had been stolen a few weeks before in a local burglary. Gonzalez told the sheriff that they did not know anything about it and he left. He and Briseno did drugs for the rest of the day and washed them down with a lot of beer.

As I continued to listen, Gonzalez said he lived in a house near the sheriff, and that they had seen him return to his residence. He and Briseno were really messed up on dope, he related, and Briseno said he wanted to go to the sheriff's house and kill him. Gonzalez said that seemed like a good idea, so he went into the kitchen and got two butcher knives. He and Briseno then walked over to Murray's house and knocked on the back door. Gonzalez said it took a while for the sheriff to open the door, and when he did, he did not unlock the screen door. He said that he and Briseno told the sheriff that they knew who had done the burglary where the jewelry had been taken.

The sheriff told them he knew who had stolen the jewelry but still needed proof. Gonzalez related that Briseno told Murray that they had gotten some of the jewelry and asked if he wanted to see it. Any officer faced with that choice would have most likely opened the door to try to solve a crime.

When the sheriff opened the door Briseno and Gonzalez attacked him and began to stab him with the knives. Gonzalez said the sheriff was a lot tougher than they thought he would be. The fight proceeded from the back door to the interior of the house. By the time they had Murray into the living room Gonzalez had the sheriff in a choke hold from behind.

Gonzalez told me that Briseno saw the sheriff's gun on the kitchen table, picked it up and pulled the slide back. That's why Coy and I had found one live round lying in the living room floor. Murray always kept a round in the chamber of his Colt. Gonzalez said Briseno walked over and put the gun to the sheriff's head and shot him one time in the forehead. The suspect told me he thought the bullet had gone through Murray's head and then through his own wrist. Only one shot had been fired in the house, he said.

Briseno and Gonzalez then ran back to the house where Briseno lived. Gonzalez said Briseno had cut his hands several times while stabbing the sheriff. When they got to Briseno's house Gonzalez didn't know what to do, so he decided to go home. The last time he had seen the sheriff's weapon, Gonzalez continued, Briseno had it with him. I then reduced Gonzalez' statement to writing and he signed the confession. As soon as he had signed it, I placed him in the county jail for capital murder.

We tried to interview Briseno again and told him that Gonzalez had confessed, but he refused to say anything about the murder. Still, we felt we had enough evidence to charge him with capital murder as well and booked him. Coy and I slept on the benches in the district court room for a few hours before we were up and running again.

We got Gonzalez out of his cell and asked if he would walk us through the sheriff's house to show us what had happened. Ranger Joe Peters had arrived and was going to make a video of the walk-through if Gonzalez was willing. He agreed, and he led us through the crime scene showing us how the murder had been done. Rangers Peters, Smith, and several other officers were there when the video was made. We worked on the case the rest of the day, then went home for some rest.

When I got back to Laredo it really sank in that Sheriff Murray was dead. I had been busy working on the case, but now it hit me hard. I had worked with him for years, but our friendship had been cut short by a brutal murder. I never realized at the time the long hours and days away from my family I would go through over the next year to put the guys that had killed the sheriff in prison. Adding to the emotional strain was knowing that the entire community of Carrizo

Springs was banking on the case that Coy and I had built to get the family some closure and most of all, justice.

We all went to the funeral a few days later and buried our friend. I worked on the case report for the next few weeks and in keeping with our agreement, Coy took care of the complicated stuff. I could have never put this case together without a lot of help from a lot of other local officers and fellow Rangers. As I had first thought, the local officers who worked the area day-to-day had made all the difference in the case. They knew the people we needed to be looking at. Most people don't think about the importance of a good relationship between officers in any given area. That relationship is what makes things happen and solves cases. My friend, Sheriff Ben Murray, would have been proud.

Over the next six months I continued to work on the case, hoping to make it airtight. I was getting ready for two trials. The DA and I met several times to review the facts, and I had learned that he had represented one of the defendants before he took office. He said he was going to have to remove himself from the case. My good friend Angel Moreno had just moved from the state DA's office to the U.S. Attorney's office. I talked with him to see if he would be interested in assisting in the prosecution of Sheriff Murray's case.

Moreno had previously tried several of my cases and I thought he was one of the best prosecutors I had ever been around. We had never lost a case together. Besides that, he was a good friend, and I knew he understood how important this case was to me. He told me he was willing to lend a hand but that I would have to write his boss in Houston and ask that he be placed on leave to work on our case. I sent the letter thinking that the Feds would not pay much attention to an ex-sheepherder like me asking for such a big favor. To my surprise, a few weeks later Moreno called and said my request had been approved. Moreno would work with Assistant District Attorney Robert Little in trying to get some payback for Sheriff

Murray.

Just when I thought I had everything lined up with the case, I got a nasty surprise. One night about six months after the murder, the DPS communications operator called me to advise that there had been a jailbreak at the county lockup in Crystal City. The sheriff's office was asking that I meet with them as soon as possible. When I got there I learned that Joe Briseno and two other inmates had stabbed a jail guard and escaped.

I was really upset, to put it mildly. Now we were going to have to go to the trouble of finding Briseno all over again. Crystal City was only forty miles from the Mexican border. If Briseno made it across the river, I knew Mexican authorities would not give him back because he faced the death penalty in Texas. Mexico has no death penalty.

Over the next four or five days every law enforcement officer in the area spent just about all their time looking for the three escapees. Unfortunately, I had to leave the manhunt to appear in court in Zapata on another case. While I was in court, Sheriff Raul Medina called me to report that they had just apprehended the three suspects. I drove to Crystal City as quickly as I could get away and along with Sheriff Medina interviewed the other inmates who had escaped with Briseno.

The two inmates told us that just after escaping they had gone to the area where Briseno had lived before Sheriff Murray's murder. Both inmates related that Briseno went to a brushy area and dug up a plastic bag containing a chrome semiautomatic pistol. I asked one of the inmates what they had done with the gun, and he said they had thrown it in the brush just before the officers apprehended them. We had never found Sheriff Murray's Colt .45 and we were thinking that this might be the missing handgun.

The following morning, supported by a large group of volunteers, Medina and I went to look for the pistol. We found it within five minutes. When I walked up and saw the gun on the ground, I knew immediately it was Sheriff Murray's gun. The grips I had given him were still on the pistol. We took photos to establish where it had been found, and I collected it as evidence. The following day I drove to the DPS crime lab in Austin to have the ballistics work done on the gun. The lab matched the gun to the projectile we had found in the living room of Sheriff Murray's house. There was no way Briseno could explain how he knew were to go and dig up the gun unless he had been the one who had taken the pistol from the sheriff when he was killed.

It's strange how things turn out in real life. In escaping from jail, Briseno actually helped us prove he was the one who had killed Murray. He had led us to the murder weapon. I think Doc may have been looking down and helped us make a case on these two *pendejos*. We filed the additional charges on the three suspects and then I started on all the new paperwork needed to wrap up the case.

Joe Briseno was tried in Laredo. Attorneys Angel Moreno and Robert Little did a great job. A jury found Briseno guilty of capital murder and assessed the death penalty. The Dimmit County DA, Robert Serna and Little tried Albert Gonzalez in San Antonio. He ended up with a life sentence for capital murder.

Again, it's strange how things work out. Gonzalez died in the penitentiary of a heart attack, and as of 2009 Briseno still sits on Death Row, awaiting execution. Sheriff Murray's family has asked that I be a witness when they give him the needle. Assuming I'm still alive at that point, I intend to be in the front row.

Bank Robbery

On July 5, 1992 I headed to lunch thinking it was going to be a normal day. But one of the things I liked about being a Texas Ranger was that you never really had any idea what you were going to be working on. You could go from some boring white-collar theft-by-check case to a murder in ten seconds. You always had to be ready to shift gears. I ate lunch and had dropped by my house to pick up something, when I got a call that a DPS trooper had been shot in a gun battle at the Union National Bank during an attempted robbery. That bank was only a few blocks from my home. I drove to the location, and arrived to find a complete mess.

A wounded Trooper Hector Rodriguez was down in the bank parking lot, and the bank robber had been shot and was dying in a drainage ditch across the street. I approached the site where the trooper had been hit, but I did not get time to talk with him because he was being loaded into an ambulance. I went to the location where the now-dead bank robber lay, and I noticed that he appeared to be a white male.

I figured him for an old convict due to the tattoos on his body. In talking with witnesses, I learned the robber had entered the bank and demanded money at gunpoint. While the robber was in the bank, some of the people who had been waiting in line at the drive-through window observed what was going on and had made 9-1-1 calls. It just so happened that Trooper Rodriguez was driving by the bank as the robbery was going down. Some of the people nearby waved him down and told him what was happening.

Trooper Rodriguez drove up to bank in his marked DPS unit and stepped out of the car. Before he realized it, he ran into the bank robber, who had collected around $80,000 and was in the process of making his getaway. The robber shot Rodriguez, who went down in the parking lot.

An unarmed bank security guard had been following the robber at a distance. When the robber shot Trooper Rodriguez, the bank guard ran to the trooper's side and picked up his .357 Magnum pistol. The now-armed security guard watched the bank robber climb down into a ditch and as the bad guy climbed out the other side, the security guard shot him right where suspenders would cross and down he went.

The Laredo Police Department, the FBI, and I continued to work the case for the following few weeks. I later identified the deceased robber as Henry Clinton Allsup. He was suspected of numerous bank robberies all across the southern United States. Allsup's record showed numerous arrests for armed robberies, felony possession of firearms, attempted escape, bank robbery, possession of heroin, and numerous auto thefts. At the time of the Laredo robbery, he was wanted by the FBI and U.S. Marshals for bank robbery.

Allsup had fourteen aliases and had been in the penitentiary in several states. During the investigation, we learned that Allsup had been living in the interior of Mexico with a Mexican female. From time to time when he needed money he would pop up along the border, cross into the United States, and rob a bank. He would then escape into Mexico with the money he had stolen. He had been living like a king in Mexico on all the money he had stolen in his bank jobs. I'll never forget the tattoo Allsup had on his stomach. It said: "*Mi Vida Loca*" ("My Crazy Life.") I couldn't have said it any better. He was a good bank robber now. No one would have any more problems with him. Some people just need killin', as the old Texas saying goes.

Trooper Rodriguez recovered from his gunshot wounds and returned to duty. The director of the DPS later gave both Trooper Rodriguez and the bank guard an award for their bravery. Rodriguez went on to retirement, passing away in February 2009.

Oklahoma Murders

On August 5, 1999 I was on vacation, just hanging around the house. Summers in Laredo verge on being unbearable. The temperature during the day may run as high as 110 degrees. And it doesn't cool off much at night. In fact, I have seen it be 100 degrees at midnight. I always tried to take my vacation during this time of year to get away from the heat. Most of the time, I would just stay around the house trying to stay cool.

About 11 p.m., I received a call from Oklahoma State Bureau of Investigation agent Joe Hogan. OSBI agents in Oklahoma basically do the same thing the Rangers do in Texas. They are state police investigators, and most of the ones that I have had dealings with were really good at what they did. Agent Hogan told me he had been working on a double capital murder that had occurred in Eufaula, a community in Oklahoma's McIntosh County.

A couple in their late 70's, Robert and Vivian Pendley, had been beaten and stabbed to death in their home. The killer had also stolen their 1988 Oldsmobile. The Oklahoma officer said he had just received information that the car had been stopped at the international bridge returning from Nuevo Laredo. Hogan told me that a male and female identified as Harold McElmurry and Vickie McElmurry had been taken into custody. He asked if I could go to the bridge, take charge of the suspects and vehicle, and attempt to interview them to ascertain if they had anything to do with the murder of the elderly couple.

I told him I would pick up the suspects and try to interview them at the Webb County Sheriff's Department. I then called Chief Deputy Meme Martinez and told him what was going on. We worked a lot of cases of this type. It was not unusual to get a call for assistance from another jurisdiction after one of their suspects got detained at the bridge. Crooks often flee to the other side of the river, only to find out Mexico wasn't what they expected. When they attempt to return to the United States they often get stopped at the bridge. Martinez and I handled the interviews on a lot of these suspects. When we first started working on these kinds of cases, I always opened a Ranger case file and wrote a report. I finally realized that if Meme wrote the report, then most of the time he would be the one to have to go and testify. So sometimes I didn't write a report. Both of us had been all over the United States testifying in cases we only got involved in because the suspect had the bad luck of being arrested in Laredo.

In this particular case, Martinez sent a deputy to pick up the suspects and transport them to the sheriff's office. I then drove downtown to brief Martinez on the case. I called the OSBI agent to make sure he wanted us to do the interviews, knowing some officers did not want someone else interviewing the suspects on the cases they were working. I also knew that the longer you wait after a suspect is arrested, the greater the chance you take that he will lawyer up. When that happens, you may never get a chance to get a confession from him or obtain useful information. Agent Hogan and I talked about this, and he said that Martinez and I should talk to the suspects and get whatever we could get.

The chief deputy and I then brought Harold McElmurry into Martinez's office, warned him of his constitutional rights and began interviewing him about the murders. It only took us about ten minutes to break him. He told us that the Pendleys had been trying to help them out, allowing his wife and him to work around their house. Unmoved by the old couple's kindness, he and his wife had decided to kill the Pendleys to get their money and car. He told us that he had stabbed Robert Pendley numerous times with a pair of scissors. When the old man fell out of his wheelchair, he continued, he found a hoe and beat him on the head with it until the handle broke. Harold said he then found a piece of pipe and kept beating Pendley in the head until he knew he was dead.

Harold told us he knew that the only way he was going to get away with the robbery was by killing Mrs. Pendley as well. He said while he was killing Robert, his wife and Vivian Pendley had been talking outside in the yard. About the time he finished killing Robert, his wife and Vivian walked up and he yelled for his wife to grab Vivian. Vivian saw what he had done to her husband and instinctively tried to run, but his wife took her down. Harold said that he and his wife killed Vivian in about the same way. Their take in the double murder was $70 in cash and an old pistol.

Harold and Vickie stole the Pendleys' car and drove to Nuevo Laredo. Finding Mexico was not as romantic as they thought it would be, after a few days the couple decided to return to the United States. That's when they had gotten stopped by U.S. Customs at the international bridge.

Next we talked with Harold's wife. Vickie also admitted her involvement in the murders, telling basically the same story as Harold. Both suspects agreed to make written statements, and Chief Martinez and I took their confessions.

The next day I called agent Hogan and told him we had interviewed the suspects and that both of them had confessed. Both of the suspects were returned to Oklahoma. We continued to work out the details of the case over the next few weeks. I had to travel to Oklahoma three times to testify against the defendants at their trials. Harold was found guilty and finally executed in 2003, four years after the double murder. Vickie remains in prison and will never get out.

I wish that they had put both of them to death. I can see no reason two people like them should be allowed to breathe the same air as the rest of us.

Chief Deputy Martinez and I had worked together for years, constantly going into Nuevo Laredo to retrieve fugitives. But this proved to be one of the last cases he worked with me. About a year after this case was concluded, Martinez had a major stroke and remains bedridden to this day. He can no longer speak. He was a good friend and a fine officer. I miss my association with him. I just wish that the people in Laredo really knew the kind of cases he worked with me and the things he did for his community. People never seem to remember.

C. J. Havrda

The best supervisor I ever worked for during my time with DPS was Captain C. J. Havrda, who took over Company D when Jack Dean retired to become U.S. Marshal for the Western District of Texas. Havrda had been a Ranger in West Texas and he and I looked on things about the same way. He tended not to get into your business unless you messed up. But you could talk to him about anything that was going on in your life and he would tell you what he thought.

Still, from time to time the captain and I would get into a disagreement about something related to how to work a case. We both would get upset, but the next day it was like nothing had even happened. He made you a better officer just being around him. You wanted to work and produce for him.

One night I got a call from the warden at the prison unit in Dilley, a small town on Interstate 35 in Frio County. He said he had a full-blown inmate riot in progress. I drove to the prison and met with the warden. When we went out into the yard it looked like the battle of Gettysburg. The black inmates were fighting it out with the whites and Hispanics. They had set fire to one of the buildings, sending smoke all over the prison yard.

I looked up and saw someone walking toward me through the smoke. It was Captain Havrda. He looked like he was taking a late-night stroll. C. J. asked me what was going on and I told him some of the inmates were having a little disagreement. We both laughed and went on with getting things back in order. It made me feel good that the captain had come out in the middle of the night to check on his men. I guess that I wasn't the only one that thought well of him. He later got promoted to senior captain, the chief of the Texas Rangers.

Progress

I came into the Rangers toward the end of an era. When I started in law enforcement, a lot of the officers were just getting over the fact that they had to read suspects the Miranda warning before they could talk with them. Some of the older guys back then thought that it was absurd that they had to spend time and effort trying to locate and arrest suspects, and as soon as they got their hands on them, they had to tell them that they had the right not to talk with them.

When I first went to work, I noticed how much the people in the community respected officers like Troopers Mike Greer and Sammy Long, and Ranger Clayton McKinney. I would watch how the older men worked a case and how they respected the people they dealt with. In those days a person knew that if he violated the law and got caught, he was going to get hammered by the justice system for what he had done. Officers like Mike and Clayton went out of their way to make a case and at the same time help the families of the suspects in dealing with the fact that one of their relatives had been arrested.

One piece of wisdom I got from Clayton just after I started work was that things change in life. And the old ways are not always better. He said that in the old days a Ranger looking for someone would saddle his horse, ride through brush, mountains, and rivers to get to the house where the man lived. He would then have to get off his horse, go up to the door and knock to see if the man he was looking for was at home only to be told that the man had left the day before. In telling that story, Clayton would laugh and say that he had much rather reach over and call a guy on the telephone and ask if he was there.

I have gone through some of the changes Clayton was referring to. Computers and other innovations implemented by the DPS have made Rangers better than they were when I came into the service. It's just harder for some of the older guys to make the changes. When I was a young Ranger, I was in San Antonio at the Company D office talking about how one of the good sheriffs that I had in one of my areas had gotten beat in his reelection bid. I was complaining that the guy who had been elected was not nearly as good as an officer as the defeated incumbent.

Captain Jack Dean, echoing Clayton, told me that one thing about life he had learned was that nothing ever stayed the same. When you were working like a red ant in July someone always comes around with a water hose and washes it all away. Some changes happen for the better and some don't. Whatever happens, we as Rangers had to make the best of the situation presented at the time. We were expected to work with whoever held office.

When I first came into the Rangers, we wrote reports by hand, and I continued to do this for years. That's the only way we did business. I would go out and spend several days working an offense and getting the suspect arrested and put in jail. Then I would retreat to the DPS office, or my kitchen table, and using penmanship that had not improved much since I had my girlfriend fill out my Highway Patrol application years before, write a report that would sometimes run fifty or sixty pages. I would mail my reports to the secretaries at the Company D office in San Antonio. They would type the report, file a copy, and send one to me to give to the district attorney.

A lot of the time I would work on cases all week, and over the weekend I would do the reports at home. I would have them done by Monday, and I could start other cases the following week. No telling how many hundreds of hours I spent working on reports on my days off. But I'm not complaining. I always thought that system worked well for me. When you have been doing something for fifteen or sixteen years you don't like change, even though you know it's inevitable.

Police officers for the most part do not like change. Six or seven years before I retired, I had to attend a computer school in Austin. They were going to teach me how to use a computer in doing my job. A lot of the younger Rangers seemed to think that was a great idea, but I had been around long enough to see the writing on the wall.

I had two secretaries that typed my reports for me, but I knew that if the department ever got us computers, at some point they were going to tell us that we had to type our own. Besides, I couldn't type. I knew that if they made me type my own reports I would spend a lot more time in the office, and at that stage of my career that was not what I wanted to do. I wanted to work cases and apprehend criminals, not do clerical work.

Well, I went to the school. I really did not pay a lot of attention because they told us at the start that we did not have to use a computer unless we wanted to. Still, they issued us new laptop computers, printers, and all the mess that goes with them. When I got back to Laredo, I used my laptop as a doorstop for the next several years. Before I knew it, I was the only Ranger in the company still doing things the old way. I realized that before long they were going to tell me that I had to do everything on the computer, so I started teaching myself to type. It took me about six months, and eventually I was doing all my reports on the computer. Truth be told, I got to the point that I liked having the computer.

E-mail was something else. Someone was always calling to ask if I had gotten their e-mail. I always told them that if they had something to tell me, to call me on the phone. If I had wanted to read something I'd read a book. I wanted to hear it from them.

Every four or five months Lieutenant Ray Cano or Jim Denman would come down to Laredo and clean out my hundreds of unopened e-mails. They didn't like having to do that, but they put up with the fact that I was kind of set in my ways. I did enough work and sent my reports in on time, so they let me be. Both supervisors did their best to take care of me and the way that I was doing business.

One of the main things that bothered me about the Rangers switching to computers was that a lot of the younger guys depended almost entirely on e-mail for communication. I had found through the years that what made the Ranger service really work was developing personal relationships with the other officers and officials a Ranger had to work with. It had taken me years to do that with my area agencies, and I worked hard to keep those relationships going. If I didn't have anything going on at the time, I would drive to one of the sheriff's offices in my area for no other reason than to eat lunch with the officers there.

By building friendships and a personal relationship in this way, when something bad happened you know the people and they know you. It just made things work a lot better when it was time to get something done on a major case. I cannot recall the number of times I would be having coffee or lunch with some local officers when something major happened. That put me in the middle of the case from the very start. During the last few years before I retired, I saw a lot of the newer guys glued to the computers in their offices, but I always thought their time would have been better spent in a face-to-face meeting with some of the officers in their areas. I hope direct communication with the area sheriffs, DA's, and police chiefs is not lost due to the new age of computers. I think it would cost the Rangers a lot.

215

The Ranger dress code was another thing I had a little trouble with. We were expected to wear a tie every day we went to work. That was okay for the guys who worked in the big city, but for the Rangers in the outstations it was a pain in the ass. I was wearing a tie one day when I was at the DPS office shredding old Ranger files. My tie got stuck in the shredder as I bent over to put some papers into the machine. That paper shredder and I had a hell of a fight. I finally had to cut my tie off with a pocketknife to win. I never did like wearing a tie.

I learned that I should always have with me what we referred to as a "throw-down" tie. Ranger Coy Smith and I always kept an old tie on the sun visor in the state car so we could put one on real quick if we happened to run into a lieutenant or the captain. You could even get in trouble for wearing a tie. The maddest I ever saw Captain Havrda was the day I came into the office wearing a Looney Tunes tie my sons had given me for Christmas. I thought he would be glad to see me in a tie but I found out real quick he was not a fan of cartoon ties, at least not around the neck of a Ranger. We had one of those conversations about my wardrobe choices in which he did all the talking. I never did that again.

I know at times I was most likely more trouble than I was worth, but Captain Havrda always stood up for me. I hope he knows what I really think of him. Well, over the time that I was a Ranger I wore a tie only on the days that I went to court or the days that I knew that some of the brass was going to be around. People in my area knew how I dressed and they didn't expect me to look any other way. Besides, if you showed up in a starched shirt, good boots, a nice hat, and starched blue jeans you were usually the best-dressed guy at the party.

It was during my initiation into the computer age that one of the *comandantes* from Nuevo Laredo called me and said he had arrested a guy wanted for murder in Texas. The *comandante* asked me to come across and meet with him so we

216

could interview the suspect. I decided that I was really going to impress the *comandante*, so I loaded up my new computer and printer and away I went to Nuevo Laredo. We interviewed the suspect for several hours and finally got him to confess to the murder. I set up my computer and printer and for the next several hours I took a long statement from the suspect.

For those of you who do not know, a statement in Texas is not any good unless the suspect signs it. When an officer gets to that point, he wants to get the signature on the statement as soon as possible. I got the statement typed out and then tried to print it, but the printer would not work. I tried everything I knew to get it to print, but no statement. I ended up getting a yellow legal pad and copying the statement from the computer screen so I would have something for the suspect to sign. I got it done, but I really don't think the *comandante* was impressed. He asked me why I had gone through the trouble of typing the statement in the computer when I could have just taken the statement on the yellow pad to start with. I came up with the story that we had to keep a record of all the statements that we took. I brought the guy back and put him in the Webb County Jail, and got him to sign a good typed statement the following day. So much for me being in the computer age.

Coy and the Colt

When Ranger Coy Smith came into Company D both of us were Colt .45 guys. After a few years, the captain sent Coy to a Sig Sauer firearms training school because the DPS was converting to a semiautomatic handgun. Well, the Sig Sauer school ruined Coy. From the day he walked out of the school he had nothing but bad stuff to say about the 1911 Colt-type pistol. Coy and I argued about the guns all the time and we did everything we could to try to change the other's mind.

Since I have carried a gun with me everywhere for years and years, it's become just another piece of equipment to me. I have always liked the Colt because it is comfortable to carry. It's slim, which makes it easy to slip inside your waistband. When you are in a car you can place it cross-draw and can still get it out if you have to. I've always liked the Government Model because of the length. The bad thing about the Colt is it will bite you if you are not careful with it.

I never will forget the day that we had the meeting where Captain Jack Dean passed out the new Sig Sauer Model 220 .45 caliber pistols. The department had finally decided we were going to get rid of the six-shot Smith & Wesson .357 Magnum revolvers and go to a semiautomatic. At the time none of the Rangers in the company carried the Smith, but we had to have a designated gun so that if we all got called to a riot or some other large-scale emergency, the same ammunition would work in everyone's gun.

I looked at the new Sig and realized that it was the same

gun that Browning had come out with around 1977. Everyone looked the gun over and most everyone decided right then that they would stick with the Colt 1911.

When I tried to carry a Sig I felt like I was wearing a shoebox on my hip. The slide is thick, and it is not a comfortable gun to carry. It also hangs up on things as you get in and out of a car. In addition, the gun just doesn't fit my hand. My right hand was broken so many times during fights and football in my high school days, that my right trigger finger is significantly shorter than my left. That makes it more difficult for me to reach the trigger.

Sig P226, .357 Sig caliber on the left,
Colt Government model .45 on the right.

Two things I do like about the Sig is the .357 caliber, and that it goes "Bang" when you pull the trigger. As Coy always said, when you buy a Colt you've only bought the kit. You have to take it and have a lot of work done to it to get it tuned up, where the Sig is as good as it's going to be straight out of the box. But I've always thought it was worth it to tinker with my Colt because that was the gun I was comfortable with and could shoot better than any other. Over the next few years we shot the Sigs a lot, and while they seemed to be a good and dependable pistol, I still carried my old Colt.

Nearly to a man, the older Rangers had no use for the Sig at all. They just put it in the trunk of their car and that's where it stayed until it was time every few months to qualify with it. Over time, as the older Rangers in the company retired, their replacements were men who knew nothing but the Sig, which they had carried while in uniform. Most of the younger Rangers are carrying Sigs now, and that's okay. I've always thought an officer should be able to carry what he wanted, since it's his own life he might someday be defending with the weapon.

When I retired, both Coy and I still held our separate opinions about Colts and Sigs. A few of the old timers still carry Colts, but I think that the Sig Sauer pistol will be the gun of the future for the Rangers. I do think that the .357 Sig caliber is the best self-defense round available to law enforcement. I just wish someone made a Colt-type gun in the .357 Sig caliber. Until they do, I'll stick with the Colt .38 Super and the .45 semiautomatic.

I've always liked to look at old pictures of the Rangers and the guns they carried back then. I suspect a hundred years from now future Rangers will be looking at pictures of today's Rangers with their computers and Sig *pistolas*. Like I said, it feels to me like the end of an era, but that's not necessarily a bad thing.

A DPS Tradition

In 1996, my son Justin decided to move to Laredo from California. He had grown up on the Left Coast with my ex-wife but had decided he wanted to live with me for a while. When he moved to Laredo, he started to take criminal justice courses at the local college. I don't think he had really made up his mind about what he wanted to be. However, the more time he spent around me, the more the kind of work that I did appealed to him.

A good friend of mine, retired DPS Narcotics agent Ray Garner, ran the Criminal Justice program at the college and assisted my son from the time that he got here. With Ray's help, Justin got more than a hundred hours of college, and that made him eligible to apply to the DPS. He went through the application process and got hired.

Justin started as a Capitol Police officer in Austin. He was a big-city type, having grown up in Los Angeles, so Austin suited him just fine. Justin stayed in the Capitol Police until he could transfer into the Highway Patrol. He stayed in the patrol until he was promoted to sergeant in the Narcotics Service.

He is also a member of the department's SWAT team, and still lives in Austin. I am very proud of him, and I think he will work for DPS until he retires. Justin and I have a combined length of service of forty-six years for DPS.

Texas Rangers

Most people don't know where Texas Rangers come from. A lot of people I have talked with over the years didn't know that the Texas Rangers are part of the Department of Public Safety. That, or they thought they were a baseball team. When I went to work, there were still a few Rangers who had not come up through the DPS. But before I became a Ranger, then DPS Director James B. Adams changed the rules so that Rangers could no longer be directly appointed from other agencies. To be a Ranger, you had to have to come from the DPS, which means you went through the training academy even if you had previous law enforcement experience.

The DPS has a certain way of training people. If they decide to promote officers, those officers are already set in the ways of DPS. They know the routine and the reporting system and are able to enter into a new service without much difficulty. As I've already noted, I was a trooper, Narcotics agent and then Ranger. By the time I made Ranger I was used to making investigative reports the distinctive DPS way, which is to number each factual point, and had a good idea where to start when it was time to do an investigation. I had been brought up in the system.

I also knew that if I did my job right, I could directly affect the lives of the people of Texas in a positive way. I liked the fact that DPS officers weren't really concerned with politics. We enforced the laws like they should be enforced. The way I looked at it, there was a victim who needed justice, and when it came to getting the justice, I was heartless about what happened to the suspect. My job was to make a case against him and turn it over to the DA and let a jury decide what kind of punishment he got. It was that simple for me, and that's what I did—get mean and try harder.

I still don't really know what it is that makes Rangers work the way they do. I have worked for years with other agencies and I have noticed that when they got tired, or it was the end of their shift, they put the case on hold and go home. The Rangers I knew never paid much attention to the clock. If they were working on a murder, they continued to work as long as they were being productive. If they were continuing to develop information on the case, they stayed at it. I have seen them go without sleep for days to follow the leads out and bring a case to a successful conclusion. I think having that kind of work ethic had a lot to do with the number of cases that we as Rangers solved. I know that it had a big impact on the crooks because we didn't give them any breathing room.

In addition, the Ranger service sends a rookie Ranger to every kind of investigative school they can think of. They also train them in working within their closed computer system in making the reports that they require. This intranet enables one Ranger to pull up reports on a suspect to ascertain if he has been mentioned by any other Ranger in some other investigation.

One of the strong points of the Rangers is that most of them know each other and have spent time together at training schools or in-service schools. One of the unwritten rules in the Rangers is that if you receive a request from another Ranger you drop what you are doing and help him in any way you can. The request may be from a Ranger in your own company or a Ranger from another part of the state.

The fact that most of the time you know the Ranger who is asking for help makes the system work much better, and you do what it takes to help him out. Don't get me wrong. All

Rangers may not personally like each other or spend time with each other after work, but they are perfectly willing to die for each other if it comes to that. They will do whatever it takes to uphold the Ranger tradition. If they tell you they will do something, then they will. It's that's simple. I always referred to them as balls-to-the-walls guys. Of all the things that I had to worry about in being a Ranger, I never had to worry if the Ranger with me would be there if things went bad.

I worked a burglary of a habitation offense in which a group of people had broken into the home of Keith Asmussen in Laredo and had stolen a small safe containing approximately $250,000 in cash and jewels. I had worked on the case for several weeks and finally obtained a confession from a female suspect who implicated several others. The woman told me that one of the persons who had assisted her in the break-in had already been sent to the penitentiary and was in a unit near Waco.

I called one of the Rangers in Company F and requested that he go to the prison and interview the suspect. The Ranger I was working with was one of the newer guys and had worked with the computer a lot more than I had. Several hours later the Ranger phoned and told me he had just e-mailed a statement in which the female inmate identified the other suspects to the offense. When I checked my computer I found that he had not only sent me a confession but as an attachment, an audio statement of the entire interview. I downloaded the audio, put it on a CD and met with the DA to let him hear the inmate's confession. He issued the additional warrants for the suspects and we wrapped up the entire group responsible for the offense.

From the time I made the request until I had the information back in my hands was less than eight hours. Again, this is what a computer can do for the modern Texas Ranger. In the old days I would have to make the request and wait several days while the Ranger mailed the statement to me. This may have allowed the other suspects to flee before I had a chance to arrest them. Things really have changed over the years.

Crystal City Riot

I was sleeping soundly when the telephone woke me up at about two a.m. I knew it couldn't be good news. The DPS communications operator said a full-scale riot was underway at the privately operated detention facility in Crystal City. The sheriff's office was calling for officers from other areas to assist in putting down the riot. It was a really cold night and I didn't want to get out of my warm bed. But I didn't have that luxury as a Texas Ranger. I made myself get up and get dressed.

I left Laredo and started toward Crystal City. It would take me at least an hour, and as I drove north I was thinking that it would most likely be over by the time that I got there.

When I was out working this time of night, I often thought how most people were home asleep and had no idea what we as state police officers went through. I thought about the hundreds of times I had been called out, remembering that my ex-wife had referred to me one time as a civil servant. She meant it as a put-down, but deep in my heart I took pride in the fact that I had a chance nearly every day to help people get through a bad experience. That's one of the reasons that I loved being a Ranger. I always felt like I could make a difference in people's lives.

As I drove on toward Crystal City I could hear from the DPS radio traffic that things were not getting any better at the private prison. When I arrived at the scene, most of the inmates stood out in the yard. They had set one of the main buildings on fire. The strong smell of smoke filled the cold night air. I met with Ranger Ray Ramon and he and I walked around so we could get a good sense of what was going on. I then talked to several of the facility supervisors to get as much information as I could.

With at least two hundred inmates going crazy in the yard, nothing but an eight-foot-tall chain link fence separated them from the outside world. There are two main rules when facing something like this in a correctional facility: Provide for officer safety and never, never, lose containment.

All it would take to bring the fence down was for a large group of the inmates to push on it. Having a couple of hundred escaped inmates running loose all over town would not be good. I got with one of the high-ranking officers from the facility and we decided to communicate with the riot leaders to find out what they wanted.

Talking through the fence, we met with about twenty inmates. All of them wanted to be the one doing the talking so I told them to go to the back of the yard and pick out two or three inmates to represent the rest of them. While I was talking with the radicals I noticed another group of about twenty or so inmates standing near a gate about fifty yards from us.

I could tell that this other group really didn't want any part of the riot, and suspected they knew it was possible to get yourself killed during something like this. A lot of times inmates have scores to settle with each other, and they don't pass up an opportunity to get even if they get a chance. While we waited on the rioters to select their spokesmen, I decided to make contact with the group near the side gate.

I walked over and started talking with several of them. They definitely wanted out of the situation. I told them that I could have the gate opened and let five of them out at a time. About ten or fifteen said that sounded good to them. I rounded up about twenty officers and told them to open the gate and let five out at a time. As the first five inmates were let out, the officers strip-searched them before moving them to a secure part of the facility.

We kept letting the inmates out in groups of five. Before the rioters knew it we had cut their strength about seventy-five percent. The instigators came back to the fence and told us that they were not going to give up. All the time we were letting the rest of the inmates out. Finally it got to the point that there were only ten to fifteen radicals left. I then told them we had more than one hundred and fifty officers available and that they were going to get their ass kicked if they didn't give up in the next five minutes. We were going to send in the prison's SORT (Special Operations Response Team) team and they knew what would happen if that occurred. The holdouts then walked over to the side gate and gave up five at a time. Just like that, the riot was over.

I really hadn't done anything but ask some of the inmates if they wanted to give up. When the first five gave up most of the rest followed like sheep. One thing I knew a lot about was getting sheep moving. I would never have thought working in that stockyard so many years ago would have helped me in a jail riot, but it did.

We had the SORT team and the Webb County SWAT team do a cell-by-cell search to make sure we had everything back under control. By the time we finished checking for hidden weapons and any other contraband it was nearly noon. The inmates had done thousands of dollars' worth of damage to the facility. It would take months before the repairs were completed.

By the time I got home I was exhausted and the clothes that I had been wearing had to be thrown away. Everyone else in the world had slept all night and was now having lunch somewhere with nice people. I had spent the night with two hundred convicted felons trying to destroy everything they could get their hands on.

High School Sniper

One day Webb County District Attorney Chief Investigator O.J. Hale contacted me about a possible murder in Laredo. A juvenile had come to the DA's office to say he had been a witness to a murder that had occurred near the Laredo Country Club in the northeastern part of town. O.J. requested I meet him at his office so we could interview the witness and find out if a murder actually happened.

The juvenile told us that a murder had occurred and said he could show us where the body was. O.J. and I contacted First Assistant DA Monica Notzon and she agreed to go to the scene with us. We loaded up the juvenile and he directed us to the location. When we arrived, we found the body of a young male who appeared to have been shot and robbed. The juvenile said that he and two of his friends had decided to rip off a small-time drug dealer—kill him for his money and drugs.

We worked the crime scene and did all of the things we normally did to collect as much evidence as we could. The juvenile provided us with the names of the two additional suspects and we spent the better part of two days rounding them up. DA investigator Louie Zapata and I began trying to locate the main suspect. The juvenile had told us that the other young man had hidden in the brush with a .22 caliber rifle and waited for them to bring the drug dealer to the meeting so he could be murdered.

As they were making the deal, the suspect shot the victim in the head. He then walked up to the victim, saw that he was still moving, and finished him off. What was shocking about the whole case was the age of those involved and the cold-blooded way they had taken a young man's life. Zapata and I finally found the suspect and interviewed him. We were able to obtain a written statement in which he admitted that he had committed the murder.

Louie and I both knew that the juvenile's father had previously been sent to the penitentiary and we played that angle when we talked to the son. We were able to convince the juvenile to tell us where he had hidden the murder weapon. The rifle was recovered and used in the court proceedings. The young man also identified the other people involved.

Zapata and I completed the investigation and both of us appeared in district court as a witness against the suspects. The young man was found guilty and sentenced to thirty-five years in the penitentiary.

One of the young people involved in the murder was a twelve-year-old girl. I thought that I had seen about everything a person could see related to murder cases. I was wrong. When I was in court and looking at the suspects that had committed the murder, they looked like they should be going to a school field trip instead of being tried for a capital murder. You never know when you start working a case what you will come up with at the end.

Roping

In the early 1990s I decided I needed a hobby totally unrelated to police work and made up my mind I was going to start team roping. I had been rodeoing since I was eight, and I loved to be around livestock. I rode bulls the early part of my life, which is why I showed up at the DPS academy with a broken right leg.

To start my new hobby, I bought a good horse and asked some friends to start teaching me to rope. I got to where I could catch most of the cattle, but I was never really fast at it. For the first time in twenty-five years I started to associate with civilians. It was like a breath of fresh air to be around people who didn't care about how many people you put in jail.

During the week I would work all day, and about 6 p.m. I would saddle up and rope until 9 or 10 p.m. On the weekends we always went to a roping event somewhere. Before long I had two good horses, a four-door pickup and a gooseneck trailer. We always laughed that we had spent $50,000 on horses, pickup, and trailer to win a $200 roping jackpot. Having horses was a great way to turn good Yankee dollars into horseshit.

A lot of the guys I ran with were really talented ropers, so I always had some good people to heel for me. Most of the guys I roped with were older like me, and I had a lot of fun being around them. I roped for about ten years, and I would have to say it was one of the most enjoyable things I've ever done.

If you mess with horses long enough, however, they will end up hurting you one way or another. In the decade I spent roping I got hurt about once every two years. At about fifty I began to notice it took me a lot longer to heal than it did when I was younger. So I decided to sell out and that's what I did. Both of my shoulders are now gone but if I could still do it, I would still be roping.

Richard Johnson, one of the guys that I ran with during the roping days, liked to play jokes on other ropers. Richard always had an ice chest full of beer. At one of the ropings, Richard took a six-foot rattlesnake he had killed, rolled it up, and set it on top of the ice inside the cooler. He spent the day sitting in a lawn chair near the ice chest. Every time someone came by he would ask them to hand him a beer. The people at the roping were good people, and they would go over to the chest and open it. Richard delighted in watching them scream and run over things while he sat in the shade. Every once in a while, he'd even throw a loop.

At one roping, Richard and I had made it to the short go and had a chance to win some money. I rode into the roping box, and waited for Richard to get into the heeling box so I could call for the steer. I knew he had been drinking a little too much, and as he rode in I saw him leaning over slightly.

Richard turned his horse and leaned a little more. As he backed into the box, I was just about to call for the steer when I saw him lean even farther. I was trying to keep my eyes on both Richard and the steer when suddenly he fell off his horse with a thud.

"The son-of-a-bitch bucked me off!" he said as he looked up at me from the ground.

Richard got back on his horse and we made the run. It was a good run and we ended up placing in the roping. We teased Richard for a long time about him getting "bucked off" in the roping box. He never would admit he plain fell off his horse.

One day we were at the barn where we stabled our horses.

We had already fed them and were sitting in plastic lawn chairs watching the world go by. Another friend of ours, Bubba Lopez, kept his horse in another barn about a hundred yards from us. Bubba always parked his pickup in the same place when he came out to feed.

Richard had killed another rattlesnake and had placed it right where Bubba would step out of his pickup. We were just waiting for Bubba to arrive. Bubba pulled up, parked, and nearly stepped on the coiled dead rattler. When Bubba saw the snake, he jumped and managed to get away from it. Richard really enjoyed the show.

We went on with what we were doing and soon forgot about the whole deal. About an hour later another friend, Burch Muldrow, pulled up next to us and got out of his truck. Burch had a paper sack with "Tacos" written on it. I thought something was wrong right from the start. Without a word, Burch set the sack on the tailgate of his pickup. Richard saw the sack. Everyone knew that he loved to eat. He would field dress at about 300 pounds.

Burch told Richard he had already eaten and that he could have the tacos if he wanted them. Richard walked over, picked up the sack and stuck his hand in to get a taco. Then he screamed and dropped the sack. Bubba and Burch couldn't stop laughing. They had put the snake into the sack and had paid Richard back for the joke a few hours before.

I told the guys that I was going to take the snake because my sons liked to make things out of the skin. I put the snake back into the sack and drove home. I really didn't think much about it when I walked into my home and put it on the kitchen counter. I went into the bedroom and in a while I heard my wife scream. I knew what had happened. That snake had scared half the people in Laredo, so I decided to put it in the freezer so the boys could work with the skin when they were ready. A week or so later, I found that one of my sons had been looking for something to eat and had opened the sack and it did the same thing to him. I finally got rid of it before it caused any more problems.

A year or so later, Richard died of cancer. I'll always remember the funny things that he did.

Doyle and horse Spot taken during roping days.

Eagle Pass

For some reason the Ranger bosses in Austin decided we needed someone stationed in Eagle Pass to work Maverick County, Carrizo Springs and Crystal City. New Ranger David Duncan got the assignment. David and I had become good friends in the early 70's and I still consider him one of my best friends.

We met when he was a rookie deputy and I was a rookie trooper in West Texas. Back then he worked for Sheriff Richard Upchurch in Van Horn. While I was stationed in Fort Hancock, I had a chance to work in Van Horn quite a bit. David was a little younger than me, but he was the kind of guy you could really depend on if things got bad.

David and I worked around each other until I left West Texas. At the time he was still working for Sheriff Upchurch. Several years went by, and I hadn't had any contact with David until I went to Austin for Ranger in-service school. I was pleased to find that David had made Ranger and was going to be assigned to my Ranger company.

David was a lot like me. He had gotten most of his early training from Sheriff Upchurch and Ranger Clayton McKinney. While David was stationed in Eagle Pass we worked a lot together. One of the things David and I often talked about was that there was something special about the border. Both of us had moved away from the border for a time but both of us found that when you had worked the border, any place else was boring. We both returned when we got the chance. He later moved to Fort Davis out in West Texas, and I still visit with him from time to time.

Another guy I enjoyed working with was Ranger Brooks Long, who also started out at Eagle Pass. I liked Brooks from the start. He came into the Rangers with a really good work ethic, and he never complained about where he was stationed. There was a lot of work around Eagle Pass, but it was not a place most officers wanted to bring their family. Everyone knew Brooks didn't really like his assignment, but he brought his wife and sons to Eagle Pass and went to work. He quickly became what I call a border Ranger.

Brooks had been raised in the Rio Grande Valley and spoke Spanish better than most people that I knew. He could talk to people in his area and knew how things worked because he had been raised on the border. He had also been a DPS Narcotics agent. I always thought that Narcotics agents made good Rangers because they conducted their own investigations and wrote good reports. Add to both of those factors that they knew how the street worked and most of the time you ended up with a well-rounded officer.

When I first started working with Brooks, I noticed he pretty much had it together when it came to working cases. He paid attention to small details and made a lot of good cases because he worked hard. I have a lot of respect for him.

One night not long after Brooks made Ranger, he called and told me that he had a murder in Carrizo Springs and asked if I could help him out. I told him I would be there in about an hour. As I drove up to the house where the murder had occurred, it started raining hard. There was a blood trail leading from the street to the front door.

Brooks had gone to a local store and bought a supply of paper cups to cover the spots of blood on the sidewalk to keep the rain from washing away the evidence. That way we would be able to obtain DNA samples if they were needed. He walked me through the house so I would get an idea of what had occurred. I noted that the bathtub was covered with smeared blood.

Brooks led me out the back door and I noticed a large mound of freshly dug dirt in the middle of the back yard. It looked as large as a pitcher's mound. Brooks scraped a little of the dirt away with the toe of his boot and we could see part of a human hand and arm. "That's a clue," I said, and we both laughed.

He told me it appeared that the victim had been killed in the bathroom and then brought to the backyard and buried. Brooks said he already had a suspect under arrest. We left the scene in the custody of the deputies and we went to the sheriff's office to interview the suspect. Brooks and I started the interview, and I noticed that Brooks had no reservations about jumping right in.

We finally got the suspect to admit he had killed the victim, and he agreed to make a written statement. The guy had killed one of his friends to take his cocaine away from him. It had been less than an ounce of dope.

I remember thinking, *What a waste!* When I worked cases like this I would always wonder how in the world someone could do something like this for what seemed like nothing. Brooks left the room, and I stayed with the suspect to keep him company. I don't know where he went, but I got tired of waiting for him so I started to take the guy's written confession. When Brooks walked back into the room and realized what I was doing, he sat down, pulled the statement away from me and started where I had left off.

Brooks was a rookie at the time. That really impressed me. He was not about to let an older Ranger take the confession on his case. We both continued to get the guy's confession, and when we were finished the suspect signed it. After we made the case, I drove back to Laredo and Brooks finished up the details. He really did a good job, and he hadn't really needed me in the first place. I formed my opinion of Brooks on this case, which we always referred to as the Pitcher's Mound Murder.

We went on to work a lot of cases together. He is a top-notch Ranger and it is a shame he no longer works the border. If he had stayed on the border, he most likely would have been the best border Ranger who ever worked for the state.

David Duncan and Brooks Long are the kind of guys I always want to see in the Texas Rangers. They both will do to ride the river with.

Republic of Texas

Things never happen when you plan for them. One night in the spring of 1997 I was at the roping arena east of Laredo. I sat on my horse in the header's box and was just about to call for the steer when my cell phone rang. It was Captain C. J. Havrda. I knew the captain wasn't calling at this time of night to wish me good luck.

He told me that Company E was having a problem with a group of radicals in the Davis Mountains, and that I needed to report to the command post at six the following morning. Be prepared to stay at least a week, he added. I looked at my watch and noted that it was already nearly 7 p.m. I would have to pack, get my things together, and drive nearly 400 miles in the next eleven hours. When I got off the phone with the captain, I called my wife and asked her to get me some money because I had to go out to West Texas for a few days. It took me over an hour to get my horse fed and put up so I could leave.

I gassed up my car, loaded my stuff and started toward Fort Davis. Ranger Coy Smith called me on the way and we made arrangements to meet in Del Rio so we could follow each other in case one of us had car trouble. I had worked around Fort Davis when I was in Narcotics and I knew that my good friend Ranger David Duncan worked that area.

Coy and I drove all night, finally arriving at the command post about 7 a.m., an hour late but the best we could do. Both of us had been up for more than twenty-four hours when we arrived. Company E Captain Barry Caver was the on-scene commander.

We were advised that a radical group calling itself the Republic of Texas had done a home invasion in a subdivision down the road from their mountain headquarters, shot one person, and had kidnapped one or two others. By the time Coy and I got there, the hostages had been released. We were told that the group had retreated to their compound and were not going to give up. The people in the group were heavily armed and would fight if we made any move to arrest them.

At least we had a lot of help. Nearly all the Rangers from company E were there and Rangers from most of the other companies had been sent to provide support. The DPS had also sent a lot of troopers and the SWAT team in case they were needed.

I was assigned to a lookout position so we could watch the group and make sure they stayed put. The first day or so I was there, the supervisors at the command post continued to negotiate with the Republic of Texas group in an effort to get them to surrender. They didn't mind talking, but said they were not going to give up.

Those of us on lookout duty slept on the ground next to our cars. It got really hot in the daytime but at night it was so cold I nearly froze. We couldn't build any fires out of concern that the bad guys would attempt to assault our position. After we had been there a day or two, we were advised that we were going to clear several houses near the compound and move up to within three or four-hundred yards of the radicals. Over the next several hours about fifty of us cleared the houses and put up a perimeter so we could keep watch on the group.

The mountains in this area are not high by Rocky Mountain standards, but Fort Davis sits more than a mile above sea level and the area where the Republic of Texas group had holed up was even higher. There are pine trees fifty feet tall in the canyons. The compound we were watching was located in the bottom of a canyon and nearly impossible to get to. The only road in the area ended at the compound itself.

Doyle, Rangers Coy Smith and Johnny Allen during the 1997 Republic of Texas standoff in Jeff Davis County.

For the next several days, Captain Caver and the command staff continued to negotiate with the group in an effort to get them to give up. The SWAT team would roll up the hill to the compound and would deliver a message. A few hours later, the group would send a message back. All the time we were trying to keep the group contained

Finally, the captain and his team talked most of the group into giving up without a fight. It took most of the day for the group to surrender. We arrested them and had to drive them into town and put them in the county jail.

As the main players were giving up, one of our observation posts related that two members had fled out the back way and headed farther up into the mountains. When we approached the vacated compound, which they called their embassy, we found that it had been booby-trapped with homemade explosives. We had to call for a military bomb squad to blow up the devices (made of butane bottles) so no one would get hurt.

I had never been around explosives before. We were working with a U. S. Army sergeant who seemed to know what he was doing. He would take a small block of C-4, put it on the device and run wires to it. We then got a long way from the charge. He would yell "Fire-in-the hole!" and Boom! We blew up a lot of devices that day.

While all this was going on, another group of Rangers was using Texas Department of Corrections dogs to hunt for the two suspects who had chosen not to give up. During this effort, one of the bad guys shot a TDC dog. It was nearly dark when that happened, so the Rangers decided to pull out for the night and start at the same point the following morning. The dog was treated for his injuries, which were not life threatening.

The canyon where the shooting had taken place was the largest in the area. Ranger Smith and another TDC dog team circled around and assumed a blocking position at the head of the canyon to keep the suspects from walking out the top end of the mountain.

The rest of us, about twenty Rangers, planned to start searching the canyons the following morning so we could push the bad guys toward Coy's group. When it got light, a group of Rangers and a TDC dog team went back into the same area. Just as the search started, one of the suspects shot another dog from some point out in front of us. Again, the injuries were not fatal, and the dog was taken back to get treatment.

Now, with the whole day ahead of us, we had a good general idea where the suspects were located. We knew that they were armed and that they were willing to shoot, because they had already done it on two separate occasions.

Over the next five or six hours we searched the mountains and canyons. Most of the guys involved in this effort were older men, most in their forties. After going after the suspects for half a day we were all beat. We called Coy's group of Rangers and TDC officers at the head of the canyon and told him to make a sweep down through the middle of the canyon and try and push the bad guys toward us. We planned to rest while Coy's group made the push.

We had just moved toward the largest canyon when all hell broke loose. Coy and a prison dog handler had been making their way down the middle of the canyon when one of the dogs alerted. When it did so, it ran up a ledge about twenty yards above Coy. As the dog neared the top one of the bad guys opened up on it and in the general direction of Coy. He hit the dog but not Coy, who took cover and fired numerous AR-15 rounds in his direction. If there is one Ranger you don't want to shoot at, it's Coy Smith. He's not at all bashful about returning the favor.

From several hundred yards away, we all started running toward the gunfire. We directed a DPS chopper to the area and several aerial gun runs were made on the suspect. Each time the chopper came in the bad guy stood up and started shooting at it. The Ranger in the chopper returned fire at the suspect.

Doyle and Ranger Coy Smith during the Republic of Texas standoff
in far West Texas. A day or so later Coy would end up in
a shootout with one of the suspects.

Meanwhile we got the suspect surrounded. At one point he stood up trying to get a shot at the helicopter, and a TDC officer got a clear shot at him with a scoped .270 rifle. When he pulled the trigger, it sounded like he had shot a tub of water. We knew he had hit the guy, but we stayed concealed in the brush for a while to make sure he was finished shooting. Finally a group of us inched up and found he was dead.

When I walked up, I saw that the TDC dog handler had pulled his dead dog's body into his lap and was hugging his K-9 friend. Of all the things I ever saw as a policeman, that was the most heartbreaking. I got choked up and had to turn away. If I live to be a hundred, I will never forget that officer holding his dead dog. I couldn't care less about the dead suspect who had been shooting at the officers. That dog probably saved an officer's life and we all knew it.

Over the next several hours Captain Caver sent several fresh Rangers into the area to work the crime scene. While they took photographs and made measurements, we tried to figure out how to get the body out of there. Finally we learned that the National Guard would be providing us with a Black Hawk equipped with a cable lift to get the body out. We waited for what seemed like a long time for the helicopter to arrive. When it did, it could not land due to the height of the pine trees on the sides of the mountain.

They finally lowered a crew member with a stretcher to remove the suspect's body. The crew member got the body ready and was in the process of removing it, when one of the Rangers, I really don't remember who, told him we were not going to remove the suspect's body before the dog's body. At this point all the Rangers on scene chimed in. We had our blood up and told the crewman that the dog was going out first.

He told us he could not put the dog on the chopper. We again told him that the dog would go out first. He radioed the chopper and then told us they had to get going because it would be dark soon. We repeated that the dog would go first. Again, he said no. We told him in that case he should get his ass back in his helicopter and leave. We would get the job done without him and his helicopter. He talked on the radio again and finally agreed to carry the dog in his arms when the stretcher went up with the dead man. That way, the dog would get on the helicopter first. We all agreed.

In all my years of being an officer, that was the most touching tribute I ever had the honor of witnessing. All these years later it still chokes me up when I think about it. The dog was later buried on TDC property and has a nice grave marker. All the Rangers who were there that day know that the dog deserved it.

Captain Caver had done what a Ranger captain was expected to do. He had brought an end to the standoff and had done what the FBI had been unable to during the 1993 Branch Davidian siege near Waco. He did one hell of a job.

Trooper Assault

On April 15, 2000 just after midnight, I was contacted by Captain C.J. Havrda and advised that Highway Patrol Trooper Sharliegh Shaw had made a traffic stop near milepost 71 in La Salle County and had nearly been beaten to death. The captain told me to go to the location and take charge of the investigation.

While on the way to the scene, I was advised by DPS communications that the suspect vehicle had been found abandoned at milepost 60. I drove to that location and met with area officers to try to get a handle on what had happened. I was told that Trooper Shaw had been airlifted to a hospital in San Antonio. Despite her injuries, she had been able to tell other officers that she had been assaulted by two males and one female. The suspect vehicle was identified as a 1989 black Mercury four-door bearing Texas plates 684-DNH. I made arrangements to have the Mercury and Trooper Shaw's DPS unit towed to the sheriff's office in Cotulla so they could be processed for physical evidence.

While we were making these arrangements, we received information from Laredo that a man had reported that two men and a female had kidnapped him at milepost 60 on the interstate in La Salle County. Now I really had a mess! I had the crime scene where the assault took place, the scene where the suspect vehicle was abandoned, and another scene where the kidnap victim had been released in Laredo.

I got with Highway Patrol Sergeant Rocky Millican and

requested that he send a unit to Laredo to pick up the kidnap victim so we could interview him and get additional information on the suspects. (Rocky would later become a Texas Ranger.) Rocky told me that he had searched the suspect vehicle and found identification for a female named Yvette Castillo of Laredo. I then contacted Highway Patrol Sergeant Don Valdez and requested that he go to the woman's address and attempt to locate her. I started toward Laredo to continue the investigation.

As I reached town, Sergeant Valdez contacted me and said he had just located Castillo at her residence. I told the sergeant to take her to the DPS office so she could be interviewed about the assault on Trooper Shaw.

When I got to the office, I started talking with Castillo. She told me she had been traveling with her boyfriend, Sergio Rangel and his brother Alfredo. As they neared Cotulla, a DPS trooper stopped them. During the traffic stop, the trooper told Sergio Rangel he was under arrest for DWI. Castillo said that as Trooper Shaw attempted to handcuff Sergio, he attacked the officer. Castillo said that Sergio had Shaw on the ground and was on top of her, beating her in the face with his fist. Alfredo then got out of the car to help his brother, and the two of them disarmed and left Shaw for dead in the ditch beside the road.

They then drove south toward Laredo for a while before pulling into a roadside park. Ditching their car, they commandeered another vehicle and kidnapped the owner. Castillo told me that once they were in Laredo, Sergio and Alfredo got their sister to help them cross into Nuevo Laredo.

I contacted DPS Narcotics Lieutenant Martin Cuellar and requested that he call some of his contacts in Mexico and get their help in locating the suspects. We continued to search for them over the next two days.

On April 17, I was contacted by some members of Rangel's family and advised that both of the suspects had gone to a sister-in-law's residence in Nuevo Laredo. The Rangel family provided me with an address where they thought they were hiding. I asked Lieutenant Cuellar to call on his sources on the other side of the river to ascertain the location of the address. At one point Cuellar and I crossed into Mexico to attempt to find the house. We located the address and returned to the Texas side.

The following day Webb County Chief Deputy Meme Martinez and I went to Nuevo Laredo and met with the Tamaulipas State Judicial Police *comandante* and advised him of our interest in the brothers. The *comandante* provided us with several carloads of *Judiciales* and we went to the address that Cuellar and I had located but the suspects were not there.

The Mexican and Texas officers talked with the people who were there and they provided another address across town where the suspects might be hiding. The multi-national convoy then drove to the second location. The second location was a large one-story apartment complex that covered an entire block. We had to search the buildings three separate times to locate the two suspects. They were finally found hiding in a small utility room behind a water heater.

After both of the Rangel brothers were arrested, they were interviewed by Martinez, the *comandante* and me. They said that they had traded Trooper Shaw's pistol to another man at the edge of Nuevo Laredo. Officers then drove to that location and recovered the trooper's service weapon. Martinez and I then made arrangements with the *comandante* to have the suspects transported to the middle of the international bridge where they could be released into the custody of DPS officers.

The two suspects were taken to the DPS office. At this point I had not had any sleep for days. I called Captain Havrda and told him that I needed someone else to interview the suspects because I was dead on my feet. He knew what I had been doing and was just glad that we had the suspects in custody. He sent Ranger Gary De Los Santos to conduct the interviews. Gary obtained written confessions from both suspects.

After getting caught up on my sleep, I continued to work on the case for the next few weeks. Several months later both suspects were tried for attempted capital murder and assault on Trooper Shaw. Sergio and Alfredo Rangel were both sent to the penitentiary and will be there for a long time.

This case was one of the most stressful I worked as a Ranger. The Rangels had nearly killed one of our fellow officers, and all of the DPS officers in Laredo did whatever it took to get them into custody. I could never have put this case together without the help of numerous DPS officers in Laredo, as well as officers from other agencies on both sides of the border. We had been able to solve the case because of all the officers working together and getting the job done. That has always been the DPS way of doing business.

Sun Murder

Most Fridays I tried to complete the week's reports and get them sent to headquarters so the lieutenant wouldn't be on my ass on Monday, wondering where my weekly reports were. Otherwise, I did my best not to get anything started, because by the time it got to the end of the week I was ready for a couple of days off.

I always tried to reserve Friday nights for my family. My wife and I worked all week, and it was important for us to have a night out. Most of the time we would go out to eat and try to take in a movie. But for some reason, on Friday May 5, 2000, I had stayed around the DPS office longer then I normally did.

I was in my unit on the way home when I overheard several Highway Patrol units getting involved in a high-speed chase on Interstate 35 north of Laredo. As I worked my way to the house, I could hear that the U.S. Border Patrol was involved, and the DPS units had just caught up with the suspect way north of town. As I got near my house it became apparent that the vehicle running from the units was not going to stop.

I decided that I had better start that way. I got on the interstate and started north to try to catch up. I was at least twenty-five miles behind them. As I drove, I heard that the chase had crossed into La Salle County, and the driver of the fleeing Toyota pickup showed no intention of stopping. I continued north, and by this time I was running somewhere around 100 mph.

As I neared the La Salle County line, I heard that the chase had finally ended just south of Cotulla, the county seat. After a short pause on the radio, the communications operator said the one thing a law enforcement officer never wants to hear. A trooper was down, and an ambulance was en route to the scene.

When something like this happens an officer's mind always races to try to figure out what happened on the other end of the radio. I didn't want to ask a lot of questions, knowing it was important to keep the airway open in case the officers on scene needed it. Obviously, there was a lot going on. All I could do was keep driving as fast as I could to get to the scene, so hopefully I could help out.

When I got there, I learned that Trooper Miguel Rodriguez and the suspect had both been airlifted to a hospital in San Antonio. Highway Patrol Sergeant Rocky Millican said the Asian male who had been driving the Toyota had cut his own wrist during the chase. Two Highway Patrol units had been involved in the chase when the Toyota pickup had finally pulled over.

The Toyota driver had opened his door and collapsed in the ditch. Both Highway Patrol vehicles pulled up behind each other. Trooper Rodriguez was in the second unit, but he got out first and started running toward the Toyota. Just as he got even with the first black-and-white, the other trooper opened his car door. The door's sharp corner caught Rodriguez in the throat, causing a severe cut.

The sergeant told me that the Toyota had been moved to a local garage. While inventorying the vehicle, they found the body of an Asian female lying in the front floorboard covered with clothing. She looked as if she had been dead for a while.

The sergeant made arrangements for one of the troopers to take measurements at the scene and we both started toward the garage. While I was on my way I called Captain Havrda to tell him what I had going on. It took me a while to run through it. I said I needed a Ranger at the hospital in San Antonio in case the suspect wasn't hurt very bad and could still talk. He was now a murder suspect, and I didn't want him to walk off if he was released from the hospital. I also requested that a DPS laboratory team be sent from Corpus Christi because I knew I was not going to have time to process the vehicle alone. The captain told me to take care of my end and he would handle the rest.

After Sergeant Millican arrived at the garage he advised me that he had identified the suspect as Eugene Hahn, who appeared to be from Georgia. When I got there, we both inspected the 1996 Toyota that Hahn had been driving. The inside was covered in blood, so much that I could smell it when I opened the door. When I went around and opened the passenger-side door I saw the body lying in the floorboard.

When I moved her, I noticed that her throat had been cut. Someone had really done a job on her. Her head was hanging by the skin from the back of her neck. We processed the vehicle for physical evidence and took photos so we could go ahead and move the victim to a local funeral home. The local Justice of the Peace arrived for the legal formality of pronouncing the victim dead. She was then taken to Peters Funeral Home.

I knew that the DPS lab team would want a search warrant for the pickup to protect the legal integrity of any evidence they found, so I decided to go to the sheriff's office and get it written. I worked on the warrant for about an hour and had a local judge sign it before the forensic team arrived. When they got there, I executed the warrant and left the team at the pickup to process it. I then returned to the La Salle County Sheriff's Office so I could contact Georgia authorities to find out as much as I could about the victim and the suspect.

While I was at the sheriff's office the lab team advised me that the victim appeared to be Kyung Sun from identification found inside the pickup. I then called Gwinnett, Georgia, authorities and told them about what we had going in La Salle County. I talked with Lieutenant Howard Beers, who agreed to try to find as much information as possible to help us with our case in Texas. I told him we were not sure that Sun had been killed in Texas, and that he should be on the lookout for a crime scene there when he contacted the victim's relatives.

By this time it was about three in the morning, so I decided to return to Laredo and get a little sleep before the Georgia investigator called me back later in the day. I went to bed about 5 a.m. and got my first call from Georgia only four hours later. I was up and running again.

Lieutenant Beers told me he had found out that Sun and Hahn had been going out for the past several months. Beers said their relationship had started to fall apart over the last few weeks, and that Hahn had started physically abusing Sun.

Apparently Hahn was a control freak, and Sun had been complaining to some of her relatives about the way he treated her. The lieutenant told me that he had interviewed some of the people Sun had worked with, and he had learned that a few weeks previously Hahn had put a knife to Sun's throat and told her he was going to kill her.

The Georgia investigator said that as far as he could tell, the last time anyone saw Sun was when she left work with Hahn at about 4 a.m. on May 5. Beers said he had checked the residences of the suspect and the victim but had not found a crime scene. He thought Hahn had taken Sun somewhere else and killed her before he left.

I asked Beers if he had come up with any reason Hahn would be in Texas. The lieutenant said he didn't have a clue why they would be in our part of the world. He told me that he would continue to work on the case, and would call if he got more information. I then called Captain Havrda and learned that he had assigned Ranger Gary De Los Santos to work the San Antonio angle at the hospital with Hahn.

I called Gary and he told me that he had done everything possible trying to get Hahn to talk, but Hahn refused to make any kind of statement. Trying to communicate with him was like talking to a wall, he said. Hahn would not respond to anything Gary asked.

At this point I was thinking, *How hard can this case be?* I knew that in Texas, in a murder case, the suspect can be prosecuted in the county where the murder happened, any county he passed through with the body, or the county where the body was finally located. I had a lot of places where the case could be prosecuted. Besides, we had caught Hahn red-handed, driving the pickup with his dead girlfriend in the floorboard. I figured the case for a slam-dunk, but I was wrong.

Over the next month I continued to work on the investigation in an effort to find where Sun had been murdered. I talked with Lieutenant Beers numerous times. He worked hard on his end, but was not able to find a crime scene in Georgia. The lieutenant had learned that Hahn had assaulted another girlfriend several years earlier, but Georgia authorities had been unable to proceed with prosecution on the case because the victim was so scared of Hahn that she refused to testify against him.

Hahn was finally released from the hospital in San Antonio and placed in the La Salle County Jail. I filed on him for the murder of Sun in La Salle County due to the fact that he had been found in that county with Sun's body. I made my report, as I usually did, and submitted it to the La Salle County District Attorney's Office for prosecution.

Several months later one of the La Salle County deputies contacted me and told that Hahn had appeared in district court in a pre-trial hearing. The deputy said he thought the judge was going to dismiss the case because the state could not prove that Sun had been killed in Texas. He said Hahn's defense attorney had put his client on the witness stand and asked him just one question: Was Sun dead when he drove into Texas with her body? Hahn had answered yes, she was dead when he drove into the state. He then refused to answer any questions from the prosecution.

At this point, I was going nuts. I could not believe a district judge would dismiss a charge of murder on a guy when we had apprehended him with the body of the victim in his pickup. San Antonio Ranger John Martin had gotten involved by this time, and both of us started trying to keep the judge from turning Hahn loose. If we didn't find something soon, the judge was going to let him go.

John and I filed on Hahn for one charge of tampering with physical evidence and one charge of evading arrest. Both of these two new complaints were filed in La Salle County. Ranger Martin also contacted Federal authorities in San Antonio in an effort to try to file Federal charges on Hahn. I continued to talk with the Georgia authorities to ascertain if they could file a murder charge in Georgia. They talked with a prosecutor there and were told that they could not file on Hahn there because they had no crime scene, and they could not prove that Sun had been killed in that state. Talk about a dog chasing his tail! This would have been laughable if it wasn't a murder case.

Ranger Jeff Robertson and I decided to interview Hahn again to see if we could get more information out of him about the murder. We drove to Cotulla and talked to him, but got nothing. I got the feeling I was interviewing one of the most dangerous men I had ever been around. At this point in my career, I had conducted thousands of interviews. This guy was like a shark. He had lifeless eyes and no facial expressions at all when I tried to talk with him.

During the interview he got very aggressive and Jeff and I let him know we would not put up with that. I could tell he was the type who would hurt you if he got the chance. The interview was terminated when it was obvious we were wasting our time and we returned Hahn to his cell.

Over the next few months I continued to work on the case with Ranger Martin. John's deal fell through with the Federal authorities so we got ready to go forward in state court on the lesser charges we had filed against Hahn. When the trial finally came along, I testified for several hours about the facts of the case. A La Salle County jury found Hahn guilty on both counts, tampering with physical evidence by carrying around his dead girlfriend's body and evading arrest in the long chase with the area troopers. Hahn was sentenced to ten years in state prison.

After the jury was released, several members wanted to know why we had not filed on Hahn for the murder of Sun. We had to explain the facts to them. Most of the jurors could not believe it, and they left thinking that our justice system had let victim Kyung Sun down. I couldn't agree with them more.

Even though I'm retired, I would still like to find a way to get Hahn for the murder offense. One thing about a murder case, it never goes away, since there is no statute of limitations. Like I said at the start, this was one of the strangest murders I ever worked.

Trooper Miguel Rodriguez made a full recovery from the injury he received attempting to arrest Hahn the night the car chase had taken place. He continues to work in La Salle County.

A Copious Amount of Blood

Rocky Millican, who I had worked with quite a bit when he was a Highway Patrol sergeant, promoted to Ranger and got assigned to Company D to work the Pearsall area. The counties Rocky worked were the ones bordering my area of responsibility.

Rocky was one of the best new Rangers I had worked with, and I liked him from the start. He had the same work ethic as the guys who had broken me in, back in my day. His fingers just flew over the keyboard when he worked on the computer. He watched (and learned) when we worked together. I noticed that when I did something during an investigation, the next time we had to do the same thing, Rocky already knew how to do it because he had been paying attention. He's a sharp guy.

Over the first year or so after he made Ranger we worked a lot together and we became good friends. When we had a company meeting, I would drive to Pearsall and catch a ride to San Antonio with him. I would make him drive. We'd always stop for diet Dr. Pepper. Both of us drank too much of it, and we both dipped too much snuff. But that kept us going when we had to work long hours.

I was in Cotulla one day and decided to go to Pearsall to eat lunch with Rocky. He had set up a small office in Dilley, and I found him there working on a case. He was just getting ready to meet with a witness. I don't remember what the case was about. After all these years they kind of all run together in

257

my mind.

Anyway, I was ready to go eat and Rocky was holding me up with his interview. He had not reached the number of years of service when, if you have the option, eating comes first. Rocky asked me to sit in on the interview, and I agreed. The guy came into the room and Rocky started his dog-and-pony show trying to get him to tell him what he wanted to know. I was just sitting back, putting my two-cents' in every once in a while.

Doyle and Ranger Rocky Millican with a Texas lizard.

Rocky asked if there was a copious amount of blood in the area where the offense was committed. The guy we were interviewing got this strange look on his face and appeared to be bewildered. I most likely had the same look. The guy looked at me for help and I kind of shrugged. I had never heard the word "copious" in my life and I was nearly fifty years old. We didn't use words like that in Rankin.

Rocky finally got the information that he was after and we ended the interview. He let the guy go, and we started for lunch. "What the hell does 'copious' mean?" I asked. Rocky got this amazed look on his face and replied, "a lot." I told Rocky that the guy most likely had an IQ of 70 and mine wasn't much higher, and it seemed that "a lot" was much easier to understand for us dumb guys. We laughed about that all the way to lunch. From that day until I retired, I used the word "copious" in my reports every chance I got, just to make everyone think I was as smart as Rocky!

259

Murder in Dilley

One day Ranger Millican contacted me about a murder that had just occurred at a small store in Dilley. He told me that a female had been stabbed to death in what appeared to be a robbery. I left for Dilley as soon as I could.

When I arrived at the scene, Rocky had already begun to process the area for physical evidence. The store where the murder had taken place was on Main Street across from the city park. It appeared that the victim had been attacked near the front door and repeatedly stabbed. It looked as if she had gone down on the floor near the door, and the suspects had dragged her from there to behind the counter near the cash register.

While Rocky and I were working the crime scene, we received information from a lady in Dilley that one of her female relatives and the girl's boyfriend had returned home and seemed in a big hurry to get out of town for some reason. The informant went on to say that she knew that the two of them had done something really bad. We started toward Pearsall to attempt to locate them and while en route notified all of the area officers to start looking for the suspects. When Rocky and I arrived in Pearsall we learned that the couple might be at a motel just west of Interstate 35.

Rocky and I went to the motel and took the female into custody. A short time later, the male suspect was apprehended by the Pearsall Police Department. We went to the Frio County Sheriff's Office to interview the couple. During the interview, we found that the male suspect had a deep cut on the back of his leg. That led us to believe that he had somehow stabbed himself in the commission of the murder. At this point the male would not admit any involvement in the offense. A while later Rocky and I interviewed the female.

The couple eventually admitted to the murder. Rocky and I got them to walk us through the crime scene and describe how the victim was murdered. Both suspects were video-recorded as they described their crime. Each blamed the other for the murder. Rocky was the lead officer in this investigation and did a really good job in putting the case together. Months later both of the suspects were sent to the penitentiary for the murder of the victim.

Blood Spatter

Over the years that I was a Ranger I was sent to almost every kind of criminal investigation school that was available. The Ranger service makes sure you have the kind of training that will help you solve the crime that no one else seems to be able to solve.

I remember when I first heard the term "blood spatter" I had no idea what that meant. I was first sent to basic blood spatter investigative training at the DPS Training Academy in Austin. By that time I had worked numerous murders. I had collected a lot of blood and blood-related evidence at crime scenes, but I had no idea what I had been missing until I went to the school.

I will not go into detail on the training except to say that there is a math formula that can be used to determine the angle a blood drop had taken before it hit a surface. By using the formula in working a scene where blood is present, it is possible to determine if a witness or suspect is telling the truth in describing what he or someone else did. An investigator can walk into a crime scene, and by just looking the scene over he can understand what has happened a lot better than he could without blood spatter training.

A short time after I had gone to the first blood spatter training school, Sheriff Darwin Avant called me and requested that I assist him with a murder investigation. I drove to Cotulla where Darwin told me that they had found the body of an old man in the driver's seat of his car. The man had been stabbed several times.

Darwin asked if I would look at the car and attempt to ascertain what had happened based on the blood in the vehicle. The sheriff and I drove to the storage lot where the victim's car was. When I walked up to look, I was surprised at what I could read from the blood patterns in the vehicle.

I told Darwin that the victim had been stabbed by a right-handed man sitting in the back seat when the offense occurred. I said the victim had been stabbed at least five times and at some point had been lying over in the front seat. Finally, I told Darwin that the murder was most likely done by someone the victim knew and trusted enough to allow to sit behind him.

After listening to what I had to say, Darwin told me he already had a suspect—a relative of the victim who had been acting strangely since the murder. Over the next few days the sheriff and I interviewed the suspect, but he would not admit that he had committed the murder.

A few days later Darwin called me late one night and told me that we didn't have to worry about the suspect anymore. He had gone to the grave of the victim and had killed himself. Darwin and I never got to the point that we could prove the suspect committed the murder, but it seem pretty apparent to both of us.

I've always been grateful for the fact that the Rangers provided me with the training that allowed me to do the job I needed to do. Getting the best training and paying attention to details allowed me to contribute to the criminal investigations being conducted by the other agencies that requested my help. The training made all of the difference.

Brotherhood

One of the fondest memories I have about the time I first went to work in law enforcement was the feeling of brotherhood among the officers that I worked with. When I arrived at my new duty station at Fort Hancock right after I graduated from the academy, I found a mix of veteran troopers and younger guys with less time on the job.

The DPS always made sure that their new troopers rode with a senior partner. In those days it was not unusual for those senior troopers to have ten to fifteen years of service and still be working the road.

When a rookie is broken in by a veteran partner, he learns a lot. The department places rookies on probation for their first six months. What that really means is that DPS can fire a new trooper at any time during those first six months if they think he's not going to be able to do the job. No matter what they teach you in a classroom, experience is the way you learn to do your job. The veteran Highway Patrol troopers had been on the road and they knew how the street works. Nothing beats experience.

It was several months before my partner even let me drive the unit. He watched everything I did and reported my progress to the Highway Patrol sergeant. Any mistakes were taken very seriously, and if you wanted to keep your job you had better not make the same mistake twice. You were taught from the start that people's lives depended on the way you conducted yourself and when you made a decision you had to take into account the people who were going to be affected.

Just after I went to work, my partner Mike Greer and I were called to a traffic accident in which a large truck tractor and cattle trailer had turned over and caught on fire. Mike and I arrived to find the trailer still engulfed in flames. The wreck had the eastbound lane of Interstate 10 blocked. In short, it was a real mess.

Before we had gotten there, a bystander had opened the back of the cattle trailer to let some of the cattle out to keep them from being burned alive. We had cattle running all over the highway. In those days there weren't any fire trucks in the area, so basically all we could do was watch the truck burn. We were busy trying to keep bystanders away from the burning truck when its big tires began to explode from the heat. The air pressure in the tires built up, and when they exploded, both rubber and metal pieces flew all over the place.

Mike told me to get the rifle out of the unit and shoot the remaining tires to let the pressure out so they would not explode and hurt or kill someone. We got everyone away from the truck, and I shot the tires out as I was told.

I really hadn't paid much attention to the way that I was acting when I shot out the tires, but I was clearly having a good time. As soon as he could, Mike got me off to the side and ripped me to no end. He told me that I was expected to act in a professional way and to not appear that I was having such a good time.

I had only been on the job a few weeks, but I learned a major life lesson real quick. As an officer, you always, always conduct yourself professionally. You never forget that.

Mike was not only looking after me, he was protecting the reputation of the DPS at the same time. We finished working the wreck and Mike told me again the way that I was expected to act. I made a mental note to watch the way I acted and to pay close attention to every detail of my job.

As I was working the area over the next few months, I

began to realize how close the officers that worked the I-10 area were. It wasn't long before I knew all the Highway Patrol troopers for 300 miles around. I also got to know the sheriffs and all of the deputies that worked for them in the two counties that I worked.

I noticed that the Border Patrolmen and local deputies worked a lot together, backing us up when we needed help. The local game wardens were good friends and rode with us a lot. One of the many things I liked about West Texas was that if you called for help, you had better get out of the way, because everyone who had a radio was coming to help you. When we went to the café everyone was friends and all agencies sat together at the tables.

Being trained and brought up through this system really did a lot for me later in my career. I was shown from the start how much more effective law enforcement could be when everyone worked together. Not only that, you are working with friends who have the same values as you. When a friend calls for assistance you drop whatever you're doing and go to his aid.

I never realized that things could be different until I moved into South Texas. When I moved to Laredo in 1977 I had no idea what it was going to be like. I assumed that it would be the same as working in West Texas.

The first thing that I noticed when I started to work in South Texas was that the area agencies did not get along. The police department did not like the sheriff's office or the other way around, and the DPS officers basically did their own thing. The game wardens didn't trust anyone. They thought we were all road hunters. The Border Patrolmen were really the only ones who appeared as if they wanted to have a working relationship with anyone. At that point there weren't that many other Federal officers in town. I found that the only way that you could work with other agencies was by building personal relationships. That way, if you needed anything you could go to your contact with that agency and

After all these years, I still ha
agencies didn't get along. It alv,
everyone spent more time trying to find ,
each other about rather than trying to fi,
everyone together. Fortunately, over the las,
things have gotten a lot better between agencies be‿‿‿‿ ‿. ‿.‿
problems that we are having with Mexico. I think everyone
now realizes it's a lot better when everyone pulls in the same
direction. It sure took them a long time to find that out.

When I was a rookie, the older officers took care of the
younger ones and showed them what was expected of them and
the correct way to do certain things. The younger officers
always showed the older guys a lot of respect. We knew that
they had experience and we took their advice, if for no other
reason than the fact that it might end up saving our life. They
taught us small things that most people would not even notice,
like the importance of holding your flashlight in your non-gun
hand or how to approach a car during a violator contact. Little
things that made all the difference in the world.

In time, I got a chance to pass on what I had learned. One
time I saw a new deputy, fresh out of training, put his new Colt
45 Government Model down on his desk on the weapon's left
side. I walked over and asked if the gun was on safety.

He reached over, picked it up and said yes, it was. I told
him if he had set the gun down on its right side, he would have
been able to tell me if the safety was on without picking up the
gun. That's the reason you should always lay down a Colt
Government Model on its right side. The deputy thought that
was a really good idea.

I walked back to my office and thought of the time that
Clayton McKinney had told me the exact same thing in 1973. It
seems strange to me that I am now in the position to be the one
giving the advice. Funny how life is. I guess there is a little
wisdom with age.

Texas Ranger Pete Montemayor and Doyle looking
for information on a fugitive.

Chepo Yanez

A Texas Ranger gets a good number of requests from local authorities to do what we refer to as special investigations. That's a "catch all" term that we used in the Rangers. An example would be any type of investigation involving an elected official. The policy related to this type of investigation is that the DPS must receive an official request from either a district attorney, county attorney, district judge or sheriff requesting an investigation.

There must also be an understanding that the case will be prosecuted if the investigation results in findings of criminal wrongdoing. After receiving such a request, a Ranger must evaluate the request and forward his recommendation, in writing, along with the written request, to his captain. The request is again evaluated and forwarded to Austin, where it is reviewed by the Chief of the Texas Rangers. The request then goes to the DPS director, who makes the final call. If the request is approved, the Ranger is notified and directed to proceed with the investigation.

Rangers do a lot of these investigations. I have arrested sheriffs, police officers, deputies, judges and county attorneys as a result of my investigations. Most of the time the DPS will make sure that the Ranger assigned to the area does not work the special investigation. This is because he most likely will know the people involved. But that is not always the case.

On one occasion I was advised that La Salle County Justice of the Peace Chepo Yanez was suspected of taking

269

money from the county by pocketing traffic fines he collected. I worked a lot in La Salle County and was friends with Judge Yanez, who I had known for years. Before being elected a JP, he had been a deputy sheriff in Cotulla. We had worked a lot of cases together and interviewed a lot of suspects. He knew how I did my interviews and that I was heartless when it came to making a case on someone that had committed a criminal offense.

When I had gotten the request, I contacted Captain Havrda and told him that authorities in La Salle County were requesting the investigation. I told the captain that I knew Yanez but thought I could handle the case because he and I were good enough friends that he would talk to me given the opportunity. The captain said he would run the request up the chain of command and let me know in the next few days.

While I was waiting, I went to Cotulla and met with some of the local deputies and tried to get a little background on the case. I learned that Yanez had never seemed to have any money until he got elected JP. Now he always had plenty of money, often insisting on paying for people's lunch.

Several days later the captain told me that the investigation had been approved. "Go and get it done," he said, adding I should notify him as soon as I made the case.

The next day I drove to La Salle County and met with several deputies to see if they had audited the Justice of the Peace accounts. I was informed such an audit was underway, but that it had not been completed. The county had, however, seen a severe drop in the amount of money being turned in by the judge. The local authorities had checked with the local troopers and found that they were still writing about the same number of tickets. If anything, there should have been an increase in revenue, not a decrease.

I decided not to beat around the bush. I would go directly to Judge Yanez and ask him how he could explain the decrease in revenue. Whenever I did an investigation of someone I

270

knew, I always felt sorry for the friend who had messed up. Yanez' election as JP was the best thing that had happened to him in years. He had a good job and people in the Cotulla area thought a lot of him. I could never understand why a man would ruin his reputation and take a chance of going to jail for money, but the judge had been down on his luck, having split up with his wife. Still, I couldn't believe he would throw it all away.

I called the judge and asked him to meet me at the sheriff's office to talk about an investigation. I could tell by the way he sounded on the telephone that he knew what I wanted to talk about. He came to the sheriff's office, and he and I went into a room. I told him why I was there, and he and I talked as one friend to another.

Knowing I would do my job no matter what, he admitted he had been stealing a lot of money from La Salle County. In fact, he said that he had taken so much he had no idea of the amount. He told me that when he first started taking the money, he had intended to pay it back. Over time, he got in over his head, having no way to get the amount of money needed to refund what he had stolen. I took a written statement at the end of the interview. I didn't arrest him at that time, but told him I would submit my report to the district attorney and let his office decide what they wanted to charge him with once the audit was completed. I returned to Laredo, called Captain Havrda and told him: "It's done." He knew what I meant.

South of the Border

I had to be able to work in Mexico, but as a Texas Ranger working on the border for years, you start to have a very bad opinion of our neighbor south of the river. Most of the bad things that happen on the border are directly related to Mexico or, more to the point, the crooks that live there. Whether it's drug smugglers or alien smugglers, neither group has any regard for law or life. We found bodies of illegal aliens every summer, drowned in trying to cross the river or dead from the heat. It always amazed me how the criminals in Mexico could treat their own people the way they do. No regard for human life. They are just after the money.

When you get up every morning for years and have to deal with this type of thing, over a period of time it affects your personality. You become hardened to things you have to see. I made up my mind that I was going to do everything in my power to put as many of these people in jail as I could to try and keep this kind of thing from spreading into Texas. That's the main reason that I chose to stay on the border my whole career.

From 1984 until about 2000 I worked a lot in Nuevo Laredo. I never got to the point that I could speak Spanish very well, but I did not let that stand in my way. I always took an officer with me who could speak Spanish, and I got along just fine. I learned from the very start that if you stayed away from stolen cars and drug cases, the police on the other side would help you do almost anything. They were good at what they did,

272

and they knew who was up to what in their area.

In those days, I would just drive across the international bridge and go to the main *comandancia* in Nuevo Laredo. I would always try to deal with the *Judiciales*. They were the state police and helped me the most. At one point, Ranger Ray Cano and I made friends with *Comandante* Franklin Barrera and he provided both of us with credentials as Tamaulipas state police officers. Barrera spoke perfect English, and I had no trouble at all in dealing with him. He dressed like a banker, and you would never know by looking at him that he was one of the most powerful men in Nuevo Laredo.

Photo of Tamaulipas credentials issued to Doyle Holdridge.

The only thing that gave him away was that he always had a lot of bodyguards with him. He gave me his personal phone numbers, and I would call him when I needed something. For people who don't live on the border the system used in Mexico

273

may seem confusing. The *comandantes* are placed in charge of an area, but they only stay for a short time. The Mexican government had learned that if you left one of the commanders in an area too long, they tended to get very powerful and hard for the government to deal with. They move them from place to place within any given state in Mexico. But while Barrera was in Nuevo Laredo, I was able to solve a lot of cases in Texas and all across the United States.

Often people commit a crime in the United States and run to Mexico because they think they can live down there and get away with whatever they have done. Most of the time the people find out in short order that Mexico is not what they thought it would be. They try to cross back into Texas and get caught by Federal authorities at the bridge. At this point, I often ended up getting called by someone to help interview the suspects and process vehicles for physical evidence related to a crime.

Other times I would be contacted by the *comandante* and advised that they had taken a suspect into custody they wanted me to identify and find out what he had done in this country. One thing that I can say for sure is that the interviewing techniques in Mexico are far more effective than the ones we have in Texas. I found that most of the time by the time I got there, a wanted person was more than ready to come back to the United States.

Working in Mexico was dangerous, but nothing like it is now. Nowadays I don't go to Mexico at all. I enjoyed the time I spent across the river and I learned a lot about the way things work over there, but I want to be able to enjoy my grandkids.

In August 1996, I was contacted by DPS Narcotics Agent Ralph Shamek and requested to assist him with locating a murder suspect thought to be in Mexico. Shamek told me he had been assisting Michigan State Police officer Doug Brooks in finding one John Kehoe. I contacted Brooks, who had traveled to San Antonio, and he told me he had been working on this case a long time. He said Kehoe had killed his girlfriend, Rose Larner. After that, Kehoe cut off the victim's head, hands and feet and burned the body. While he was at it, he had eaten part of his victim. Then he fled to Mexico.

The Michigan investigator said Kehoe's brother, Tim, had helped him clean up the crime scene and had since moved to San Antonio. Brooks had been in San Antonio for the past couple of days trying to find Tim Kehoe only to get a call from Michigan that the brother had been located there and arrested for accessory-after-the-fact to murder.

Tim Kehoe confirmed that his brother was hiding out in Mexico. He told officers in Michigan that on two occasions he had made trips to Nuevo Laredo and met with his brother at a bar about two blocks from the international bridge to give him money. Brooks said he needed all the help he could get in trying to get John Kehoe returned to the United States and would be driving to Laredo to meet with me to see what could be done.

I contacted DPS Motor Vehicle Theft agent Joe Morales and we made arrangements to meet with *Comandante* Juan Muniz in Nuevo Laredo. Agent Morales and I explained the facts of the case to the state police commander and he agreed to help us locate the suspect. Now, when a *comandante* agrees to help you, the extent of the help always relates directly to how much heat it will cause. Morales and I had worked in Mexico together a lot of times, and both of us knew a lot of things could go wrong. We knew a suspect that had been involved in the murder of a Federal Drug Enforcement Agency agent had been brought back to the United States by DEA in, let us say, an unusual way. There had been a lot of heat on that deal, and we both knew that we did not want an international incident. In addition, if Joe and I had John Kehoe in a DPS unit when we crossed back into Texas, it might be perceived as kidnapping in Mexico. We were walking a very fine line but Morales and I had made up our minds that we were going to do everything in our power to get the guy back into the United States for the Michigan authorities.

Later that day, Morales and I met with investigator Brooks. He told us two additional Michigan officers were en route to Laredo with the brother of the murder suspect. He said they had already had Tim Kehoe contact his brother in Mexico, and that John Kehoe was on his way to meet with his brother at the bar to pick up some more money. Brooks said the other officers would be arriving at 11 p.m.

We spent the rest of the day making arrangements with the Mexican authorities to assist with the arrest. The one thing that the Mexican authorities did not want to do was deliver Kehoe to us on our side. They would help us arrest him, but they wanted us to drive him across the river. That way, if there was any heat we were going to be the ones who took it. I had talked with Senior Ranger Captain Bruce Casteel several times and he had instructed me not to take part in transporting the suspect to the United States. We were at a stalemate and I could not figure a way around the hang-up.

During the day, I learned that one of the highest officials from the state of Tamaulipas, Mexico was to be at the International Airport in Laredo in the afternoon. Morales and I went to the airport, contacted the official and told him about our dilemma. We also told him what Kehoe had done to the victim. I gave the official the telephone number of the *comandante* in Nuevo Laredo. The official called the *comandante* and told him to help us any way he could.

At this point, DPS Narcotics Lieutenant Rick Gonzalez and Special Crimes agent Hector Herrera agreed to assist with the investigation. The Michigan officers arrived in Laredo with Tim Kehoe, and we all met at the DPS office to come up with a plan to arrest his brother John.

The following day, Morales and I, along with the Michigan officers, crossed into Mexico and met with *Comandante* Juan Muniz. It was decided that the Michigan

276

officers would turn Tim Kehoe loose to walk from the U.S. side to the bar in Nuevo Laredo where he was supposed to meet his brother. This was risky. If Tim Kehoe ran or warned his brother while he was in Mexico, it was going to be a major problem for us. We decided that the two Michigan officers and I would cross the bridge in front of Tim Kehoe and set up surveillance of the bar before he got there.

We were going to try to keep Tim close in case he changed his mind. DPS agents Gonzalez and Morales would follow Tim across the bridge and set up surveillance after he entered the bar. DPS agent Herrera and the remaining Michigan officers would stay on the U.S. side and receive the suspect if we could get him across the river. *Comandante* Muniz would provide the undercover officers to be in the bar and an arrest team to take the suspect in custody if everything came together.

During the entire process I kept in constant contact with the captain in San Antonio and Senior Captain Casteel in Austin. We just wanted everything to go as planned. John Kehoe was supposed to show up at the bar at 4 p.m.

At about 3 p.m. we started the operation. The Mexican officers basically took over the bar where the meeting was to take place. The *comandante* put several *Judiciales* inside and went so far as to dress one of his officers as a waiter.

On our end, we stopped at Wal-Mart and bought a bright red jogging suit for Tim Kehoe to wear when he crossed into Mexico. We got him dressed, and away to the bridge we went. One thing everyone was worried about was the fact that none of us were carrying guns. The *comandante* had offered all of us Beretta 9mm pistols, but we knew that if something went wrong, we would be better off unarmed. Technically, even with the *comandante's* permission, we would still be breaking the law in Mexico if we carried weapons.

The two Michigan officers and I walked across the bridge with nothing but a radio. A short time later, we observed Tim Kehoe cross the bridge and head toward the bar. This was a first for me—helping a wanted fugitive get to Mexico. We had told Tim Kehoe to walk up to the bar and to take off his baseball cap if he saw his brother inside.

Just as we were all getting set up, Tim Kehoe walked up to the front of the bar and after a few seconds took off his baseball cap. The Michigan officers and I were standing a few yards from the bar when the *Judiciales* arrived in about six vehicles. There must have been fifteen Mexican officers running into the bar with machine guns. In only a few seconds a large group of men came out of the bar like they were playing Australian-rules football. A few moments after that, the *Judiciales* emerged with John Kehoe and Tim Kehoe, threw them in the back of a jeep and headed toward the international bridge. As we all started toward the bridge we saw the jeep crossing into the United States on the wrong side of the road, driving like a bat out of hell. The Jeep skidded up to the officers on our side of the river, both of the Kehoes came flying out, and away the Jeep went, back to the Mexican side. The whole operation did not take more than two minutes.

When we got back to our side, the Michigan officers could not believe what had happened. They had been looking for the Kehoes for months and we had got them back to the United States faster than a minnow could swim a dipper.

We all returned to the DPS office and made all the phone calls to let all of the bosses know that everything had gone as planned. The Michigan officers took the Kehoes back to Michigan, where they got convicted. I don't think that John Kehoe will ever get out. One of the Michigan officers was within a few days of his retirement, and he told me he could not think of a better way to end his career. All of the DPS guys that took part in the investigation did a great job. A day or so later, Morales and I met the *comandante* and thanked him for the help he had given us. Had it not been for his blessing and assistance we could have never gotten the guys back.

Agent Morales and I would continue to work in Mexico

for the next several years and we crossed a lot more fugitives over, but none with the drama this case had.

Fugitive Lawman

While I was working in Laredo as a Ranger I was aware of most of what happened in the area. That's because I knew a lot of people. One was a casual friend named Joe, a Webb County deputy. He had been to my house and was a close friend of one of my best friends, Wayo Ruiz.

I started hearing rumors that Joe might have gotten into a problem somewhere near Houston. I heard that he had been to a party, and that someone had shot and killed two men at a store near that party. Joe fit the physical description of the shooter. Over the next few weeks, I learned that Joe had returned to the Laredo area. I also got word that investigators from the Houston area had traveled to Laredo and had hunted for Joe for several days.

No one seemed to know where Joe was, or if he had really done the murders. I had heard that he had been stopped by two different police units while heading back to Laredo on the night of the murders because his vehicle fit the description of the suspect's vehicle. However, the Deputy had shown his law enforcement credentials, and the officers had let him go because they did not think a Deputy would have committed the murders. When the detectives arrived from the Houston area, they had gone to the Laredo Police Department, and not the DPS. I was not aware of the details of the investigation, but I knew that if the Webb County Deputy was hiding, he was most likely in Mexico.

For about a year, I would periodically hear that they were

still looking for Joe, but he had disappeared from the planet earth. No one ever asked me to get involved, so I assumed that they had some idea where he was and were trying to get him arrested. I was at the DPS office one day when a good friend of mine from Company A, Ranger David Maxwell, called to talk to me about the case. He said he had been asked to get involved and wanted to bring me up to date on the investigation. Ranger Maxwell and I had gone to the DPS Academy together. I told him that I would help him in any way I could.

He said the officers working the murders had developed information that the Webb County Deputy was hiding in Nuevo Laredo. Ranger Maxwell provided me with the address of a small rent house in Nuevo Laredo. I told him I would contact some people I knew there and attempt to see if Joe was at that location.

David sent me copies of two capital murder warrants for the former deputy. He said that they had been having a lot of trouble getting information from the Webb County Sheriff's Office, and believed that some of his friends there were feeding the suspect information about the investigation. I told David I would work on the case and let him know what I found out. Later that night, I got into my personal vehicle, crossed into Nuevo Laredo, and found the address David had given me.

The following morning I talked to some people I knew in the Laredo area and got the names of Joe's mother, father, and wife. I knew his family did not have a lot of money. If he was living in Nuevo Laredo, his family had to be crossing over to visit him and provide him assistance.

The next day, I again crossed into Nuevo Laredo and drove by the house. It appeared that someone lived there, but I had to be careful because there was no reason that a "Gringo" should be riding around the neighborhood. I then went to the *Comandancia* and met with the *comandante* of the *Judiciales* to fill him in on the case. I knew I was taking a chance by telling them, because sometimes in Mexico the family of a fugitive pays a fee not to be bothered by the authorities.

The *comandante* seemed to be truly interested in the case. He loaded up about ten *Judiciales* in three Chevrolet Suburbans and away we went. We drove to the neighborhood and I showed them the house where I thought Joe might be hiding. We were all out of the vehicle, and I asked the *comandante* if we were going to hit the house. He said that in Mexico we either had to have a search warrant, some kind of suspicion of a crime, or be in hot pursuit before we could enter a residence. I figured that this was his way out and that nothing was going to be done.

The *comandante* then called his *jefe de grupo* and spoke to him in Spanish. Then I saw a very young officer taking off his gun, his belt, and his shirt. I had no idea what was going on. As we stood around the vehicles, the now shirtless *Judicial* started walking down the block toward the house. When he got within about fifty yards of the house, he broke into a run. At this point, the *Judiciales* standing around the vehicle started chasing him. The shirtless *Judicial* ran up to the house that we were looking at, opened the front door and ran through all the way out the back. All of the other *Judiciales* chased him right up into the house. A short time later, the shirtless guy showed back up at the vehicles and put his clothes back on.

After a while, the group of *Judiciales* returned to the *comandante* and told him that the fugitive Deputy was not at the location. The *comandante* looked at me and just winked. It was their country, and I let them do their business their way. While we were at the location, I took out the photos of Joe and his family members. Several neighbors said Joe had lived at the house but had moved a few weeks before. They identified Joe's family members as people that would visit him and bring things he needed. A few of the neighbors even knew that he was wanted in the United States for something.

After the raid, I thanked the *comandante* for his assistance and returned to Laredo. The following day, I contacted my friend and former state prosecutor, U.S. District Attorney Angel Moreno. I told him about the case and asked if there were any Federal charges that we could file on Joe's family for helping him in Mexico.

Moreno told me he did not think there was anything we could do because the help was being provided in another country. I asked Moreno for one favor: If anyone from Joe's family called, tell them only that I had met with him about a capital murder case in which Joe was the suspect. Moreno said he had no problem telling the truth, since that's what I had done.

I left Moreno's office and contacted members of Joe's family to arrange for a meeting. I told the family members that I knew what they had been up to, and I showed them the driver's license photos I had obtained of the family. I told them that I had been to the house across the river, and that the neighbors had identified them as the persons who had been helping Joe. I told them that they had ten days to turn Joe in to me, or I was going to go back to the Federal prosecutor.

I reminded the family that Joe was going to prison one way or the other whether they helped or not. If they cooperated, at least they could provide for Joe's family while Joe was in the penitentiary. I then got up and left the room. The following day I drove by one of the family member's house and put one of my business cards in the mail box with "DAY 1" written on the back. The next day I did the same thing, except the card said "DAY 2." About the fifth day they locked the mailbox, but I just taped my card on the outside of the box. This went on until Day 9.

On that day, I was sitting at the DPS office when Joe, the fugitive Deputy, called me. He and I talked for a while and then he asked if I would forget the charges against his family if he gave up. I said getting him in custody was all I wanted. He said he would call me at nine o'clock the following morning and tell me where to meet him. At this point I didn't know if he was really going to give up or not.

As promised, at 9 a.m. the next day Joe called. He asked one favor: He did not want to be put in jail in Laredo. I told him that if he gave up, I would have Ranger Maxwell meet us in San Antonio and he would be taken back to face the charges where the offenses had occurred. I told him I would keep my word. He then told me to meet him near the Border Patrol checkpoint on Interstate 35 just north of Laredo. I drove to the checkpoint and there he was. I kept my part of the bargain and drove him to San Antonio where I turned him over to my friend in Company A.

A few months later I testified against Joe at his trial. A jury found him guilty and he will spend the rest of his life in the penitentiary.

Pigtails

I was at home late one night when the *comandante* called me from Nuevo Laredo and told me some of his officers had arrested four suspects from San Antonio who had been stealing cars and taking them to Nuevo Laredo. He said they also had recovered four stolen vehicles. The suspects were all U.S. citizens and the Mexican authorities were willing to release them into my custody if I would come pick them up.

I crossed into Mexico and drove to the *Comandancia*. The *comandante* said he wanted to talk to some of the suspects to ascertain the names of the people who had planned to purchase the stolen vehicles. We interviewed two or three of the suspects and the *comandante* got the people to talk. When we brought in the last suspect I noticed he had one of those hair cuts in which he had cut all of his hair except for a six or eight inch pigtail right in the middle of the back of his head. After the *comandante* started his interview I began to notice that when the suspect moved his head while responding, his pigtail would swish back and forth. I could tell that the *comandante* had also become aware of the swinging pigtail.

Suddenly he stopped the interview, reached across his desk, pulled the guy toward him and cut the pigtail off with a pair of scissors. He then sat down and continued his interrogation as if nothing had happened. I got so tickled I had to leave the room. It was kind of like being in church when you are not supposed to laugh and you can't help it. I finally got my act back together and returned to the interview. A short time

285

later as we were loading the suspects into my car, I told the *comandante* he had just done something I had wanted to do my whole life. We both got a good laugh and I took the four men back to Texas and placed them in the Webb County Jail. The guy who had gotten the free haircut never said a word.

Updating Files

I never have understood why on earth we've made some of the rules and laws we have that dictate the way we do business in our court system. When Rangers make a criminal case against a suspect, the first thing we do is tell the suspect he has the right not to talk to us. We have just spent a lot of time and effort catching the guy, and then we tell him that!

The work really starts when you arrest someone. After placing the suspect in jail, for the next few days or weeks you work on making a case report that is then submitted to the district attorney's office. Of course, your lieutenant and captain have to check it first. Several months later, you have to appear as a witness for the state before a grand jury to testify about the facts of the case. If the grand jury decides to indict the suspect, you start getting ready for the trial.

Several months after that, you again have to appear in district court to testify about the case before a jury. When that happens, a defense attorney does everything in his power to make you appear to be the most over-aggressive, stupid, racist, uneducated officer who ever coerced a confession out of his client. A defense attorney would have a jury believe that the only reason you arrested his client was that you needed to clear a case and you decided to pick on him.

In our system, the young lawyers who work for a DA's office are fresh out of law school. As soon as they get some good trial experience as a prosecutor they can later go to the dark side and become defense attorneys. That's where the money is. While they are still learning the ropes as state prosecutors, they will sit back and let an experienced defense attorney rip you to shreds while you are on the witness stand. They don't seem to know they can object and keep you from getting eaten alive.

If the suspect is found guilty, you then have to wait for the appeal process to proceed so you can send in a final disposition on the scumbag and quit making six-month updates on that case. You see, after a Ranger makes a case and submits it to a DA, he is required to turn in a report to his supervisors on that case every six months until the case is disposed of. That may not seem like a big deal, but if you file a case every one or two weeks, over a period of time you may have to update twenty to thirty files a month just to keep up with the cases that you have pending. That's not counting all the investigations you may have underway at the time.

You find that most of your time is spent either working on a case, doing the case report, or updating cases that you may have handled years ago. The more cases you make, the worse it gets. It gets to the point that you don't want to turn on your computer because you know that your lieutenant is going to be sending you your update list. It's like a wagon wheel, it never ends. Ask any Ranger in the state. If he has been around for a while, he hates the monthly updates more than anything else about the job.

Now try calling a DA's office and see how much interest you get from a clerk when you ask about a case that happened two years ago. Most of the time they can't find the ones that came in last week. The DA offices have thousands of cases and the state expects you to report on every case that you worked over the length of the statute of limitations.

I had a case several years ago where I ran a search warrant on a heroin dealer in Crystal City. I had developed information on the drug dealer and the sheriff had asked me to help him with the investigation. I drew up a search warrant and the sheriff and I hit the house. We arrested seven people and seized a small amount of heroin. I went back to Laredo and worked for a day or two on the report. When I completed the report I submitted it to the DA. Several months later I appeared before a grand jury and testified about the facts to the case. The seven defendants were indicted for possession of heroin.

For the next three years I checked the status of the case and I would have to submit a six-month's update on each defendant as to what action had been taken on the case. Each six-month period that I called, I was told that the case was still pending. This went on forever. Well, after three years I wised up and I quit calling. When it got time to update the case, I figured that I had better things to do than waste my time getting the same answer. I had always gotten some girl on the phone who had no idea what information I was trying to obtain. So, to save time and still play by the rules, I just reported that the case was still pending.

I knew I would have to testify against the defendants if the case ever went to trial, so I would know if any action was taken related to the case. I really didn't pay much attention as to how long I had been reporting the case as pending until I submitted a report to Lieutenant Ray Cano. A week or so after I had reported that the case on one of the defendants was still pending, the lieutenant called and asked if I had called the district clerk's office.

I smelled a rat real quick. He said he had called and found that the man whose case I had reported as still pending had died three years ago. Now how do you respond to something like that? I told the lieutenant that just because the guy was dead didn't mean that I was not going to convict him for what he had done while here on earth. The lieutenant failed to see the humor in it. An ex-Marine, he did things by the book. A lot of the other guys thought it was funny that I was updating a dead guy's file, but he didn't.

Over the next few months I tried to be a little more careful in updating the old files. To this day I think that it would be much better to have the office staff in the company headquarters update the files so the Rangers could be out on the street putting crooks in jail, but that's just my opinion.

Ranch Rescue

In March 2003 I was at the DPS office trying to catch up on the never-ending paperwork when I received a call from one of the deputies in Hebbronville, Jim Hogg County. Ram Garza, a good friend of mine, told me that they had an aggravated assault that occurred on a ranch east of Hebbronville. The deputy asked if I had time to come over and give them a hand in conducting the investigation. I told him I would be over in a few hours.

I left the office and headed that way not really knowing about the mess that I was about to get into. Hebbronville, fifty miles southeast of Laredo, had been in my area since I had made Ranger back in 1982. I liked the people and the town. Hebbronville never really had the meanness the other towns that I worked had. The main problems they had always seemed related to the drug or alien smuggling trade. Most of the time the sheriff and his deputies took care of their own problems but every once in a while they called and when they called, I went.

When I got to Hebbronville I met with Sheriff Erasmo Alarcon and Deputy Garza. They told me that one of the patrol deputies had picked up two illegal aliens, a male and female, walking along the highway west of Hebbronville the night before. The sheriff said the deputy intended to take them to the Border Patrol checkpoint located just a few miles from where they were found. After they arrived at the checkpoint the two aliens began to tell stories about being confronted by soldiers while they had been walking through the brush. Both aliens

291

said they had been assaulted by soldiers while on the Sutton Ranch. The Border Patrol knew their men had not been in the area so the incident got reported to the sheriff's office.

The sheriff and Ram began to bring me up to speed on the whole story. Over the last few days they had become aware that Joseph Sutton, a local rancher, had brought members of a para-military group onto his property to help with his illegal alien problem. The name of the group was Ranch Rescue. At the time that didn't mean much to me. I had heard of the group and knew that they had been in and around Laredo, but the only people who seemed to pay much attention to them were the news media. After seeing several members of this group interviewed on TV, I remember thinking that those fools were going to plow up a snake if they ran into the wrong people. The bad guys we messed with along the border played for keeps. It wouldn't bother any of the drug cartels at all to blow so many little round holes in their ass if Ranch Rescue got in their way while looking for drug smugglers or illegal aliens.

Sutton's place was located a few miles west of the Border Patrol checkpoint. Over the past few years he had been having a big problem with smugglers letting their loads of dope and illegal aliens out on the highway so they could try to avoid the checkpoint by walking through Sutton's ranch. The illegal aliens tore down Sutton's fences and left a lot of trash. Sutton was also concerned about the danger the illegal traffic posed to him and his family. The sheriff said that over the last few years Sutton had become so frustrated with both smugglers and illegal aliens that he had begun to take matters into his own hands.

Sheriff Alarcon went on to tell me that he had received information that the members of Ranch Rescue were heavily armed and thought to be carrying illegal fully automatic weapons along with night vision equipment. He said Sutton would not allow any Border Patrolman or deputies on his place. When Sutton found illegal aliens on his property he always had the officers meet him at the front gate to the ranch. At this point in the investigation all I had were two illegal aliens who had reported that they had been assaulted by "soldiers" while they were attempting to avoid a Border Patrol checkpoint.

I talked some more with the sheriff and we decided the best thing to do was locate the victims and interview them about the assault. We contacted the Border Patrol and learned the aliens were still at the checkpoint east of Hebbronville. The sheriff and I drove there and took custody of the aliens so they could be interviewed and hopefully identify whoever had assaulted them. On most of the offenses I worked, if possible, I liked to start by taking a statement from the victim. That always gave me a good idea as to what was going on.

About this time one of the sheriff's patrol units radioed that two men thought to be involved in the Ranch Rescue group were eating at the Dairy Queen. That demonstrates one of the things I always liked about working in a small town. The local officers knew most of the people in town. Outsiders were easy to find. The sheriff and I talked it over for a while and decided to ask the two men to come over to his office so we could talk with them about what was going on at the Sutton Ranch.

But first I interviewed the male and female victim and got their story. They had been traveling in a cargo type truck when the truck stopped east of Hebbronville. The smuggler or "coyote" told them to cross the fence onto the Sutton Ranch and walk east. They needed to cross two fences, he said. Once they had cleared the second fence, they were to work their way back to the highway. There the same truck they had been smuggled across in would pick them up after it cleared the Border Patrol checkpoint.

The couple said they had been walking through the brush when they saw what they thought were soldiers. The female told me that they tried to hide but that the soldiers found them with a large dog. Both victims said they were held at gunpoint and that a large bald-headed fat man hit the male in the head with a pistol. The man said he nearly passed out from the blow. I looked at his head and saw that he had a large knot about the size of my fist on the back of his head. Both victims said they had been in fear of their life. The victims told me they were forced into the back of a van where one of the men, an older gray haired guy, guarded them with a machine gun. They were held for a while and then taken back to the highway where the soldiers released them.

When I finished interviewing them I met with the sheriff. He said he had been talking with the two men who had been at the DQ. One of the men, Casey Nethercott, told the sheriff that a large group of men with fully automatic weapons was conducting security at the Sutton Ranch.

When I started interviewing them, I noticed that Casey did all of the talking. The other man, Henry Conner, had the good sense to keep his mouth shut. I saw that both of them fit the physical description given by the assault victims. I told the sheriff that we should make a photo lineup of both suspects and have the victims look it over to ascertain if they were the ones who had committed the assault.

While the photo lineups were being put together I had a couple of the deputies take a written statement from both victims so we could have the facts of the assault down on paper. When the photo lineups were ready I showed them to both victims and both identified Casey as the person who had struck the male in the head with a pistol. Both victims also picked Conner as the one who had held them at gunpoint and guarded them in the back of a van while they were transported off the ranch.

At this point I felt that our case was made. But I knew there were always two sides to every story, so I wanted to give Casey and Conner the opportunity to tell what had happened. I interviewed both of them and both told the same story as the victims. Conner said he had sat in the back of the van guarding the two victims with an AR-15 while they were taken off the ranch. Casey admitted he had been the one with the dog and that he might have accidentally hit the male alien with a flashlight when he took him into custody. But the injury I had observed on the male victim was no accident.

The sheriff and I contacted the Jim Hogg County District Attorney's Office to see if they felt the case was strong enough to issue warrants. They said it was. Both defendants were charged with two counts of aggravated assault and two counts of unlawful restraint.

Just after we booked them into county jail, a reporter from Canada showed up at the sheriff's office and wanted to know the details of the case. I remember thinking *what in the hell is a reporter from Canada doing in Hebbronville, Texas?* We gave him the information that we could on an active case and sent him on his way. Little did we know that the reporter had been at the ranch with Casey and Conner and that there was no way he was going to see things our way.

Happy that I had been able to wrap up the case in just one day, I returned to Laredo and really didn't think much more about it. But the next morning the telephone started ringing at the DPS office. I had people calling from all over the United States. They wanted to know how I could protect illegal aliens and put U.S. citizens in jail. I got call after call after call. All of the calls referred to what a worthless SOB I was and how I was a traitor to my country. It was as if I had stirred up all the mountain people from the movie "Deliverance." Then other news media got involved. I could not hang up the phone before I got another call from some nut in Kansas, Alabama or wherever. I received several death threats and was told that something bad was going to happen to me and my family. I found out that Ranch Rescue had put the information about the case on their web page and somehow gotten my picture and posted that. They were referring to Sheriff Alarcon and me as the Texas Taliban. This went on for the next week or two. It finally got to the point that I quit answering the phone.

The Ranch Rescue folks were not interested in the truth. They were mainly trying to get people stirred up about the case so they could ask them to make cash donations to their group via their web page. You would have thought that it would have mattered to the group that Casey was a convicted felon and should not have had any weapons when he was on Sutton's ranch. Ranch Rescue apparently didn't mind the small things like that. All that seemed to matter to them was to try and make the sheriff and me look as bad as possible.

Over the next few months things finally settled down and the case went on through the court system. Casey was found guilty and sentenced to five years in the penitentiary. The case against Conner was dismissed by the DA's office. I thought at this point it was over. Wrong again.

I was contacted by the Southern Poverty Law Center and told that they were in the process of suing Casey on behalf of the two victims. I knew that the Southern Poverty Law Center was the group that had taken the KKK to court and won on behalf of a victim. Sure enough, they won the case and took a small piece of land away from Casey. Again, I started getting calls from people telling me how worthless I was. And the news media attention started up again. I finally told the media that in Texas we didn't allow people to sic dogs on folks and pistol whip them no matter where they were from. They finally got the point and left me alone. However, after putting up with all this for more than a year I got to the point that I refused to talk with the media at all about anything.

Murder by Illegal Aliens

I was working on reports at the DPS office in Laredo when I was contacted by my old friend, Company F Ranger John Aycock about a missing person case. John and I had both been Narcotics agents and made Ranger at the same time. He is the most highly decorated officer that has ever worked for the department, having won the Commissioners' Medal of Valor on two occasions. When you work for DPS, you know how hard it is to win it one time, much less twice.

John was the kind of officer you wanted around if things went wrong. He had been with Ranger Stan Guffey when he was killed and John killed the guy who had killed Guffey. After that incident, he had come to my house in Laredo and spent several days with me trying to unwind. I always knew that if my family and I ever needed anything, John would be there in the time it took him to make the drive. He was that kind of friend.

But this phone call wasn't to catch up on old times. He told me he had been working on a case in which an elderly man had disappeared. The missing man had lived out in the country, had a lot of goats and had hired several illegal aliens to help him out on his place. The old man's car was gone, as well as several items from his house. John said he had been looking for the man and his car, but could not find them.

He had learned that the illegal aliens who had been working for the old man were from Nuevo Laredo. He also had obtained some photos of the illegal aliens from the house that

297

they had been staying in. John and I made arrangements for him to forward the photos to me. He also said that the Crime Stoppers program in his area had offered a reward for information that produced results on the case.

At about 3 p.m. on the day I received the photos of the aliens and the missing man's car, I crossed into Nuevo Laredo, met with the *comandante* and told him what I was working on. I also told the commander that he could get a reward from Crime Stoppers if he developed information on the case.

Seven hours later the *comandante* called me at home and told me that he had located the suspects, recovered the elderly man's car and some items that may have been stolen from his house. The *comandante* wanted me to come over and interview the suspects about the case.

I again crossed into Nuevo Laredo and over the next several hours we interviewed the suspects. Eventually they admitted they had murdered the man in Texas. One of the suspects drew me a map of the area where they had dumped the elderly man's body. I called John at 2 a.m. and described to him where the body could be located. About two hours later he called me back and said he had found the body. Unfortunately, I was unable to return the suspects to Texas due to the fact that they were Mexican citizens, and Mexico very rarely will give up one of its citizens, especially when they could face a death penalty in the U.S.

Over the next few months John had the entire case report translated into Spanish. He came to Laredo and he and I submitted the case to the Mexican prosecutor in Nuevo Laredo. John succeeded in getting the suspects convicted in Mexico for the murder they committed in Texas. Most officers don't know it is a violation of Mexican law to kill a person in another country. I'm happy we were able to get closure for the victim's family.

Nuevo Laredo

When you live and work on the border for nearly four decades you begin to understand how and why things happen along the river. In my opinion, the Mexican government has had a bad problem for years. Mexico has been allowing people in their country to run dope into Texas a long time before I started working. The problem only became visible to the outside world when the two drug cartels went to war with each other.

Smuggling on the border is a way of life. Generations of people have made their living slipping everything from endangered wildlife to alcohol and drugs into Texas. But now things have gotten completely out of control.

The desire for money complicates things on both sides of the issue. Mexico has never paid its police officers enough to live on. That means they have to come up with some way to supplement their income. Stolen cars and drugs have always been a way that the officers could bring in enough money to feed their families and allow them to have some of the good things in life. That's just the way business is done south of the border.

A policeman on our side of the river knows, just by living and working in the Laredo area, that there is always a lot of drug smuggling going on. Most of the murder cases are related to the drug trade in some way or the other. John Doe citizens going about their daily lives really have no idea what's going on in the town they live in. People tend not to think about things like that until they affect them or their family directly.

The drug cartels on the Mexican side have nearly ruined Nuevo Laredo. Nowadays, I will not go to Mexico for any reason. There have been hundreds of murders there and nearly all have gone unsolved. A lot of the businesses that were in Nuevo Laredo have moved over to the Texas side in an effort to make a living without being extorted.

This is how things work along the border these days:

The drug smuggler's right to cross their product through Nuevo Laredo is referred to as the "Plaza." A few years ago the Nuevo Laredo Plaza was controlled by one cartel. There was no dispute as to whom you had to pay if you wanted to pass drugs or illegal aliens into the U.S. Smugglers paid a percentage of their profit for the right to pass through the Plaza.

When you look at a map of the U.S. you will see that Laredo sits at the end of Interstate 35, which cuts through the middle of the nation from Texas to Minnesota. Because of that, Laredo is one of the biggest inland ports in the U.S. Six to eight thousand truck tractors and trailers cross from Nuevo Laredo to Laredo on a daily basis. The U.S. Customs Service won't publicly admit it, but they can normally only inspect a fraction of these trucks each day. If you are a drug dealer in Nuevo Laredo and you hide your drugs inside a normal load of cargo, you have a very good chance of getting your drugs into this country without them being seized. When you have the drugs in Texas, then all you have to worry about is getting them through the Border Patrol checkpoints. Once the drugs are past the checkpoints they end up all over the U.S.

The problems started when a rival cartel wanted to acquire the Plaza in Nuevo Laredo. In 2004 they started fighting each other for the right to own the Plaza. Nuevo Laredo has turned into a battleground and hundreds of people have been killed. The only way we have been able to keep a lid on the problem in Texas is that all of the local, state and federal law enforcement agencies have started working together as never before. The Mexican government also brought its military into the fight, but the problem has spread throughout Mexico.

The cartels have now started killing anyone in the Mexican government that they can get to try to keep the government from taking action against them. The cartels have also silenced the press by attacking newspaper offices and broadcast stations and killing journalists whose reporting was a little too accurate.

If this problem is not aggressively addressed by the state and federal government in the U.S., in a few years we will have a problem on the border that will be out of control. We had better do whatever it takes now to stop this or we will pay for it in the long run.

Driving to Zapata recently, I passed a roadside park that sits next to the Rio Grande. In 1977 I was working in a black and white DPS unit as a drug task force officer when I drove into that same park and busted about 1,500 pounds of marijuana. I was twenty-five years old. As I drove by the park I started thinking that I had been fighting the drug cartels nearly half my life and things were worse now than ever before. It really makes you think that you didn't really accomplish much with your life when the problem is worse than ever.

People who do not live on the border do not realize what kind of people we are now dealing with. In the old days it was more or less like a game. The drug smugglers tried to get their drugs through, and we tried to stop them. We busted a lot of dope and I'm sure a lot got through. From time to time we would see the drug dealers kill each other, but it was always in a way that the only people that got hurt were the people that were involved in the drug business.

It's not like that any more along the river. We now have people in Mexico who kill without regard for anyone. They will hose down a carload of people with an AK-47 just to get one guy in the car. They will kill men, women and children with no regard to who gets hurt. They will kill a whole family just to get one guy's attention. If they can't kill who they want, then they will kill a member of his family to get their point across.

Over the last few months the cartels have begun to use the same methods being used in the sand box wars. They have begun to decapitate people. They not only cut people's heads off, they do it and then post a video of the whole thing on the Internet. They do this for no other reason than to get the attention of their enemies. If I was working for one of the cartels and I watched one of my friends getting his head cut off, that might make me want to find another way to make a living. And that's what they want. Make everyone so afraid that no one will stand up to them and do the right thing.

Now they are killing police officers, military officers, soldiers and elected officials in Mexico. One police chief in Nuevo Laredo lasted just six hours in office before they killed him in a burst of automatic rifle fire in broad daylight. The way the cartels operate, if they have a problem, they kill it.

Ironically, Mexico does not have a death penalty. It's not legal, but for all practical purposes you can kill anyone you want. The cartels are now using the prison gangs on our side of the river, particularly the Mexican Mafia and Latino *Pistoleros*, to do things for them because these local gangs know how to work in the U.S.

Most of the officers who work the border have a lot more concern for their security then ever before. You never go out unarmed. You have to watch your back and you have to tell your family to be careful as they go about their lives. You go to work a different way each day. You do not set a pattern in the way that you do business. The thing that bothers me the most is the fact that public officials do not want to talk about the problem. They try to give the Chamber of Commerce line that everything is under control.

But the problem needs to be aggressively addressed in the state of Texas. If we don't do it, it will be that much harder to fix later. The border with Mexico is the first line of defense for our state and nation in slowing down the poison that is being shipped into our country and is destroying the lives of so many of our citizens. I hope that some of the people we have elected to public office will have the sense to fund our police agencies in this state and give them the tools and personnel to make a difference. I hope I live long enough to see that happen.

Drug Dealers on the Border

Through my law enforcement career, the one thing that has bothered me the most is the drug dealers. People just don't seem to realize the effect illegal drugs have on our lives. But police officers see what it does to families and communities. Drug dealers don't care about anything but guns, girls, cars and money. Not in that order. They will do whatever it takes to keep the money flowing.

When the citizens of a community read in the newspaper about a thousand pounds of drugs being seized, they don't stop to think that most likely several officers risked their lives in making the seizure and arresting the people involved. They also don't stop to think of the risk that the officers face, days and weeks later, when the drug dealers realize that because of these officers, they have lost hundreds of thousands of dollars. John Doe citizen just reads his newspaper, drinks his coffee, and forgets about the whole deal before lunch. The drug dealers never forget.

If you want to get someone really upset with you, mess with his money. The drug dealers work for no other reason than to make as much money, as fast as they can, selling their poison on the streets in the good old USA. People have no idea of the huge amount of money involved.

The cartels run their business just like anyone would run a business. They have overhead. They have got to get their loads through to make the money they need to pay the people who work for them. The more product they send north the better the

304

chance that some of it will get through to make the money they need for their operation.

After fighting these people my whole adult life I have come to understand that we are never going to stop them. But we have to continue to fight them to preserve our way of life. We have to continue to put them in prison. We have to spend the money it takes to do the job. If we don't, we will regret it later when it will cost more money and lives to get back to where we are now. We need to get the politicians to do the right thing.

A load of approximately 3,000 pounds of marijuana seized by the Webb County Sheriff's Office in Laredo at the height of the drug cartel wars in Nuevo Laredo, Mexico.

I attended a trial in 2007 in which a seventeen-year-old was being tried for the murder of a man in Laredo. The defendant had been hired and trained by one of the cartels in Nuevo Laredo, and had been assigned to a hit team working in

Texas. Now, understand what I just said. A seventeen-year-old man was hired and assigned to kill people in Texas for money by the Mexican drug cartels.

More than one million in cash and assorted weapons
seized by the Webb County Sheriff's Office.

We had received information from our contacts on the other side of the river that this teenager might have killed around thirty people in Mexico and Texas. The cartels have silenced the press in Mexico by killing reporters and bombing news media outlets, and they don't like negative publicity in the U.S., either. We soon heard that the cartels were going to try to kill the young man *and* his defense attorney because he had not agreed to plead guilty to avoid a trial. The information indicated that the cartels did not want all the facts of the case to come out in open court where the news media would pick up on the story. The Webb County Sheriff's Office had to double security in the Justice Center and call out our SWAT team to provide security for the courtroom and the district judge in this case. After a few days of the court proceedings and the death threats the defendant decided to cop a plea and got forty years in the state penitentiary.

This sounds like something that might happen in some foreign country, but it's happening on the Texas border. Most people don't stop to think what a situation like this costs local government, or the fear it creates in the community. In this case, we had to assign twelve additional officers to the Justice Center to provide security. As a result we had to remove officers from patrol to assign them to the courts.

People do not realize that the drug wars in Mexico have spilled over into the United States and that it will be costly to try to keep our way of life.

DPS and the Border

Most of the men and women who stay and work on the border are people raised there. But the federal and state agencies continuously send people fresh from the academy. When those guys get down on the border they don't even know where the Rio Grande is. They are not from that part of the state, don't know the customs and don't know the methods the crooks use to operate. On top of all that, if they happen to be federal officers they seem to think they are the only honest guys working in law enforcement.

When they get to Laredo and other border duty stations they are already counting the days until they can transfer back to wherever they came from. I had seen so many of these people come through the DPS office that it got to the point I no longer even tried to learn their names. I knew it was a waste of time trying to teach them how things worked in the area because they would be gone before they knew their way around.

I know this because I was once one of those guys. I most likely would have left the area myself if it weren't for a certain green-eyed lady I met in 1983. I think that the best way to solve the problem of transient border law enforcement officers would be for the agencies to pay additional money for officers to live and work on the border. We need good seasoned officers who know how to handle their business. The border is where the problem starts and that's where we should have our best officers.

Assign the officers to the border for several years. When they have completed their time, give them the choice of where they want to go. Try to hire people from the border area and allow them to stay in the same area if they promote, so the knowledge that they have developed won't be wasted by working in a part of the state where nothing is happening.

Living in Laredo

After all these years living on the border, I can still remember how I felt the first time that I moved to Laredo. When the DPS told me that I was going to be working in Laredo, I had to get a map to find out where it was located. I had never been there before, and I had no idea what it was like. In fact, I had never been south of Del Rio.

When I drove into town I noticed palm trees all over. I had never seen palms up close and personal before. I remember thinking that it was kind of a useless tree because it didn't provide any shade. After all, I was from West Texas. We didn't have trees—or water. One of the signs in Rankin said: "GOOD FISHING, ANY DIRECTION 100 MILES".

At that time Laredo was a lot different than it is today. A lot of the streets were not paved. Most of the people spoke Spanish and you could tell that they were really not too friendly towards Anglos. I had been raised with most every kind of people, and I never really paid much attention to what race a person was. To me it always was more important what the person was like on the inside.

Well, I started to work the area and I began to learn about some of the local customs and how the people lived their lives. Most of the people I came into contact with were crooks, or people directly related to the legal system. The locals looked at us as just another one of the Anglos that had been stationed in Laredo by the DPS. They were of the opinion that we would stay a year or two, and then leave. Why go to the trouble of getting to know us? We wouldn't be here long. One thing that I hadn't counted on was that the longer I stayed the better I liked it.

One of the first things I began to notice in the Hispanic culture was how the younger generations always seem to take care of the older people. I'd be sitting in a restaurant and see a large family walk in. The younger folks always went out of their way to help the old people get seated. You could tell there was a lot of love and respect there. I also noticed that Hispanic families always showed a lot more affection toward each other than families did where I grew up. The grown children would hold their parents' hands and openly show them that they cared for them. That made an impression on me, and I really liked what I saw. When I think back, I realize I was raised a lot differently. I cannot remember my mother or father ever telling me that they loved me. I knew they did, but it wasn't something that we told each other.

I also found that it was really hard as a police officer to deal with a Hispanic mother if you were going to arrest her son. In the Anglo culture you might have a little problem, but if you crossed a Hispanic mother there was no telling what was going to happen. I have actually had to fight the mother and the rest of the family just trying to arrest one of the sons. The local Hispanic officers would refer to these encounters by saying the mothers had "an MA." I first heard that term years ago and it still brings a smile to my face. MA stands for "Mexican Attack." The term refers to a mother faking a heart attack or fainting while officers are trying to arrest one of her family members. Most of the time all they are trying to do is buy time so the son can get away. I always tried to deal with the mothers directly and explain to them what was going on. If they understood, most of the time I didn't have any problems. Being an Anglo it was just one of the many things I had to learn about the culture in South Texas.

When I made Ranger and returned to Laredo I was very

much aware that the Rangers had a bad reputation in South Texas. There were still a lot of hard feelings about the way the Rangers had treated people years ago. With that in mind, I decided I was going to be as fair to everyone as I could be. It took me several years, but I made a lot of friends and got along just fine with the people in the area.

There are a few people who don't like me just because I am Anglo, but I think that a Ranger would find that in any part of the state that he works in. As a whole I have been treated wonderfully over the years and most of the friends I have are Hispanic. I have grown to love the Hispanic culture and I don't want to live anywhere else. People are just people. Some good, some bad. I now have a large family in the area and I enjoy every day that I get to spend in Laredo. I am just glad that I made the decision to stay all these years ago.

When I came to Laredo I never ate Mexican food. I was a meat, potatoes, and cornbread kind of guy. When I started dating my future wife she began to cook a lot of things for me that I couldn't even pronounce. We have been together for more than a quarter of a century and now I only eat Mexican food. When I go out of town I have trouble finding the kind of food I've gotten used to eating.

It strikes me as funny how things change in life. I just wish more people would be more open to change. It sure would make it a lot easier to get along.

Chicago Murder Case
(AKA Flying Baby Case)

On March 4, 2004 I was contacted by Rocky Millican, the Ranger stationed in Pearsall. Rocky told me he had been contacted by several Chicago Police Department detectives about an old murder case they had been working on for several years. Rocky said that the Chicago officers were requesting the assistance of the Texas Rangers to help them locate a murder suspect thought to be in the Carrizo Springs area. The Chicago officers told Rocky that a man named Raul Tijerina was thought to have killed his fourteen-year-old girlfriend. She had been eight months pregnant at the time.

Carrizo Springs was now Rocky's area, but it appeared that it would take several officers to conduct a surveillance of the suspect's house, so he decided to call me. I didn't have much going on at the time so I drove to Carrizo and met with Rocky and the Chicago officers. The Illinois officers told us that they had information that Tijerina had been hiding out in the Carrizo Springs area for a long time. They also had an address where Tijerina was living.

We started watching the residence to determine whether he was home. We all knew that if we hit the house and he wasn't there, he would be on the run again and it would be hard to find him. It wasn't easy to conduct a surveillance in Carrizo Springs, because everyone in town knew everyone else and a strange car just sitting in a neighborhood attracted a lot of

313

attention. After sitting on the house for several hours we were able to confirm that Tijerina was indeed inside. We held a quick meeting and decided that we would raid the house in an effort to serve the murder warrant and take the suspect into custody. We divided the officers into teams and decided to have one team hit the back and another to hit the front of the house. Rocky and I were going to go in the front door.

As we went in both Rocky and I noticed that the inside of the house was a real mess. The place smelled and you could tell that no one was making any kind of effort to keep the place clean. Clothes, trash and anything else you could think of was just piled up along the walls. Rocky and I searched the living room and found no murder suspect. We then entered a long hallway and went inside a dark, front bedroom of the house. Again the bedroom was in terrible condition. Piles of dirty clothes, blankets and pillows were waist high all along the walls and on top of the bed. We actually had trouble walking into the room it was so crammed with stuff. When I looked at the bed it appeared that someone was hiding under the covers. I reached down, grabbed the end of the bedspread with both hands and jerked the bed covers off so I could see who was in the bed. Rocky and I were amazed to see a small baby go flying across the room. The child landed in a pile of clothing and pillows along the wall. It was a small child, about a year old. Apparently someone had placed him on the bed and piled clothing and pillows around him to keep him from falling off the bed. I waded through the clutter, picked him up and found he was not injured. In fact, he didn't even wake up. We put him back on the bed and continued to search the house. The house was a pigpen, but all the piled clothing had kept the baby from being injured.

Rocky and I then checked the garage, where we found the suspect hiding behind a refrigerator. He was placed under arrest and transported to the sheriff's office. The Chicago officers interviewed Tijerina and he confessed to beating his pregnant girlfriend to death in Chicago. Rocky and I were glad that the case had been solved and no one had gotten hurt in the process. One thing about being a Ranger, you never knew what you were going to get into. Local officers always referred to this case as "The flying baby case."

Retiring from DPS

When Captain Clete Buckaloo and I heard that retired Ranger Clayton McKinney had passed away in August 2004, we both decided to attend his funeral. I drove to Del Rio, met Clete, and he and I made the trip together in one of our units. As we drove for miles and miles across West Texas, we told each other the stories we knew about Clayton. Up until that point I don't think either one of us had realized just how much of an impact he had had on our lives. He also had a big influence on Ranger David Duncan.

Capt. Clete Buckaloo at the old Marathon jail
while attending Ranger Clayton McKinney's funeral.

316

I knew when I was a rookie that Clayton was one of the most respected guys in the communities he served. I made up my mind then that, at some point in my career, I wanted people to think of me in the same way.

After the services, a friend of Clete's gave him one of Clayton's Colt .38 Super Commanders. I know that Clete would not take anything for that pistol.

As we were driving back from the funeral, I decided it was time for me to retire from the Rangers. Senior Captain C. J. Havrda had retired in June, and I had been thinking about doing the same thing for the last year or so. On our way home I told Clete that I was going to Austin the following week to check on my retirement. He told me he really didn't want to lose me from Company D, but that if that's what I wanted to do, to go ahead.

It's strange how things are when you start to get older. One day I went in to renew my driver's license. A few weeks later I got the DL and looked at the photo, I thought, *Who in the hell is that old guy in the photograph?*

I really don't remember noticing when I started getting old. It's like one day I woke up and realized, *Hey, I'm an old man.* No warning. I just noticed that I couldn't do the things that I used to be able to do. I had gotten to the point that life was no longer giving me things. Life was now starting to take things away. Friends, family and health. When I was younger I could work for days without going to bed. Now if I worked all night it nearly killed me. It took me days to get over it. Add the fact that I needed a purse to carry all my accessories. I had reading glasses, seeing glasses, medicine for if I couldn't get home, my hearing aid, my book with all my telephone numbers, badge, pocket knife, gun, extra mags, cell phone, pager, and handcuffs. It took me longer to get ready in the morning than it did my wife. Now on top of all that, most of the time I couldn't remember where I had left all my stuff. I spent most of the time trying to find my car keys or my pistol, which I had hidden in case someone broke into the house.

I finally decided that it was time for me to go. I had noticed that a lot of the older guys seemed to start getting sick somewhere around sixty. I was fifty-two and had already started to have some health problems. I knew I had a window of about five or ten years that I might be able to enjoy my retirement before I started having the same kind of problems everyone else my age would be having.

Doyle and Captain Buckaloo in front of the old Dimmit County Jail
a short time before Doyle retired from the Rangers.

I turned in my paperwork and retired from the Texas Rangers on August 31, 2004. It was the hardest decision that I ever had to make. Working for the DPS was the only real job I had ever known. For a few days after I retired, I didn't know what to do with myself. I knew that the Texas Ranger part of my life was over, and it gave me a sick feeling in the pit of my stomach.

The End of the Story

Not long after I retired, Webb County Sheriff-elect Rick Flores asked me if I would be willing to run the department's Criminal Division. What impressed me about Rick was that he wanted to improve the sheriff's office to better serve the community. After spending the last twenty-two years working as a Ranger in Webb County, I thought, *What better way to end my law enforcement career than to help make the community a better place to live?* So I accepted Rick's offer, going to work when he took office on January 1, 2005.

Rick also hired my good friend Louie Zapata as Chief Deputy. Louie and I had worked together for more than twenty-five years and I knew that he knew what he was doing.

The new sheriff and I made up our minds that we were going to improve the way that the department did business. I explained to the sheriff how the Rangers had a system set up where they had laptop computers for use in taking statements, obtaining photos and making reports. The sheriff bought each of our investigators new laptops and printers. We set up our system in the same way as the Rangers. The end result was a much better work product for the DA's Office.

One case I worked with Ranger Robert Hunter, who took over my area when I retired, really brings to light what a computer can do when it is used in the right way. A Border Patrolman was shot by a suspect in South Laredo. We set up a command post in the college near the scene.

Ranger Hunter and I ran a registration check on the

320

suspect's vehicle and got the name of the owner. We then called the Ranger office in Austin and asked for a driver's license check on the name, and had them e-mail a DL photo to us. The photo fit the description of the suspect, and we called Austin again and had them make us a photo line-up.

The problem was that the Border Patrolman was at the local hospital with the possibility of being transferred to San Antonio, and we needed him to give us a positive ID on the suspect. We had the Rangers' office e-mail the photo line-up to us and to the Laredo Police Department, which is located across the street from the hospital where the Border Patrolman was being treated. A police officer walked over to the hospital and the victim picked the suspect out of the lineup. We then contacted Ranger Frank Malinak in College Station and he ran a search warrant on the suspect's apartment. Frank found the pistol box with the serial number of the gun used to shoot the officer. The following day Frank went to the gun store and picked up the yellow form indicating the suspect had bought the weapon.

We had identified the suspect within twenty minutes and later put the gun that was used to shoot the officer in the suspect's hands. That's what a computer can do for you if you know what to do with it.

One of the first things I learned when I went to work for the sheriff was that I had a real job. I had around seventy men and women working for me and something was always going on.

About two weeks after Sheriff Flores took office, we had a double murder on our hands. We found a car that had been parked and set on fire on a dirt road just east of Laredo, off Highway 359. When the fire was put out, the officers found that two young males had been placed in the trunk. Both had been shot numerous times with a .40 caliber pistol.

When I received the details about the offense I knew that this was the way the Mexican Mafia did business. I had worked a lot of cases like this and knew they were hard to solve because fire destroys most of the evidence in the case. At the time that the offense occurred, I was in the hospital and not able to assist in working the crime scene. Ranger Hunter had gone to the scene and he and sheriff's investigators had started the investigation.

A few days later we got a lucky break when a man jumped off a bus at the Border Patrol checkpoint and told them that people were after him. One of the Sheriff's Office patrol deputies headed to the checkpoint to find out what the problem was. When the deputy picked the guy up he started talking about having been in a house in Laredo when two guys had been kidnapped and killed. This was the break that we needed.

Over the next several hours we were able to identify the residence and the people who lived there. We eventually identified all of the suspects in the double murder and got all but one of them arrested. After several trials, five people got sent to the penitentiary for the murders. Only one suspect remained on the loose, probably in Mexico.

Over the next four years, the Webb County Sheriff's Department seized more than $60 million worth of drugs and around $6 million in cash from the dopers. A lot of the drug seizures came through the Sheriff's Office Crime Stoppers program and were the direct result of Captain Ted Garcia's work and that of his small group of people. Likewise, the Sheriff's Office Patrol section, headed by Captain Benny Botello, was always taking loads of dope down.

About the time I went to work for Flores, two drug cartels started to fight for control in Nuevo Laredo. As the violence escalated in Nuevo Laredo, we had some spillover violence in Laredo as well, but we were able to keep a lid on it with the local, state and federal agencies working together as never before.

Sheriff Flores and Zapata County Sheriff Sigi Gonzalez helped form the Texas Border Sheriffs' Coalition. They both took it upon themselves to do the right thing for their communities in asking for help from the state and federal governments to combat the cartels. Whether people know it or not, they really made a difference. All sheriffs along the border joined Sigi and Rick in their efforts. The pressure paid off and the government increased law enforcement funding along the border.

Seizure of 1,000 pounds of cocaine and weapons made by
Webb County Sheriff's Office Crime Stoppers Program.
Seizure made during the bad times of the drug cartel wars in Mexico.

After living on the border all these years, I finally got to see officers from all agencies working together like they did when I first went to work out in West Texas.

The cartels in Mexico are the biggest threat to law enforcement and to our way of life that Texas has faced in a long time. We have to keep up the fight no matter what it costs or how long it takes. I don't even want to think about what it would be like if we don't do the right thing. If for no other reason, we need to do it for our children and the people of Texas.

Sheriff Flores lost his reelection bid in March 2008 and I decided I would retire for good in November. So now we come to the end of the story and the end of the career of an ex-sheepherder from Rankin, Texas. With this book I hope that I have given an insight into what Texas Rangers go through in protecting the people of the state of Texas. As for me, I am going to sleep late and find something else to do.

To order additional copies of this book,
contact the author at his website
www.workingtheborder.com
or e-mail him at
dholdrid@stx.rr.com

About the Author:

Doyle Holdridge grew up in West Texas and attended San Angelo State University before joining the Texas Department of Public Safety. As a Trooper, Narcotics Officer, and a Texas Ranger for the Department of Public Safety, and subsequently as a Major in charge of the Criminal Division at the Webb County Sheriff's Office, Doyle worked the Texas-Mexico Border area from El Paso to Brownsville for nearly four decades. Some of his experiences working this area are highlighted in this book.

9 781933 177250